WRITING LONDON

Also by Julian Wolfreys

BEING ENGLISH: Narratives, Idioms, and Performances of
National Identity from Coleridge to Trollope

THE RHETORIC OF AFFIRMATIVE RESISTANCE: Dissonant
Identities from Carroll to Derrida

DECONSTRUCTION • DERRIDA

VICTORIAN IDENTITIES: Social and Cultural Formations in
Nineteenth-Century Literature (*co-editor with Ruth Robbins*)

APPLYING: TO DERRIDA
(*co-editor with John Brannigan and Ruth Robbins*)

LITERARY THEORIES: A Case Study
in Critical Performance (*co-editor with William Baker*)

RE: JOYCE: Text • Culture • Politics
(*co-editor with John Brannigan and Geoff Ward*)

THE DERRIDA READER
(*editor*)

writing London

the trace of the urban text
from
Blake to Dickens

Julian Wolfreys

palgrave

Published by
PALGRAVE
Houndmills, Basingstoke, Hampshire RG21 6XS and
175 Fifth Avenue, New York, N. Y. 10010
Companies and representatives throughout the world

PALGRAVE is the new global academic imprint of
St. Martin's Press LLC Scholarly and Reference Division and
Palgrave Publishers Ltd (formerly Macmillan Press Ltd).

ISBN 0–333–73686–9

This book is printed on paper suitable for recycling and
made from fully managed and sustained forest sources.

A catalogue record for this book is available
from the British Library.

Transferred to digital printing 2001

Printed and bound in Great Britain by
Antony Rowe Ltd, Chippenham, Wiltshire

For
John Abercrombie
and
James Kincaid

Contents

I could tell you how many steps make up the streets rising like stair-
ways, and the degree of the arcades' curves, and what kind of zinc
scales cover the roofs; but I already know this would be the same as
telling you nothing. The city does not consist of this . . . .

Italo Calvino

At times we can become possessed by some compelling obsession with
transmutation – by dint of studying some spectacle, walking in its vicinity,
entering blind substance that shines with knowledge.

Jacques Réda

But it is not a principle just to avoid writing architecture. When I
speak of writing or texts usually I insist that I don't just refer to writ-
ing words on the page, for me building is the writing of a text. Even if
there are no apparent words in it, I call this writing, and I call this
text.

Jacques Derrida

Acknowledgements

Writing London is very much a labour of love, and it is largely due to the kindness and interest of friends and colleagues that it has been completed. Chiefly I was surprised by the enthusiasm of people otherwise antipathetic to the idea of London, who formulated remarks such as 'why don't you read this', or 'I think you'd be really interested to see this'. They were right, I was, and nearly everything offered has ended up somewhere in this book. The exact location may be imprecise, but then, that's only fitting to the subject.

I would like to thank the following people for their help and input during the writing and researching of this book: for reading the work on Dickens and enthusing over the idea of architextures, Virginia Mason Vaughan; the staff at the British Library, who found everything which was misplaced; the anonymous reader who put me on to Bill Readings's reading of Blake's London; Claire Jones, Jenny Bourne Taylor, Mark Currie, Andrew Roberts, Jessica Maynard, Burhan Tufail: all have, indirectly or in passing, offered helpful hints and useful photocopies; Helen Debenham, for introducing me to the novels of Charlotte Riddell; Jane Stabler, for her positive response to the chapter on De Quincey, Engels and Wordsworth; everyone who commented so helpfully on a presentation of an early form of the Dickens chapter at the 'Victorian Literature, Contemporary Theory' conference, held at the University of Luton in the summer of 1994; Alec MacAulay, for the idea in the first place, even though he never envisaged the book becoming what it has; John Brannigan, for countless fruitful conversations, and for walking around London on a very hot day in search of places which didn't exist and boundaries which seemed to erase themselves, and for his comments on several of the chapters; Moyra Haslett, for reading various drafts, suggesting certain inclusions, and also for walking; Ruth Robbins, for comments and encouragement, and the eleventh-hour loan of Arthur Symons; and Jane Goldman, whose particular helpful hints (and photocopies) have always been of immense help. Also, I really must thank beyond all formal politeness David Hearn,

Brian Niro, and Leah Wain, who have offered invaluable editorial assistance, and feel all the better for having done so (at least, so they inform me). Charmian Hearne at Macmillan deserves thanks and has, once more, been the best of editors to work both for and with, as has Julian Horner; I would also like to thank John Smith at Macmillan, whose help has always been invaluable and whom it has been a pleasure to work with over the last few years. I would also like to extend my warmest thanks to Nita and Jim Kincaid, whose enthusiastic and often comic discussion one sunny afternoon, in a place as unlike London as it's possible to get, helped me to see the shape of this project. I should also like to thank Peter Ackroyd for his generosity and for confirming all my own most cherished prejudices concerning London.

It cannot be often that a book is dedicated to two people six thousand miles apart, who have never met; this one is, and I hope they'll not mind sharing (knowing them as I do I know they won't). *Writing London* is dedicated therefore with affection to Jim Kincaid, who has taught me more than I can ever acknowledge *or* repay (and in so generous a fashion), and to John Abercrombie, who introduced me to architectural theory in the first place, who has maintained humour and scepticism ever since, and *despite* the fact that he prefers Paris. . . .

An earlier, shorter version of the Dickens chapter appeared in *Victorian Identities: Social and Cultural Formations in Nineteenth-Century Literature*, ed. Ruth Robbins and Julian Wolfreys (Macmillan, 1996); the author gratefully acknowledges the publishers' permission to reproduce that material in this book.

JULIAN WOLFREYS

Introduction:
imagining London or,
Rainbird was sure of it

Now let me call back those who introduced me to the city.
Walter Benjamin

London must ever have a great illustrative and suggestive
value ... it is the single place in which most readers, most
possible lovers, are gathered together.
Henry James

I saw and felt London at last.
Charlotte Brontë

In 1862, at a point shortly after which this book concludes, Charles
Baudelaire asks a rhetorical question in the dedication to Arsène
Houssaye which prefaces *Le spleen de Paris*:

> Quel est celui de nous qui n'a pas, dans ses jours d'ambition,
> rêvé le miracle d'une prose poétique, musicale sans rythme et
> sans rime, assez souple et assez heurtée pour s'adapter aux
> mouvements lyriques de l'âme, aux ondulations de la rêverie,
> aux soubresauts de la conscience?

> Which of us has never imagined, in his more ambitious moments,
> the miracle of a poetic prose, musical though rhythmless and
> rhymeless, flexible yet strong enough to identify with the lyri-
> cal impulses of the soul, *the ebbs and flows of revery*, the pangs
> of conscience?

He then responds immediately to this question in the following
manner:

3

C'est surtout de la fréquentation des villes énormes, c'est du croisement de leurs innombrables rapports que naît cet idéal obsédant.

The notion of such an obsessive ideal has its origins above all in *our experience of the life of great cities, the confluence and interactions of the countless relationships within them.*[1] (emphases added)

The shift between question and answer, call and response, is instructive. From reflecting in an abstract fashion on the desires of the artistic imagination, Baudelaire locates the very idea of an implicitly *modern* poetic prose not in the artist but rising out of the experience of the life of cities. The cities transform the artist as s/he becomes the creative conduit. In that phrase, the undulations (or 'ebbs and flows', as translator Francis Scarfe has it) of reverie, there is caught and anticipated what has subsequently become something of a commonplace image in the urban text. Yet Baudelaire brings together in a prose that is both musical and poetic, though rhythmless and rhymeless, the intimate sense of the spirit of the modern metropolitan space, which it is the purpose of this study to pursue.

Writing London is, of course, not merely confined to a study of more or less 'poetic prose', but also to the performance of London in poetry and essays during the first half of the nineteenth century. What Baudelaire captures here for me is a comprehension of the city space beyond the merely real or everyday. Reality and its representation are not my concerns here. The 'reality' of London which this study seeks to open to its readers, is a reality beyond the experience of the empirical and quotidian. Even though these are in part inscribed in the texts with which we are concerned, the texts of the writers here considered are read as translating and transforming the real and the everyday beyond themselves. The London of this book is, if not a sublime site, then at least a *hyperreality*. The texts which are herein analysed are read in their efforts to inscribe a sense of the city, instead of merely recording a representation.

Thus 'London', as it is understood here, is not a place as such, even though we may say that the London being read here is that which *takes place* in the texts in question. The structures of the city which the texts perform are read as part of a continuous constitution of the city, as writers strive to come to terms with a city quite unlike any other on the planet in the first fifty or so years of the last century. The meaning of the city is not (yet) fixed in place, either *for* or *by* the writers in question. London does not define itself in its naming. Its performance defies the absolutism implied in the pronominal act, even as the proper name quite improperly signs and guarantees an excess beyond what the proper name can signify. For William Blake, Anna Laetitia Barbauld, Percy Bysshe Shelley, Lord Byron, Thomas De Quincey, Friedrich Engels, William Wordsworth and Charles Dickens, the city has meaning as unexpected event which takes place constantly. The city is reformed with each encounter. London for these writers and in their texts is a taking-place of mystery, mutability, catachresis and ineffability. Their acts of writing respond differently in every example. What they share, though, is a development of a heterogeneous rhetoric and poetics of the modern city which has continued to impress itself as the often spectral *imprimatur* of the city on writers from the 1850s to the present day, some of whom are quoted and discussed in brief or in passing in this introduction, and given further consideration in the afterword to *Writing London*. Given this, it might be well to suggest that this introduction is really, and already, an 'afterword' which reverses the movement of history in order to bring its readers to the point of departure, William Blake. My 'Afterword' may well come to seem like an introduction, if not an invitation to reacquaint oneself with the city in all its strangeness.

I have already suggested, and will continue to suggest throughout *Writing London*, that London understood through the writings in question is perceived as a modern city. London of the nineteenth century assumes a central importance to the world and in the minds not only of its inhabitants but of people everywhere. It is not the purpose of this study to pursue a sociological analysis of the city, thereby fixing its range of meanings within a given cultural context and historical moment. Certainly, London becomes more than merely 'real' in the minds of the writers in question, and, because of this it assumes retrospectively – when read at the end of the twentieth century – a quality of 'supermodernity', to use Marc Augé's phrase.[2]

'Supermodernity' avoids the temporal progessiveness inherent in '*post*modern', and the problems attendant in such a term, while hinting at a possible or imagined quasi-transcendentality (much as I have tried to intimate in my use of the term 'hyperreality', above). Augé defines 'supermodernity' through a reading of the function of airports, shopping malls, supermarkets, motorways and a host of other late twentieth-century urban phenomena, describing these as 'non-places'. The non-place is a place of transition and transformation, to which we have been, and continue to be, drawn. For Augé, there is something more and more in the non-place which is inexhaustible in terms of comprehension and analysis. Non-places are composed of a certain play of images. Yet, as Augé warns, in rejecting a postmodern epistemology:

> It would be a mistake to see this play of images as nothing but an illusion (a postmodern form of alienation). The reality of a phenomenon has never been exhaustively understood by analysing its determinants. What is significant in the experience of non-place is its power of attraction, inversely proportional to territorial attraction, to the gravitational pull of place and tradition.[3]

The literature of London in the early nineteenth century has not yet become simply a unified text, much less a work, where the principal purpose of the city is to provide a backdrop to action, a stage on which action happens to take place, or a key to the moods, psyches or personalities of particular characters. While the writing of the authors read here does partake of such uses of the city, it also does much more. In its play of images it maps the condition of the city onto the text itself, so that the text assumes in a variety of ways the shape, the contours, the architecture and the 'ebbs and flows' of the city. The writing of the urban text is thus a response to a projection coming from some other place. The writing of the city is at once real and more than real. The city text imposes on the reader a reconsideration of what is meant by the 'real'.

Augé's description of supermodern phenomena is, in this case, an accurate registration for the ways in which London is understood in the period in question. The 'London' in which we are interested cannot be exhaustively understood, to use his words, because the attempts to write the city's sites and spaces carry in them an understanding, at the level of grammar, syntax, rhetoric and enunciation – in short at all levels of form – of the excess beyond comprehension which is the modern city of London. London is iterable, it returns as never quite itself, each and every time providing a singular example. Augé's theorization of supermodernity gives us a key to understanding how London is neither merely illusion nor merely real. It hovers beyond the possibility of simple representation, but is never yet reducible to a series of simulacra. 'London' does not name a location or base. Instead it names a multiplicity of events, chance occurrences and fields of opportunities. The significant 'power of attraction, inversely proportional to territorial attraction, to the gravitational pull of place and tradition' named by Augé, is that very same attraction which first drew Charles Baudelaire in his considera-tion of Paris, one hundred and thirty years before Augé. It is the 'impulse of the soul', as Baudelaire puts it, which the writers considered in this study recognize in their different fashions, in their attempted responses to, and poetic considerations of, the 'confluence and interactions of the countless relationships' which the city performs.

The city is therefore simultaneously a performance and gener-ator of the architecture and poetics of 'writing London'. In assigning the city a history we overwrite a past onto what has always been a city in the act of becoming, a city always in the process of self-transformation. Such an overwriting erases the transformative becoming-modern, the city's constant movement towards a future which is yet to arrive. To the extent that this will to modernity has been forgotten, we might say that we have lost the means of access to London which the texts in this study provide. We have lost the city codes, to use a phrase of Hana Wirth-Nesher's.[4]

Richard Jefferies, the late-nineteenth-century agricultural essayist and novelist, understands the code when he writes:

> London is the only *real* place in the world. The cities turn toward London as young partridges run to their mother. The cities know that they are not real. They are only houses and wharves, and bricks and stucco; only outside. The minds of all men in them, merchants, artists, thinkers, are bent on London. Thither they go as soon as they can. San Francisco thinks London; so does St. Petersburg.
>
> Men amuse themselves in Paris; they work in London. Gold is made abroad, but London has a hook and line on every napoleon and dollar, pulling the round discs hither. A house is not a dwelling if a man's heart be elsewhere. Now, the heart of the world is in London, and the cities with the simulacrum

of man in them are empty. They are moving images only; stand
here and you are real.[5]

In saying that London is the only *real* place, Jefferies can be read
as suggesting that there is something more than real, something
hyperreal about the capital, hence his emphasis in the first line.
Ordinary reality is the conglomeration of houses, wharves, bricks
and stucco; on the other hand, Jefferies reads London as being
reality + *X*. It is this equation which connects Jefferies in his
comprehension of the city's partial incomprehensibility back to
Baudelaire thirty years earlier, and forward to Marc Augé, a century
later (especially in Jefferies' description of other cities being
composed only of 'simulacrum' and 'moving images').

Reality + *X* : this is the non-conceptual, aprogrammatic term
or equation by which I want to define provisionally the London-
effect on the writers who I read in *Writing London*. Arthur Symons
acknowledges the ineffable expression of London when he writes
that the city was 'for a long time my supreme sensation',[6] or
when he suggests that London 'exists, goes on, and has been
going on for so many centuries', even while it 'makes no display; it is there, as it has come'; London has for Symons an 'atmosphere which makes and unmakes' the city.[7] It is this simultaneity,
the continual rhythm of the city, and the response to that rhythm,
that movement, which can be expressed as *Reality* + *X*. It is that
which informs their texts beyond mere acts of representation or
mimesis; it is that which we need to remember in reading London.

Another person who does remember the condition of London
in relation to the writing of that city is the intriguingly named
Rainbird, encountered by Jonathan Raban in his travels across
the United States of America. This character, whose name seems
to invite Dickensian comparisons, made the following comments
to Raban, which the author transcribed:

In 1831, when Dickens was 19, London had a population of
1.65 million, and there was a relationship (Rainbird was sure
of it) between the demography of the city and the plot of the
19th-century London novel. A city of less than two millions
was big – plenty big enough for people to disappear into it
without a trace for years at a time. It was also small enough to
ensure that chance meetings, coincidences, would continually
happen in it, *unexpectedly and out of context*. Twentieth-century

critics had sometimes complained of the way in which Dickens's plots were kept moving by these surprise encounters, with X and Y suddenly bumping into each other around the next corner. . . . It was various, sprawling, a place full of secrets and dark corners; and yet it was contained . . . *it would fit inside the covers of a book.*[8] (emphases added)

Forgetting London, we are in danger of making the same mistake about the writing of the city, its rhetoric and narrative architectures, as those shadowy critics who complain of what *they* mistake as Dickensian contrivance, rather than understanding – as does Rainbird – that the city dictates its writing. London, simultaneously both big enough and small enough, real and yet more than real; a city where X does not mark the spot, but where X may (or may not) name that which can never quite be described; a city then which, on the one hand, belongs to a book while, on the other hand, can never be determined absolutely by a context, whether historical, factual or cultural.

This book is not then a history of London. To reiterate, it does not pretend to provide a sociological study of the development of London as that development is either 'revealed' or 'represented' in the literature of the first half, roughly speaking, of the nineteenth century. 'London', as considered in this book, is not necessarily the city which one can visit, walk through, inhabit. However, it may be for some readers that 'real' London evokes the 'unreal city'. Hopefully, the question of the 'real' as opposed to the 'unreal' city is a binary distinction which will collapse for the reader in the progress of this study. Instead of making such distinctions and the epistemological frameworks by which they are supported, or relying on empirical evidence, I am concerned with the construction and mediation of a range of phenomena which come to figure London in imaginative writing in the period in question. I look at the ways in which poets, novelists and essayists grapple with the problem of finding new ways of expressing the spirit and the nature of a city which is, for them, a protean, labyrinthine and Babelian site.

In examining the writing of London from William Blake's poem 'London' (c. 1789) to Charles Dickens's *Our Mutual Friend* (1865),

I am not concerned with issues of mimesis or verisimilitude in representation or realism, other than to question such notions as being appropriate to an understanding of the material under consideration. Indeed, most of what I have to suggest about the configuration of the city of London and its environs in nineteenth-century textuality is either implicitly or explicitly anti-realistic (unless the 'real' is comprehended in that 'unreal' fashion of Richard Jefferies). As I hope I have already made clear in this introduction, I do not take the images, figures and tropes to be more or less direct representations of what is out there. Instead I am concerned with offering a series of close readings of the rhetoric of imagining London, the uses to which that rhetoric is put, the forms it takes, and the ways in which such various and diverse rhetoric can be read as allowing us access to a greater comprehension of 'what London feels like', 'how London creates an impression on the mind', rather than 'what London looks like', to rely momentarily on such imprecise phrases. To this end I shall be reading the various texts considered from a range of theoretical positions, all of which aim to dispel the possibility of mimetic or realistic interpretation, and offer ways of *explaining* rather than *interpreting* textual representations of London.[9]

These theoretical positions are drawn from literary theory, continental philosophy and various strands of what is termed 'post-structuralism' (principally Jacques Derrida, but also Michel Foucault, and Jacques Lacan, amongst others), Freudian psychoanalysis, and certain areas of architectural theory and writing (the work of Bernard Tschumi, Anthony Vidler, and Peter Eisenmann). Realizing that not all these areas are necessarily compatible, I nevertheless draw on them as a way of helping to make visible in the texts in question the formations of London, and also as a way of bringing into focus questions of the purpose behind the very structure of such formations. Assuming mimetic or realist qualities for a prose 'description', we tend to naturalize and normalize the figure as representation, as merely the figural painting of what is supposedly there.

Thus we get drawn into an unquestioning relationship with the text in question while engaging in a curious paradox, whereby the form and content of the so-called primary text becomes, through the act of reading, a secondary or subordinate matter which apparently allows us access to our supposedly true primary subject or object. In Dickens's case this has tended to mean that we merely marvel at the veracity and vitality, the vibrancy of the author's description of a particular area of the city, the site of which we can locate on the map, trace its streets and, even, walk down those selfsame streets, comparing in our minds what we have before us with what the novelist has shown us; either marvelling at the similarity between 'then and now' or lamenting the loss of particular features which 'made that area come alive'. While I have used Dickens as the particular example here (and he is the novelist with whom I conclude, if only because, inevitably, if asked to connect 'London' and 'Literature', we tend to cite Dickens as *the* novelist of London), the same attitude exists when we come to consider other writers in their relationship to the city.

Literary tourism aside however, my purpose in drawing on the various theoretical discourses and models already mentioned is done not so as to reveal the power, the truth, the mastery of 'theory'. Instead my purpose is to show, through theoretically informed arguments, how each writer makes manifest a quite different London from his or her contemporaries; how each novelist, while drawing on similar notions, ideologies, topographies, architectural models, works with an effort to map London in a manner which unfolds, folds back into view for our comprehension, the contemporary networks of power, discourse, ideology, belief, doxa, all of which flow through the sites and locations of London and which are as much a part of London's constructedness, the structuration of its structures, as are squares, streets, parks, offices, houses, names.

For example, William Blake figures London through acts of reiteration, inversion, re-naming. In reading Blake for these acts of writing the city, this study draws on the work of Jacques Derrida (perhaps more explicitly and directly in Chapter 1, than elsewhere in *Writing London*). This is not to suggest that Blake is a 'deconstructionist' *avant la lettre* (as I discuss at the beginning of Chapter 1), but to facilitate a reading always focused on the act of writing itself. Theories of writing such as those proposed by Derrida make possible an understanding of the differences in the 'representations' of London between writers in a manner which allows us insights, not only into the context in which the texts are produced, but also into the ways in which London, as an imaginary site, serves an integral part in the construction of the narrative itself. 'London' comes to be seen to be integral to the shaping of narrative, determining and mediating both the rhetoric which composes the narrative and the shape which the narrative eventually assumes. And a simpler, even obvious point (yet one worth making): we would not assume similarity in the theoretical terrains of, say, Michel Foucault, Pierre Macherey, Bernard Tschumi and Jacques Derrida, even though there are discernible overlaps in the contexts of their discourses, as I have already stressed; so why should we assume that the London of William Blake is necessarily the same London as that of Charles Dickens, Thomas De Quincey or Lord Byron? Of course we don't, or shouldn't, unless we merely read London as the stage on which narrative is enacted (which, arguably, is much easier to do with Henry James, Joseph Conrad, Conan Doyle, Oscar Wilde, and George Gissing, for example, than the authors with whom this study is concerned). Another problem is that, in reading these writers, we may have a tendency to conflate the symptoms of London as revealed in the various texts with a finitely knowable London, a real $(- X)$ London, a historical London.

London is diverse, rich and strange, estranging and alien; real and yet hyperreal, babbling and yet ineffable, apocalyptic and yet also banal, quotidian *and* exotic at one and the same time. What can we ever say about London except that there is always more to say about London? We can never say anything about London which does not fall short of the experience of imagining London as a sensual and sensory plenitude of qualities, such as the ones named above. These qualities and these paradoxes find their register in the writers in question in this study; and it is the purpose of this study, then, to bring back such qualities, such ephemera and esoterica, to show them alongside of the everyday, the mundane, the brutal. To borrow a formula of Joseph Conrad's, I want to make the reader 'feel' London through this study, to feel it in quite new and strange, hopefully exciting ways. From this feeling emerges a sense that, when one considers the effect which London has on writing in the period which this study considers, that effect has important ramifications for modernist concerns with the city as a fragmentary and mutable space.

Although I do not pursue this thought fully – it perhaps being a consideration for another study – I have come to think in the writing of this book that any consideration of the modernist representation of the city owes much and must return to the writing of London in the early part of the nineteenth century, and that, subsequently, those who write on the development of a modernist aesthetic may have to reconsider the origins of that aesthetic, at least in terms of urban representation and mapping. Indeed, one critic at least has already begun this process in the context of London. In his recent study of Robert Louis Stevenson, Alan Sandison makes claims for Stevenson as modernist or proto-modernist writer, while arguing in the chapter on *Jekyll and Hyde*, that '[t]o those aspects of Stevenson's writing which give it its Modernist cast, there should be added his representation of the city in *Jekyll and Hyde*'.[10] Citing Malcolm Bradbury's assessments of the city and the subject and discussing both Gustave Doré's etchings and illustrations and the Baudelairean *flâneur*, Sandison puts forward a convincing case.[11] He does, however, own up somewhat grudgingly to the influence of Dickens on Stevenson's representation of the city.[12] In doing so, he points towards our own understanding of the city's modernity. Modernity erupts through the very act of writing the city, and the writers which we study engage in rhetorical events of poetic cartography. Such cartography does not reveal the city. Instead it suggests the limits to which mapping can extend, beyond which representation cannot reach.

Let's move back, from 1956 to 1848, with four passages from very different texts. The first is by Sam Selvon:

One grim winter evening, when it had a kind of unrealness about London, with a fog sleeping restlessly over the city and the lights showing not as to blur as if is not London at all but some strange place from another planet, Moses Aloetta hop on a number 46 bus at the corner of Chepstow Road and Westbourne Grove to go to Waterloo to meet a fellar who was coming from Trinidad on the boat-train.[13]

J.B. Priestley comes next:

He found himself staring at the immense panorama of the Pool. Dusk was falling; the river rippled darkly; and the fleet of barges across the way was almost shapeless. There was, however, enough daylight lingering on the north bank, where the black piles and the whitewashed wharf edge above them still stood out sharply, to give shape and character to the water front. Over on the right, the grey stones of the Tower were faintly luminous, as if they had contrived to store away a little of their centuries of sunlight ... two church spires thrust themselves above the blur of stone and smoke and vague flickering lights: one was blanched and graceful ... the other was abrupt and dark .... Then his gaze swept over the bridge to what could be seen beyond .... Lights were flickering on along the wharf, immediately giving the unlit entrances a sombre air of mystery .... Two minutes later, he had gone hooting into the lights and shadows of the city, which sent whirling past the windows a crazy frieze, glimmering, glittering, darkening, of shops, taverns, theatre doors, hoardings, church porches, crimson and gold segments of buses, little lighted interiors of saloon cars, railings and doorsteps and lace curtains, mounds of chocolate, thousands of cigarette packets, beer and buns and aspirin and wreaths and coffins, and faces, faces, more and more faces, strange, meaningless, and without end.[14]

Now, Richard Jefferies once more:

... on, on, the one law of existence in a London street – drive on, stumble or stand, drive on – strain sinews, crack, splinter – drive on; what a sight to watch as you wait amid the newsvendors and bonnetless girls for the 'bus that will not come! Is it real? It seems like a dream, those nightmare dreams in which you know that you must run, and do run, and yet cannot lift the legs that are heavy as lead, with the demon behind pursuing, the demon of Drive-on. Move, or cease to be ....[15]

Finally, a passage from *Mary Barton*:

'Do tell us about London, dear father,' asked Mary, who was sitting at her old post by her father's knee.
    'How can I tell yo a' about it, when I never seed one-tenth of it. It's as big as six Manchesters, they told me .... They're sadly puzzled how to build a house though in London .... For yo see the houses are many on 'em built without any proper shape for a body to live in; some on 'em they've after thought would fall down, so they've stuck great ugly pillars out before

'em. And some on 'em (we thought they must be th' tailor's sign) had getten stone men and women as wanted clothes stuck on 'em. I were like a child, I forgot a' my errand in looking about me'.[16]

These passages serve to illustrate the protean nature of London, along with its enigmatic and baffling qualities (they also register the extent to which novelists and essayists over a hundred year period remain indebted to earlier writers of the city). Each passage speaks of London in a different fashion, yet there is also registered a shared sense between the excerpts of the idiomatic nature of that which the writers attempt to describe, whilst also understanding they cannot put into words that which is London.

Allowing for the Trinidadian idiom, Sam Selvon relies on what is recognizable as an almost Dickensian tone in his mapping of a city simultaneously unreal and yet geographically ascertainable. J.B. Priestley's invocation of the city acknowledges a debt to acts of imagining the city which stretch back from modernism to the beginning of the nineteenth century, with images of juxtaposed light, mobile confusion, immensity, and endless, unorderable detail. As in Byron's *Don Juan* or Dickens's *Oliver Twist*, London is first seen at twilight in all its crepuscular strangeness,[17] and Priestley's prose moves through rhetoric which is identifiably Dickensian or Byronic (or even Conradian) in its descriptions of the dock, the lighting, the plethora of unrelated items and the blur of impressions as the protagonist moves through London in a taxi, recalling Juan's first carriage ride through the streets of the city over one hundred years earlier. Richard Jefferies seemingly anticipates phenomenological concepts of being in his mobile trope of Being-in-the-city. Elizabeth Gaskell uses John Barton's lack of worldly experience to register the incomprehensibility of London, an incomprehensibility which is figured all the more vividly by the comparsion of London with 'six Manchesters', which renders the observer awestruck and childlike, and which does not lessen with familiarity.

These passages, and many others like them, lead us to ask questions which motivate this particular study. From where is such an urban rhetoric generated? How did nineteenth-century writers respond to the capital? How did they mediate its presence as a cultural, political and psychic force within which to situate their narratives? Was the city imaginable or otherwise and, if unim-

aginable, ineffable, how did writers come to terms with attempting to express the inexpressible? Where and how might we locate
provisional departure points for the modern language of the city,
language which is still in use in novels and other writings of the
present day? When reading the multiplicity of forms that the
city comes to take in various texts, the question of what we can
ever know about London from nineteenth-century textuality and
how that textuality constructs and mediates our knowledge today
of what we now call Victorian London seems repeatedly
foregrounded.

A response to such questions might be that we need to be sensitive to the structures informing such images and tropes; in order
to 'sensitize' ourselves, we need to consider new ways of looking at the material in question, moving outside the field of literary studies on occasion. One of the ways this might be effected
is to consider the writing as a form of architecture or topography,
rather than only narrative, for example. The writing of London
in the first sixty years of the last century offers a map of
unknowability, a map which, to paraphrase Jean Baudrillard,
precedes the territory.[18] That the map does precede the territory
suggests that we turn our attention to the ways in which the
map is drawn, rather than trying to see what the map supposedly represents. Understanding this means that we can also
comprehend how a degree of unknowability is put in place already
by the difficulties of the writers in question in finding an adequate
language for their subject, and in order to comprehend this we
must find different ways of reading drawn from different
disciplines.

However, even though, as suggested above, there will be
recourse to various theoretical models, there will most often be a
return to the work of Jacques Derrida and those influenced by
him, either directly or indirectly, whether in the fields of architectural or literary theory. The constant return to Derrida and to
his writings is also a response dictated coincidentally enough by
the very nature of London. This return and response is not only
prompted by the fact that, in the words of Mark Wigley, a 'rhetoric
of the house can be found throughout Derrida's texts without it
ever being their ostensible subject', even though this 'rhetoric of
the house' is itself suggestive for any discussion of urban poetics.[19]
Derrida's work has in recent years become influential amongst
leading architects, architectural theorists and writers; to ignore

his indirect contribution to this discipline and the unexpected interpretations to which this has led, would be to miss much of value for analytical purposes in considering the writing of the city, not least Derrida's complication of the architectural and spatial metaphors of inside/outside. Amongst many things, Derrida has taught us that no reading can be pre-programmed; there can be no theory which does not do violence to that which it reads. Derrida teaches us to await the event of reading, the unpredictable in the text. Writers in the nineteenth century understood the event of London, and responded in their writing of the capital by writing of the city's very unpredictability.

Thus Derrida is returned to, as is London, in order to offer readings alive to the chance encountered in the writing of London, readings not dominated ahead of the event of reading by a carefully worked out theoretical programme or model. This may also help to explain my choice of texts from the sixty-year period to which we turn our attention. It is not that writers such as Henry James, Joseph Conrad, Arthur Conan Doyle, George Gissing, Arthur Morrison, Robert Louis Stevenson or Oscar Wilde might be said to be less 'original' or less 'interesting' writers than Blake, Wordsworth, De Quincey, Engels, Barbauld, Byron, Shelley and, of course, Dickens. It is just that, after Blake and after Dickens, the act of writing the city is to a large degree overdetermined by the experimental forays of the earlier writers. There is readable in these writers' texts a more open-ended sense of adventure and exploration in the act of writing London.

Why should this seem to be the case? In the face of a rapidly changing capital, writers were faced with certain paradoxical situations revolving around centrality and marginality, stasis and metamorphosis, rich and poor, and so on. London as both a real city and a place of the imagination, a symbolic construct always already something other than that which its mere presence indicated, needed a writing necessary to its paradoxes and contradictions. London was distinct from other large English cities in that, while it was a centre of money and power, it was not a manufacturing centre. Thus it was of a different order. It had a cosmopolitan heritage, yet also was a new type of city. Its heritage and tradition emerged out of its constant reinvention and transformation. This combination of newness and inheritance affected the city's planning, development and architecture, along with the ways in which the city came to be mapped out. Pragmatic concerns as to the swift re-establishment of the city as a centre of power after the Fire of London in the seventeenth century meant that Wren's great plans for the co-ordinated and coherent aesthetic model for the city's rebuilding were put on one side. Similarly, in the first years of the nineteenth century the Prince of Wales's plans to have John Nash rebuild the capital so that it rivalled Napoleon's Paris, came only to a limited fruition; the cost proved too great, and so London remained resolutely heterogeneous. The beginnings of the modern, everchanging city may be said to have started with these arbitrary changes of plans, so that London as a static monument to the vision of one man never came into being, unlike Haussmann's Paris.

These changes are perhaps accidentally fortunate for the development of imaginative writing in the nineteenth century, and show the extent to which the real space of the city is intimately connected with the shaping of the writing. Furthermore, physical and geographical concerns, concerns with living areas, domestic spaces, and issues of class, also brought about by chance events, not only had an impact on the city and the lives of its inhabitants, but also suggested new possibilities for writers. The city, having a cultural and historical context, but being always in the process of developing and changing, was fundamentally a *textual* place, a place of non-static intersections, weaves, interconnections, recurring traces and remarkings. As Elizabeth Grosz comments in a theoretical statement about the nature of cities, '[t]he city brings together economic flows and power networks, forms of management and political organization, interpersonal, familial and extra-familial social relations, and the aesthetic/economic organisation of space and place to create a semi-permanent but everchanging built environment or milieu'.[20] It was, as we have already commented, a city of the event, city-as-event, a city always on the way to becoming, but never coming to a standstill. Never finished in its formation, London in the texts being analysed is always readable as antithetically positioned to the closure of narrative. London as both discourse and place of the imaginary flows in and out of, through the various narratives in question, barely containable, even as those narratives flow through the city (at least this is how we are used to reading such novels).

This of course dictates a range of responses, not all of them positive. London fortuitously becomes the space – it names the *taking place* – at the end of the eighteenth century and the beginning of the nineteenth century, where issues of aesthetics, textuality, power, economics and the discourse of class come to be intricately mapped and most powerfully focused in the writing of the period in a particularly forceful fashion. This is not to say that such concerns are not already gathered together in poetry or prose of the eighteenth century. Arguably, one could turn to Pope's *Dunciad Variorum*, commentaries on the city and politics in *The Spectator*, or Smollett's *The Expedition of Humphrey Clinker* for ample evidence of this concatenation of interests. What one notices, however, in texts such as these which engage with the city in the eighteenth century (as distinct from their nineteenth-century counterparts) is that London *can* be visualized, described, depicted and represented, and all of this quite confidently.[21]

On the other hand, it is perhaps the sense of millennial disruption occurring at the end of the eighteenth century which may be said to mark a profound change in sensibility, allied to the immeasurable effects of the French Revolution on the British psyche, which inevitably comes to find itself mediated in the writing of the period, albeit in, at times, highly indirect ways.[22] The issues of ideology, power, and radical social and religious dissent are, of course, inseparable from aesthetic concerns in the writing of William Blake. In William Wordsworth's *The Prelude*, but also in the texts of writers such as De Quincey and Engels, we come to see the concatenation of discourses of the sublime and the outgrowth of terror in the face of urban immensity, the perplexing question of the formation of an urban bourgeois identity in the face of anonymity, the concern over proximity between East and West, rich and poor, and the fear of contamination in both a literal and metaphorical sense because of the connections afforded by sewers, roads, public transport, and so on. Matthew Arnold's focus and concern in his short poem 'West London' is the incursion of a beggar woman into the streets of a more 'fashionable' part of town.[23] She sits within the poem, on the street, making passers-by, the poet and readers alike, uncomfortable, a constant reminder of the proximity of the poverty that the wealthy part of town has helped to create, whether directly or indirectly. Such uneasy proximity is explored increasingly by writers towards the end of the century.

An important aesthetic point which emerges from the study of the representation of London in nineteenth-century writing is that the writers of the nineteenth century, caught up as they are in the myriad ideological and philosophical concerns of their day, produce a range of discursive models for the representation and mediation of the space and architecture of London in the act of writing which has dominated the construction of imagined city spaces within narratives of the twentieth century. Even though the architecture may have changed, especially during the major redevelopments of the 1820s, 1880s and, then again in the late 1950s and 1960s, the writing of the city, its rhetoric and form, has remained dictated by the innovations and experiments of the nineteenth century. We can certainly see this effect in the passages above from Sam Selvon and J.B. Priestley, but we also encounter this in novels by writers such as Muriel Spark in *A Far Cry from Kensington* (1988), Iain Sinclair's *White Chappell, Scarlet Tracings* (1987), *Downriver* (1991), *Radon Daughters* (1994), *Lud Heat and Suicide Bridge* (1975, 1979), and *Lights Out for the Territory* (1996), virtually all the novels of Peter Ackroyd including his most recent, *Milton in America* (1996),[24] Martin Amis's *London Fields* (1989), and Graham Swift's *Last Orders* (1996), which, like Selvon's *The Lonely Londoners*, seems indebted in equal measure to Charles Dickens and James Joyce. *Diamond Geezers*, by Greg Williams (1997), is only the latest London text, as I write, to be haunted by a certain urban trace.[25]

These titles, and many others, celebrate London's unknowability, its hidden recesses and the chance encounters with the other that they suggest, and which Jonathan Raban's Rainbird comments on so astutely. Dickens, of course, adores the idea of a hidden space amidst the uproar. Priestley, already quoted above, utilizes the obscure space in *Angel Pavement* as a non-place (to recall Marc Augé) which may possibly just exist within 'real' London (rather like the wardrobe that leads to Narnia), were we only to notice it, as a disproportionate place of attraction:

> Many people who think they know the City well have been compelled to admit that they do not know Angel Pavement. You could go wandering half a dozen times between Bunhill Fields and London Wall, or across from Barbican to Broad Street Station, and yet miss Angel Pavement. Some of the street maps of the district omit it altogether; taxi drivers often do not even pretend to know it; policemen are frequently not sure; and only the postmen who are caught within half a dozen streets of it are positively triumphant.[26]

Priestley's introduction to his principal setting owes more than a little to Dickens's description of the unlocatability of Todger's in *Martin Chuzzlewit*, even to the detail of the postmen as keepers of the topographical secret. The overarching debt aside, what we see here is the romance of the hidden, the 'arcana' of London being architectural and geographical details of the city itself.

The now neglected novels of Charlotte Riddell from the 1870s and 1880s also celebrate the hidden court, the forgotten square, the unobserved portico, from which romance is waiting to emerge. Take the following passage from her *Mitre Court. A Tale of the Great City*:

> In a courtyard that might well escape the observation of passers-by, entered as it is through an archway of the most unassuming appearance, there stands even to this day an old and most beautiful house.[27]

Or, here is a similar passage from another novel, *George Geith of Fen Court*, two years later:

> Quite close to Fenchurch Street – within a few yards of that noisy and crowded thoroughfare – there lies hidden away as quiet and forsaken-looking a spot as the heart of man need desire to see.[28]

Riddell, like Priestley, finds hidden London within the financial heart of the city itself, opposing the workaday world with the imaginary space necessary for romance and narrative. Arthur Morrison perhaps typifies and subverts the narrative of the imaginary and hidden space in his *A Child of the Jago* (1896), and there are of course documentary works such as *Unknown London, its Romance and Tragedy* by A.T. Camden Pratt (1897), *Unknown London* by Walter George Bell (1920), and *The London Nobody Knows* by Geoffrey Fletcher (1962). The hidden, obscured topography is, it must be remembered, no mere fictional or rhetorical device for the purposes of romance and mystery, terror and the sublime. Obscurity is part of the very fabric of London itself, as the opening of *Bleak House* should remind us, or as we are informed by architectural theorist and historian M. Christine Boyer.

Writing of London in the 1870s, Boyer remarks: 'A haze hung over the horizon of London; smoke belching forth in hydralike fashion from its hundreds of thousands of furnaces. London might have many fine architectural specimens around Hyde Park, or in its Pall-Mall clubs, yet they were *hidden in narrow streets and darkened courts*, isolated in style and character from their structures' (emphasis added).[29] The critic's language in representing historical London cannot but help assume the imaginative register of the nineteenth-century writer. This is a singular feature of Boyer's writing on London, the chapters on other cities never assuming such a tone. The remarkable thing is that, after nearly two centuries of exploration, London still seems to remain a 'dark continent' for novelists, essayists, poets and critics. It is perhaps that London ultimately cannot be expressed; as I suggest in the chapter on Dickens, the city is ineffable, and Charlotte Riddell's apostrophe – 'O City! once interesting beyond all power of speech'[30] – still captures the spirit of the city despite the novelist's feeling that all that was interesting is now torn down, even though the hidden squares and 'darkened courts' may perhaps hold what we most desire: an anachronistic curiosity, a delight out of time suggesting the eternal.

This last comment suggests one reason why London is written as it is, with all its sense of ineffability and secrecy. We only have to recall Dickens's earthquake-like transformation of North London by the incursion of the railroads in *Dombey and Son*, to realize that the city was being made over as fast as writers could register their sense of what was often passing before their very eyes. The imaginary space, the unknowable architecture, intimates and in so doing preserves the spirit and the secret of the city. What once had been, now mapped otherwise in writing, may yet come again, if the spirit is charted in all its unpredictable manifestations. There is, then, often a sense of hope and longing in the act of writing the city and imagining its spaces and buildings; a hope and longing rooted not only in nostalgia, but arising out of a sense of the spectral quality of eternal city, to which 'real' buildings are merely incidental. Very few writers respond with unalloyed animosity to the Capital. Even those – De Quincey, Wordsworth, Engels – who respond with anxiety and fear, are also inextricably caught up in the motions of desire and awe which the city generates.

The chapters which follow are in roughly chronological order. This is not to suggest a progression or linear narrative, for neither necessarily exists. Nor should it be implied that I am seeking some sort of continuity. Indeed, in concluding with Dickens, I began to get the sense of returning to Blake, to an understanding of Blake as being, along with Dickens, one of the most 'modern' or 'contemporary' of the city's biographers and cartographers. Dickens's and Blake's texts figure for this reader of the city two complex aspects of a particular spirit and energy which the city projects. Their creative responses change the stakes for representing or imagining the city forever, after they have written and we have read (see the Afterword, below). Their contribution to the rhetorical urban register may be taken as somewhat analogous to the changes brought about in musical composition by J.S. Bach and Arnold Schoenberg. After Blake, after Dickens, the city can never be read or written in the same manner. Although the 'after' in phrases such as 'after Blake' and 'after Dickens' implies a temporal moment later than the instance of a supposedly 'first' writing and reading, I am thinking here of 'after' in different senses, senses which Nicholas Royle alerts us to in his discussion of his own title, *After Derrida*.[31] Such possible senses or meanings are 'in the manner or imitation of' or 'in agreement with', or 'in search of', all of which Royle pursues in all their problematic possibilities. Thus it is possible to read Henry James, Joseph Conrad, J.B Priestley, Charlotte Brontë in the 'London' chapter of *Villette*, Sam Selvon, Peter Ackroyd, along with the other authors so far quoted or mentioned (as well as many others), who read and write either in the manner or imitation of Blake and/or Dickens, or whose own writing to a greater or lesser extent goes in search of Blake/Dickens through the act of writing the city.

If I take liberties with chronology this occurs in places where this is dictated by a sense of an abiding and shared response to London, and a return of particular interests in the city from writers who are appreciably dissimilar. This is most immediately apparent in Chapter 3. This chapter discusses the different manifestations of anxiety felt by Thomas De Quincey, William Wordsworth, and Friedrich Engels. Anxiety in the texts of these writers is approached by a theoretical turn to essays by Freud on anxiety and the development of phobias. De Quincey, Engels, and Wordsworth are not the only writers to feel anxious in the face of the capital's immensity and its powers (as they perceive those

powers) of alienation; but they are most typical in their registration of perplexity and fear of a certain sense of anxiousness at
the possible loss of personal identity. Anxiety is as important a
response to the city as wonder and is found in equal measure
throughout late-nineteenth-century, modernist and post-war urban
texts. If Blake and Dickens set the scene for the miraculous, then
De Quincey, Wordsworth and Engels make available to writers
and readers a recognizably modern monstrous urban tone.[32]

When beginning work on this book, I had originally intended
that it should be concerned with those writers narrowly conceived
as being Victorian, but, for the reasons outlined above and
considered in more detail in the various chapters of this study, I
changed my focus to examine the writing of the city in the first
half of the nineteenth century, which necessitated including
William Blake, Percy Bysshe Shelley, Lord Byron, Anna Laetitia
Barbauld, and extending – at least through the gestures of this
Introduction, and the Afterword – my reading of the imagined
city into the twentieth century, as a means of prefacing this study.
Blake's writing offers the reader interested in the response to
London one appropriate, though admittedly arbitrary, departure
point into the writing of the city, because it can be said arguably
to break quite radically with all prior urban representations in
the eighteenth century. With Blake, though each in obviously
different ways, Barbauld, Shelley and Byron encounter the city
in fragments, in ruins even, rather than seeking to convey the
whole picture, or to employ the city as mere backdrop, either for
the development of narrative or for the revelation of psychologi-
cal or characterological trait. London for the writers of the nineteenth century is no longer merely a sounding board or distorted
mirror in which might be seen reflected certain aspects of 'human
nature' already comprehended; instead we see and read responses
to the city as itself composed from a range of phenomena. The
city in the first part of the nineteenth century is written as a
series of subjects (always plural) always in excess of expression
and comprehension.

Again, when beginning *Writing London*, I had thought of
concentrating on the representation of architecture in novels and
essays on London. Given the unknowable nature of London as
expressed in many of its narratives, however, I soon found that
this also would be a restricted task. As I argue below in the chapter
on Dickens, the idea of architecture implies a knowable, finite,

often monumental and static structure or form. This very idea is deconstructed by the act of writing the city, according to the city's dictates. Writing London is not writing Paris, for reasons both obvious and obscure. There does not exist either a Zola or Balzac, or even a Simenon, to give us the definite sense of the city, despite what is conventionally known and assumed about Charles Dickens and his representation of the city. It is a somewhat obvious observation, of course, to say that when the reader encounters Paris in, say, Zola or Balzac, the reader is likely to be able to identify the location exactly. The same cannot be said of the representation of London in the novels, narratives and poetry of the nineteenth century. In purely mimetic terms, the writing of London may be said to 'fail', if by this we might imagine a writing which accurately records the material city. Yet, I want to suggest that the writers of the city of London are not merely documentarists; or rather, their writing, responding to the nature of London, cannot help but be transformed into something other than a mimetic or realistic medium. Representational verisimilitude is not an issue in the writing of London. Instead, it is important to recognize that the writing of modern London is a writing which acknowledges what Carol Bernstein calls 'the transformation of city into text. The city becomes the scene of writing . . .'.[33] This in turn leads, quoting Bernstein again, to 'new correspondences between urban and verbal creation . . . the artist's capacity to insert himself into a city now conceived of as a text'.[34]

Instead of writing about architecture, then, I came to see writing as a form of architecture which incorporates and connects presence and absence, inside and outside, building and space; and that architecture I understand, in the words of architect and theorist Bernard Tschumi, as being 'always the expression of a lack, a shortcoming, a noncompletion'.[35] This is not to say that the novels, poems, and essays which form the basis for this book are incomplete; far from it. What they describe, what they represent, what they imagine, however, is the sense of incompletion, the unendingness, the ineffability and lack which is always at the heart of London and any faithful attempt to represent or imagine it. Thus, in the most unimaginable and surprising ways, I found that the writing of the city was also an architectural tracing of the city, at least in the sense of 'architecture' as defined by Tschumi above, and other architects and architectural theorists discussed in particular chapters. This way of talking about architecture – and perhaps, by extension, literature – may be, to borrow and paraphrase Tschumi's own words on the subject, intolerable to those 'who want to objectify the subject'.[36] But London refuses objectification due to its multiple personalities, amongst which is the labyrinthine.

Tschumi identifies the labyrinth as a resistant figure typical of a city such as London: 'a total revelation of the Labyrinth is historically impossible because no one point of transcendence in time is available. One can participate in and share the fundamentals of the Labyrinth, but one's perception is only part of the Labyrinth as it manifests itself. One can never see it in totality, nor can one express it. One is condemned to it and cannot go outside and see the whole'.[37] It is precisely this condition which Dickens celebrates. It is precisely this labyrinthine quality which Mr Pecksniff finds so intolerable and unnerving, as do Wordsworth, De Quincey, and Engels. It is the feeling caught in a phrase from H.G. Wells's *Love and Mr Lewisham*, where Clapham Junction, in South London, is described as 'a hazy bristling mystery of roofs and chimneys, gliding chains of lit window carriages and vague vistas of streets'.[38] The labyrinthine architectural, topographic nature of the city space and site resists mastery and totalization, involved as it is, and emerging from, mystifying, semi-obscured fragments and mobile figures.

To write about the city faithfully one must write on its terms, according to its non-presentable order and responding to the city as it appears to dictate to you, rather than seeking to master it. The city cannot be reduced to its name. This is recognized in the opening word of *Bleak House*, 'London' (see Chapter 4). Giving the name names all that cannot be spoken, except by indirection. The city cannot be reduced to a single order or objectified definition. In order to see and remember the city, in order to read and write it, one must be inside its text, which, by definition means that one cannot read it from the outside and close the book on the city. There is no structural model or order, no programme which can define London as an entirety. One can have the illusion of order with New York or with Paris, because of geometric regularity or the stateliness and symmetry of Haussmann's conception. But London remains unknowable and ineffable, and it is this which leads to the textual form equivalent to Kant's mathematical sublime (see Chapter 3). In this quality, only Los Angeles today comes close to the celebratory disorder and disunity of London. And even then it 'fails' in a certain manner because the often elevated presence of freeways apportions and ghettoizes, carving up the city according to imposed class- and race-determined boundaries, financial interests and political concerns. With London, however, the act of representation becomes swallowed up in its own efforts, like the snake eating its own tail on the Sealy Tomb in St Mary's, Lambeth (see the photograph of the snake in the photo-essay included in this book).[39] As Neil Hertz puts it in writing of Book VII of William Wordsworth's *The Prelude*, representation becomes subsumed by what one seeks to represent: 'representation comes to seem like the very pulse of the machine'.[40]

The city then takes over acts of representation, determining the various modes of production and performing the city otherwise. Writing the city becomes, in Raphael Samuel's words, a theatre of memory[41] in which takes place, over and over, the struggle for power. The city itself, as well as being an improper stage, also offers a barely comprehensible range of images, a Symbolic Disorder over which no single power structure can dominate. The act of writing in all its textuality, all its reference and allusion, testifies to the resistance which the modern city signifies, a resistance which affirms its own nature and which haunts the act of writing about the urban space and experience with specific reference to London. I use the metaphor of 'haunting' with good reason, not least because of the concomitant rise of the modern city and the sense of the uncanny, first noted by Walter Benjamin.[42] For London, from the beginning of the nineteenth century to the present day, presents writers with an always unanswerable question, asked in another context by Bernard Tschumi: 'How to assert the character of a city at the very point where it negates itself?'[43] This study does not hope – or pretend – to answer the unanswerable. What I do hope to show, instead, are the ways in which the writers in question in this book manage to articulate this question in a variety of ways. They do so, I believe, in ways which are as unexpected as the experience of London itself; in ways which acknowledge a certain 'truth' of London given voice by Henry James, who, talking of the weather – which often amounts to talking of the city, as Dickens knew – said, with a telling accuracy that '[i]t is bad for the eyesight, but excellent for the image'.[44]

1

Blake's London • London's Blake: an Introduction to the Spirit of London or, on the way to Apocalypse

The ever fluctuating colour[,] the spectral pigmies, rolling, flying, leaping among the letters . . . made the page seem to move and quiver within its boundaries.

Samuel Palmer

. . . Albions city . . .

If thought is life . . .

William Blake

Beginning a study of the ways in which London is written and read in the first half of the nineteenth century, we hope the reader will indulge us for a moment if we consider the first part of this chapter's title, as a way into what follows. This is not merely a self-referential gesture, but is dictated out of an attempt to comprehend the ways in which William Blake writes himself into his vision of London, as a figure in writing, and as a figure inscribed by the condition of the city itself, as that condition is perceived by the poet. As the second of the three epigraphs to this chapter suggests, Albion is not only a place but also a personification, if not a person, and for Blake that person is as much himself as another or the other of, within his identity, as readers of Blake will understand. So, to the title:

Blake's London ● London's Blake.

- The grammar of this is strange; it estranges even as it recirculates its terms, doesn't it?
Yes, it opens the reader onto undecidability, rather than appearing to do some of the reader's work for her, or him.
- How then might we read this strange and estranging phrase?

We might propose, given that bullet point, that the phrases are, if not identical then at least endowed with a certain symmetry, a fearful symmetry even, given the play of meaning, which is also marked – as are all symmetries – by displacement and inversion, by the haunting of a meaning yet to come; on its way but not yet having arrived. And what we read from this symmetry is that Blake's (sense of) London is also informed by Blake having a sense of belonging to, being part of, London, in the most intimate sense, as though the city had written on his body. This is then reversible. If Blake is part of London, and part of our sense of what it means to imagine the city, then Blake's London is, perhaps, our London also even though it is peculiarly his.

　'London' is in this double context of Blake-writing and reading-Blake what Jacques Derrida has described as 'that something, "X", which does not have a stable meaning or reference, [but which] becomes indispensable in a certain finite, but open, context, during a certain period of time, for a certain number of actors'.[1] The lack of stable meaning or reference in Blake is not restricted to the writing of the city, as is well known by Blake scholars, although we may say that the writing of the city takes on an emblematic condition for Blake's writing in general as a practice without predetermined form. If the event of reading Blake's later poems such as *Jerusalem* is an encounter with what Vincent De Luca calls a 'wall of words',[2] that wall is curiously mutable, for all its materiality. It is perhaps that the difficult form of Blake's 'wall of words' can enclose us, as well as closing us off from access to certain meanings or areas. Like being in the city itself, we can lose ourselves at any moment and yet be next to the very location we had sought. It is as if, caught up in the intertext of city and writing, site and citation (*sitation?*), we find ourselves within what David Wellbery terms in another context the 'inadvertent traces and remainders of cultural production'[3] which, though legible, are not wholly comprehensible. The potential multiplicity of meanings is simultaneously a sublime resistance to mapping and yet a strangely familiar, if not knowable topography. The labyrinth of the city translated through signs transforms cartography into cryptography. Thus comprehending the nature of Blake's London is analogous to the experience of looking at Blake's texts.

This tension or paradox is noted in the first epigraph to this chapter by Samuel Palmer, Blake's disciple and friend.[4] Palmer's 'reading' of the material text is instructive. We see and understand through Palmer's eyes and memory that the page 'seemed to move and quiver within its boundaries'. At once this is both a response to Blake's text and an implicit acknowledgement of the experience of 'reading' London, specifically, though not exclusively, Blake's London. The city, though having definite and definable bounds, all of which are traceable on a map, can have a powerfully disorienting effect on us when we are immersed in its weaving passages. Like the page and the book, the city has both stable referents and locations and vertiginous traces. Blake's encounter with the city effects a transformative textual production.

This transformative quality is in some ways similar to the transformative critiques of Derrida's writing, where a text is not so much read as it is performed otherwise.[5] Such an understanding of Blake's text and its reconfiguring of or indebtedness to the urban space is not to imply any simple correlation between the texts of Blake and the thought of Derrida, any more than is the introduction of Derrida above a suggestion that we read Blake in a particular fashion. We are not trying to find here what Dan Miller has called 'the critical path . . . which finds deconstructive motifs in Blake's poetry or [show] . . . how Blake anticipates Derrida . . . . [A] reading of this sort would only relapse into thematism, which is exactly not the purpose of deconstruction'.[6] Blake and Derrida are brought together in this chapter (as are other writers and Derrida in subsequent chapters) because both writers may be read as proscribing thematization, whether implicitly or explicitly. Both can be read as desiring the avoidance of the programme. For Blake the figure of London provides that chance. It happens to name that which cannot be programmed but which offers a field of opportunity for the *aprogrammatic* writer. The meeting of Derrida and Blake is to allow these writers to 'meet on the way', in the words of Simon Critchley,[7] as a means to explore what we perceive as a shared resistance to thematics or conceptualization. Blake and Derrida can be read in this chapter as happening to meet on the way in the figure of London, where the relationship to the other is explored without the designation of a final location or meaning for London.

Perhaps (and, for me, most importantly) London provides the opportunity for Blake to pursue the political: the politicization of the city's mapping; the radical politicization of verse and the politicization of Blake *in* London. What Blake may be said to produce is what I have described elsewhere as both an other politics and a *politics of the other*, performing for us the other within the identity of politics. Blake's texts may be seen to transform political thought as such in conventionally defined ways through a production of the aporetic within political discourse, that about which political discourse is traditionally silent. Rather than retreating from political engagement, as some critics have suggested (see my discussion of Marilyn Butler's critique, below), Blake 'awakens politicization', to use a phrase of Derrida's. Through London, Blake grants 'us the space necessary . . . to think the political'[8] as an act of writing which places the subject in the necessary place – London, thereby creating the potential to think of the political as taking place. Such location is strategically necessary to the rewriting of the subject and as the deconstructive gesture which avoids the traps and gaps of conventional political thought at the end of the eighteenth century and the beginning of the nineteenth. The deconstructive move occurs in the rewriting of London, from the poem 'London' to *Jerusalem* and *Milton*.

It is this trajectory which interests us here. With this in mind, we might want to take these introductory suggestions on the title further, forcing the reading only just a little, and using those possessive apostrophes as hooks on which to turn the meanings against the grain. We might usefully wish to read the phrase in the following manner:

Blake *is* London ● London *is* Blake.

This still doesn't solve the problem of meaning for us, although it does now impose a new grammatical topography which alters the sense of those reiterated terms, Blake, London. Is Blake London? Is London Blake? Most immediately, is there perhaps a 'personification' or an imagination on Blake's part of the city as a figure named for and after the city it – he – walks? We have already proposed a tentative answer to this question. Those familiar with Blake's later poems are aware that the answer to this question is 'yes'. This raises a further question in relation to the issue of politicization, which we take to be at work constantly in Blake's writing, however obliquely: to what extent does Blake see himself – if at all – as this other figure, as the *figure of the other*? Is London, in fact, and in writing, in the imaginary topography of Blake's London, the figure of the other for Blake? Is it Blake's other, coming through Blake to write the city as always other than itself? Blake's writing of the city in the early 1800s disturbs all received opinion about London, while also disturbing the idea or discourse of forms of political power which are based on a fixed and stable meaning for 'London'. Blake's text remaps and reimagines London and the idea of the city in quite startling ways which force us to reconsider the 'Four-fold city eternal'.

Any study wishing to consider London cannot exclude William Blake, therefore. Blake is, along with Turner and Dickens, 'one of the great artists of London', as Blake's most recent biographer, Peter Ackroyd, has put it.[9] Furthermore, his sense of and feeling for the city is quite unlike any other writer's, even though many are indebted to him, and we could trace his influence on the writing of London in numerous places, were that the project at hand. Blake's London is recognizably of its moment, while simultaneously knowable as a 'modern' city. Certainly it reaches in all its paradoxical being forward to the end of the nineteenth century to haunt the words of Henry James, who calls London 'a great grey Babylon [which] easily becomes, on its face, a garden bristling with an immense illustrative flora'.[10] James's garden of illustrative flora is highly suggestive itself of Blake's Edenic and so-called apocalyptic verse and etchings, while the image of Babylon is, of course, apposite, given Blake's revelation of the multiplicity of languages within language. If London for Blake *is* the eternal city however, then eternity is not analogous with unending, unchanging sameness, but with flux, flow, change and movement. It is precisely through the workings of displacement and inversion, along with the iterable seriality out of which Blake writes London that this city is unfolded as the eternal city, already there awaiting Blake's *cartocryptography*. Blake's London is modern precisely because its vision pushes at the limits of knowability and comprehension. No mere knowledge of London streets and places will ever allow us to 'know' London, and Blake acknowledges this throughout his performances of the city in 'London' from *Songs of Innocence and Experience,* in *Milton,* and in *Jerusalem.*[11]

And Blake's vision of London is modern because, as Peter Ackroyd points out, Blake's understanding of the city is 'preoccupied with light and darkness in a city that is built in the shadows of money and power'; Blake's is an art 'entranced by the scenic and spectacular in a city that is filled with the energetic display of people and institutions . . . [Blake] is often preoccupied with the movement of crowds and assemblies . . . if Blake understood the energy and variety of London, he was continually aware of its symbolic existence through time'.[12] London is thus central to Blake's art, as much as is his knowledge of the arcana of the Old Testament, and his knowledge of the dissenting religious and radical groups of his period.[13] Furthermore, we may suggest that his understanding of the city's spaces and shapes is as much architectural and topographic, as it is visual, given his own knowledge of spatial layout and relationships, first learned as an apprentice to architectural engraver James Basire.[14] It is then not going too far to suggest that to begin understanding Blake we should begin by attempting to understand London as a textual and constructed form, a form of writing no less. For London marks Blake's identity as much as Blake remarks his own perception of London. This chapter attempts to introduce the vision of London in Blake's work. It does not presume to offer a thorough reading of Blake. A rigorous study of *Jerusalem* alone would constitute a lifetime's work, if not more, as would a thorough reading of *Milton,* and it is with the knowledge of the immensity of Blake's work that I approach the London of these poems, without seeking to make larger claims for Blake's work as a whole. Blake is that writer in whose texts we encounter most forcefully both the alterity of the city and what Arthur Symons called in an essay on London 'the poetry of cities'.[15] Such writing effectively doubles the city, responding to its already spectral status, a condition which is irreducible through writing to any simple 'mimetologism'.[16] Blake's London is, to recall a neologism of Derrida's, profoundly 'idiophantasmatic'.[17] This term, invoking simultaneously the idiomatic, the ideological and the phantasm or spectre, expresses precisely that to which Blake responds in his appreciation of the city text, as he seeks to write the city otherwise, defying simple definition through the singular, the idiomatic, while addressing the issue of the contest of ideologies within London.

It is precisely over the question of the idiomatic/ideological matrix that I turn to Marilyn Butler's reading of Blake. In *Romantics, Rebels and Reactionaries* Butler offers convincing arguments for remembering the historical context of European revolution, and domestic radicalism and religious dissent, for much of Blake's writing.[18] Butler, discussing Blake's 'deliberate naïveté' and his constant recourse to 'models of the primal' (one of which, we may suggest, is the model of London itself),[19] argues that Blake's texts 'emanate at a particular time from a society which believes it is seeing the end of the old world and the coming of a new dawn'.[20] Or, as Steven Goldsmith puts it, in summarizing the critical tendency to accept Blake's text as apocalyptic: there is an 'understanding that Blake is a political poet whose interests coincide with those of the late eighteenth-century democratic revolutions'.[21] This model of irrevocable change put forward by Butler and others, similar in its perceptions of cultural upheaval to Michel Foucault's analysis of an epistemic shift at the end of the eighteenth century concerning the power of representation in *The Order of Things* (discussed below in Chapter 2), allows us a possible means of comprehending how Blake's vision of London comes to be formed.

Blake's London is simultaneously real and unreal, it derives from and reinvents a multiplicity of millenarian discourses of the period. It builds London out of the indirect translation of radical oppositional politics and nonconformist discourse, while attempting to 'unbuild' the mainstream manifestations of London's political power. Certain material conditions in the capital as a result of economic and political policies come to find themselves figured next to apocalyptic and sublime mythological remappings of the city as an imaginary site for the rebuilding of Jerusalem. Real locations are named and doubled, as other than they are. They are figured and refigured as the geographical locations and signifiers of a desired, apocalyptic topography. Yet at the same time as Blake works on his major 'London' poems he appears to ignore the opulent development of central parts of London, as part of George III's and the Prince of Wales's (later George IV) design to build not the new Jerusalem but the new Rome.[22] Blake's topography is thus composed, quite possibly as a radical reaction, of non-sites, places which, strictly speaking are not places – at least not locatable places in any real sense – but from which emerge the enunciations of the other: the other of the city, the city as other, and the city as the constantly rearticulated coming-into-being of otherness. In this scheme, this topography or, more correctly, *u-topography* (the paradoxical mapping, marking or siting of non-locatable sites and places) maps Blake's conceptualizations in the name of London (which, it might be suggested, is also a name for Blake's Imaginary). As J. Hillis Miller puts it (in discussing Wallace Stevens), Blake's poetry – and poetics – of London is concerned with demonstrating the transformative and 'performative power of poetic language'.[23] Blake's words deconstruct the purely real, purely representable London in order to transform it into a world of words and discourse, with a topography which resists mapping in the conventional sense, and yet which Blake himself maps without fixing it in place.

What this seems to suggest is that, as Blake is perceived to turn away in his writing from the failures of overt manifestations of political radicalism (as Marilyn Butler supposes), to a more private, cabalistic expression of apocalyptic identity, so London becomes increasingly important as a mediating topography for radical identity through which Blake filters his millennial desires. London is that which allows Blake to keep his feet on the ground, as it were, while also giving him a location from which to launch his project. London is that place where, in Blake's writing, tensions are foregrounded between what Steven Goldsmith calls 'political apocalypse and formal apocalypse'.[24] In *Jerusalem* at least – but also, I would argue, in *Milton*, given the one poem's echoes of the other's configurations of London,[25] and given received opinion concerning Milton's own radical politics – in the attempt to build Jerusalem on London, relying on the names of places where dissenting groups met, Blake, it might be argued, is seeking to mobilize London as a figure beyond the containment which conventional ideological discourse effects, whether conservative or progressive. Blake imagines the pillars of Jerusalem rising out of locations such as Islington. 'Apocalyptic' London is, in this case, not a wall but a city of words, its architecture in *Milton* and *Jerusalem* constructed by the naming of liminal and marginal sites, and built on the foundations of the words of other dissenting voices. Whether this is a move beyond or a retreat from the limits of the political on Blake's part is open to debate, and the formal radicalism of Blake's writing is not going to help us solve the matter easily, because that radicalism strains at the very limits of intelligibility in the later works.

Yet to see London as purely an apocalyptic figure is surely a

misreading, a retreat in itself into idealist formalism, which locates
our own desires concerning the city, rather than suggesting
anything about Blake's writing and mapping of London.[26] The
figure of apocalypse does bring to the fore the question of
representation, as Steven Goldsmith explores in *Unbuilding
Jerusalem.*[27] What we can say for now though is that, in the face
of Blake's own self-deconstructive writing ('technique' and 'method'
are not words we can properly apply in this case, for reasons
already discussed in the context of 'theme' and 'programme', and
which I will consider below), London at least remains, if not
knowable, then strangely familiar and familiarly strange. The
familiar strangeness of the city is that which, as demand of the
other, calls us to return to it.

Of the three texts with which I am concerned, the short poem
'London' is the shortest and, apparently, amongst the most
accessible of Blake's poems. It is also the earliest, composition
having occurred somewhere between 1789–1793. In looking at
this poem, I shall be following readings of the poem by E.P.
Thompson and Bill Readings:

LONDON

I wander thro' each charter'd street,
Near where the charter'd Thames does flow.
And mark in every face I meet
Marks of weakness, marks of woe.

In every cry of every Man,
In every infants cry of fear,
In every voice, in every ban,
The mind-forg'd manacles I hear

How the Chimney-sweepers cry
Every blackning Church appalls,
And the hapless Soldiers sigh
Runs in blood down palace walls

But most thro' midnight streets I hear
How the youthful Harlots curse
Blasts the new-born Infants tear
And blights with plagues the Marriage hearse

E.P. Thompson, who also acknowledges the directness and apparent simplicity of 'London', devotes a chapter to this poem in his last work, *Witness Against the Beast*. Thompson's is a substantial and convincing reading in many ways, and serves as a useful departure point for my own reading, which is, in many aspects, indebted to his. As he points out, 'London' is not a poem clearly paired with any other text in *Songs of Innocence and Experience*,[28] although certain other poems, such as 'Infant Sorrow', 'The Human Abstract', and 'The Chimney Sweeper' may be read as flowing through 'London'. They can be said to flow inasmuch as their scenes and characters are recognizably of London, moving through the city. Certainly it is not a poem which immediately gives up a specific, concrete or unified vision of London, although there are recognizable sounds and sights in Blake's verses. Yet there is still that which retains its strangeness even as we believe we recognize or understand the signs, asking us to reconsider London otherwise. One of the reasons for this is, as Thompson asserts, a 'literal reading does not fit the poem's meaning'.[29] This lack of specificity is important; it points to the constant simultaneity of Blake's writing, all figures, images, visions having a double meaning at least. Such doubleness is important to the construction and imagining of the (other) city.

The constant re-marking of doubleness is borne out by Thompson's own assertion that '[E]very reader can . . . see London simultaneously as Blake's own city, as the image of the state of English society and as an image of the human condition . . . it is one of those foundation poems upon which our knowledge of [Blake's] verse can be built'[30]. Blake, Blake's London, clearly leave their mark on Thompson's own prose, here. Thompson's language is marked by a certain architectural register – 'foundation', 'built' – which captures nicely the foundational importance of London to Blake as a site on which he can build, or imagine the building of, Jerusalem. Thompson's phrase 'every reader' picks up on Blake's repeated use of every in the poem, and this is important, for this reiteration on Blake's part marks the formal condition of the poem with a sense of the city's infinite series of sights and sounds. 'Every' works in complex ways in the poem. Every 'every' repeats the one(s) before, but every time it is used it refers to another subject, and so its meaning becomes displaced. This is the experience – as well as being the vision – of London: walking through London one will encounter thousands of people, hundreds of buildings, countless streets; one will hear endlessly the variety of sounds (also something which the poem emphasizes and which Thompson's reading directs us to hear)[31], all of them part of the series 'London', a series without causal connection, other than the city itself or the title of the poem, which is also the city's proper name of course. The text thus possibly maps the experience of walking the streets. The peripatetic act, discussed at length in relation to the representation of the city by Deborah Epstein Nord,[32] unfolds London through its layered walkways without seeking to represent them through anything but the merest impression. This in itself might be read as hinting at the – ultimately – unrepresentable condition of London. The effect is cumulative and confusing, rather than narrative and seeking a resolution or closure. The text does not sum up 'London'; rather it enters it, passes through it, immerses the reader in it.[33]

Thompson's chapter moves through an important considera-tion of Blake's use of the word 'charter'd', showing how the poem is historically and politically determined, to examine next, Blake's employment of 'mark' – again, another of Blake's doubling signifiers – and the use of sound, to the effect that, in all but the first verse, 'we *hear* many things simultaneously'.[34] The sounds, sights and marks all leave an indelible impression of London on us. London marks us even as we 'mark' – observe and write about – it. I have already traced this impression briefly in E.P. Thompson's writing, and it is equally re-marked within my own discourse. But, before this, what we must realize, as a necessity of reading Blake, is that Blake is marked as he does the marking, as he both writes and observes, as he traces the city with his steps, his eyes and ears, and then reproduces in other words that trace in the act of writing itself. What Blake's wandering, what his taking the city into himself makes clear for us, is that simultaneously London writes us as we write (about) it.

But this is not to suggest, as does E.P. Thompson, that Blake 'offers the city as a unitary experience', whether that unitary experience be located in the strolling observer or in the experi-ence of reading a unified text.[35] Certainly 'London' seems, as Thompson asserts, a 'theatre of discrete episodes'.[36] I do diverge from Thompson's reading of 'London', however, over this ques-tion of unity and unification. As I comment above, the various 'series' which trace the city and the poem are not connected except by the most coincidental causality or other relationship; which is

nothing other than to say that Londoners, such as chimney-
sweepers, soldiers, infants and harlots, are only connected in that
they are a group of different people living in the same place (to
misquote Leopold Bloom, and to offer a definition of the city
against Bloom's definition of a nation). Similarly, the cry of 'every
Man' is not the same cry as that of either the infant or the Chim-
ney-sweeper. Reiteration and seriality do not necessarily create
unity, nor do they suggest sameness. Instead, they can be read
as impressing on us the architecture of difference. The sounds of
London are only sounds which happen to be heard in London –
and in 'London' – and Blake's text should not be construed as
providing the unitary experience by bringing them together. These
sounds are the chance events which the city writes on Blake's
writing, and in Blake's name. That there is the possibility of a
partial palimpsest through the event of sounds transcribed into
text does not mean that the city becomes rendered whole. Such
an argument makes Blake a little too safe, and makes apparent
the desire on Thompson's part to impose a unity-in-oppression
onto the poem, as a gesture of radical solidarity with the poet –
or to claim the poet's voice for the critic's own ideology.

Such a desire to impose and control Blake's 'London' manifests itself in Harold Bloom's reading of the poem.[37] Bloom's
argument concerning Blake's prophetic anxiety which manifests
itself as Blake wanders the streets of London, rather than passing
directly through it, seems both misdirected and, once again, to
bear the mark of a desire for unity, this time under the heading
'anxiety'.[38] The problem lies with the idea of proceeding directly
'through' London, as though such a thing were either possible
or even desirable. Wandering is not the remarking of anxiety but
the act of giving one's self up in aleatory perambulation to chance;
which is to say the chance of the city, and the chance of encountering the city, and the visions which might be immanent in such
a city and such a chance passage. Blake's meandering gives its
self up to the possibility of an encounter with the other. Only in
this manner does Blake come to allow the city to speak through
him, without attempting to master it. Blake's writing resists unity,
and does so at every level, even down to the single word, which,
as I am going to argue, can hardly be read as 'single' in meaning.

The peripatetic figure of the implicitly bourgeois wanderer[39] –
the 'rambler, the stroller, the spectator, the flâneur'[40] – who
effectively hides himself and his construction as observer in the

act of showing us the city's others, such as the poor, the criminalized, the traders and shopkeepers, is of course a dominant figure – and *fiction* – in nineteenth-century writing. Reading this character, this self-erasing trace in the discourse of the city has provided fascinating readings of nineteenth-century urban textuality, such as those of Carol L. Bernstein and Deborah Epstein Nord, both of whom deal with the latter part of the nineteenth century and its urban fictions into which this study does not extend.[41] We can also find an exemplary model for this fiction in Thomas De Quincey's *Confessions of an English Opium-Eater*.[42] To read such a character as *there* is a fiction, for it provides a supposed unity through the twinned acts of observation and representation. But I want to resist this unity, especially with Blake, if only for the fact that such a unity embodies or can embody – and thereby hide – an ideology, as Bernstein has, herself, acknowledged.[43] Indeed, Blake resists a single, unified ideological position in the construction of London in *Milton* and *Jerusalem* by never acceding in those texts to a unified subject position. London is itself the 'subject', but it is a subject without a unified or unifiable identity. The effort to construct such a 'subject-without-identity' is arguably present in 'London', and I wish to offer a possible alternative reading to the reading which insists on the 'real' peripatetic experience or, at least, to complicate such a reading through an admittedly naïve supposition.

Blake-wandering through the city, Blake-writing, Blake-remembering London; all are different figures within our imagination. Every one is easily imaginable as the other of the other. One moves, the other moves only his pen, while allowing London to flow through him. The dominant sensory response to the city is an aural, rather than a visual, one. Certainly the first verse's 'I wander' and 'I meet' suggest 'real' experience, rather than the recalling of that experience; but if, as Blake suggests in 'The Fly' 'thought is life'[44] (and Blake, like myself, is offering no more than a hypothesis), such 'wandering' and such encounters are equally plausible as the meanderings of the mind, which reading in turn suggests alternative readings for the 'mind-forg'd manacles', which are themselves heard 'in every ban' (and which are the figures in opposition to Blake's ceaseless 'mental fight'). However one construes 'ban', the sense of it is something written, some form of text which authorizes or prohibits; the mind is thus manacled by writing, discourse and textuality, which is then reproduced in hegemonic enforcement and social coercion (see the discussion of Bill Readings's reading below). If we posit London as a possible identity for 'I', an always already textual, decentred identity, an identity without centre, the poem becomes a text which militates against coercive and repressive textual forms, through a self-opening of the city's identity as being composed of the human sounds which are the results of such prohibitive texts. These suggestions all become clearer if we turn to *Jerusalem*:

> He [London] says . . .
> My Streets are my, Ideas of Imagination . . . .
> My Houses are Thoughts . . .
>   . . .
> In Felpham I *heard* and *saw* the visions of Albion
> I write in South Molton Street, what I both *see* and *hear*
> In regions of Humanity, in Londons opening streets.
>
>   (Ch. 2, Plate 34; emphases added)

> I behold Babylon in the opening streets of London, I behold Jerusalem in ruins wandering from house to house . . .
>
>   (Ch. 3, Plate 74)

The writer in South Molton Street, just south of Oxford Street, and adjacent to South Molton Lane, would certainly have been capable of imagining 'Londons opening streets' from the sights and sounds which surrounded him in that location. The lines referring first to Felpham (near Bognor on the Sussex coast) and then to South Molton Street mark the division in identity, the doubling of Blake's identity as wanderer and writer. This doubling and splitting is marked in the shift from past to present tense in the verbs for hearing and sight: experience and memory thus mark the subject as always already doubled, as other within himself. Significantly, while Sussex is the place of visions, London is the scene of writing, the writing which engenders disunity, heterogeneity and textuality. This is the effect which the city has upon one, and it is this which Blake comprehends so startlingly about the city and the ways in which the city moves through the subject, displacing unity. The lines from Ch. 3, which repeat the figure of the 'opening streets', placing Babylon there and then envisaging the wandering of Jerusalem recall very strongly, while still in other words, the cumulative effect of 'London', and can be brought to bear in support of the argument against the actual experience of wandering and meeting, and the literal interpretation of the first verse (while there is little doubt that Blake did wander through the streets, and that this is not merely a romantic fiction on Peter Ackroyd's part). And this is further supported if we read the first-quoted lines from *Jerusalem* above in the light of this reading of 'London'. Here Blake personifies London, and London states that the streets are the ideas of his imagination, while the houses his thoughts. South Molton Street may be 'real', and so may – and so are – the poor and the oppressed. Certainly Blake never shies away from the problems of the city and society – indeed, he endlessly reinvents them so as to defamiliarize their image and make the case for their sufferings with ever-increasing urgency in *Jerusalem*. But what Blake forces us to acknowledge is that if there is to be a London imagined which can affirm its own spirit and which can resist its real and appalling (Blake's own word) horrors, that city has to be imagined through acts of writing which do not unite into a single vision.

London for Blake is, then, a disseminating scene of writing and textuality, beyond polyphony and polysemy. If it were merely polyphonic or polysemic careful reading could reduce the city to the number and sum of its traces, its marks, its signs. But Blake registers in his writing the otherness which exceeds definition. As he himself hears the simultaneous, myriad sounds of the disturbing and violent city, so his words catch within themselves, sometimes consciously, sometimes unconsciously (and who can tell which is which?), the traces of the other. And what this serves to do is put us 'in London'. As Thompson remarks, we do not observe the city from the outside, as William Wordsworth appears to in *The Prelude*.[45] 'Charter'd' locates us in London. The word is very carefully explored by Thompson. What his reading does not take account of, though, is another city-related word, which I think it is reasonable to speculate on, offering a tentative hypothesis. 'Charter'd' shares its etymology with 'charted', having their origins, so the OED informs us, in the related Latin words, *cartula* and *carta*, respectively (of which the former is a diminutive of the latter). These, in turn, mean 'small paper or writing' or 'leaf of paper'. We can of course hear the absent 'charted' in the present 'Charter'd'. If it is accepted that the poem offers the reader a meandering trace through London, then the text both charts and writes, it maps and cites the city. Blake writes the other London, he charts London as other, in indirect opposition to all restricting, cheating, dishonest, commercial charters, of which E.P. Thompson writes.[46]

It is not that what Thompson argues is incorrect. His reading of the draft versions of the poem, where the words 'dirty' and 'cheating' come to be replaced with 'charter'd' in the final version, is wholly convincing.[47] But reading – and, more importantly, given the poem's emphasis on sound, *hearing* – the nearly simultaneously sounded 'charted', brings us a moment of displacement and dislocation in the text which opposes a general sense of writing to the restricted and restrictive sense of writing installed by 'Charter'd'. Thus it may be speculated that writing's *différance* offers at the levels of both form and content a political resistance to the dishonesty and oppression foisted on Londoners by the business men and politicians. The possibility of this dissonance undoes the fixing-in-place of oppression (which Thompson's reading ultimately seems to do, thereby making the sense of oppression even more despairing); it does so, furthermore, through a figure which directly intimates the city-as-writing, and the writing of the city as the writing of the other. Mapping the other city as the spectre haunting the 'Charter'd streets' affirms the city's uncontainable dissonance, difference, and alterity. And all of this can be read from within: from within the city, and from within the text.[48]

But who is the 'I' who speaks? Is it Blake? Is it London? is it Blake-as-London? Thompson connects 'London' to its illumination in *Songs of Innocence and Experience*, and sees the illumination as an illustration of a line from *Jerusalem*, where London is personified as blind and 'age-bent'.[49] The connection is a reasonable one. But, yet again, this seems to impose a sense of unity. London is certainly personified, and on more than one occasion in *Jerusalem*, but then, in 'London' London 'speaks' in many voices, in sighs, cries, and curses. It is, in short, a Babelian din, and the multiplicity of dissonant sound is itself folded into the 'Harlots curse', her figure being, clearly, a figure which doubles as the whore of Babylon, Babylon being one of London's *other* cities. To hear these voices is to hear the other and to hear the event that is London, the other London to which this book seeks to be responsive. Blake's writing of London, in 'London' and elsewhere, is the series-iteration of London writing itself as simultaneously (to borrow a double-phrase of Derrida's) 'hermetic and totally open – secret and superficial'.[50]

This doubleness is not available in Bill Readings's analysis of London.[51] Readings reads Blake's London as part of his effort to 'read work' in the wake of Jean-François Lyotard's writings, asking 'what it might mean to read, after Lyotard'.[52] What it might mean it seems is the ability to read figures and tropes without governing them by making them into concepts or master signifiers. Even though Readings goes on to reject 'post-structuralist' playfulness, his interpretation of Lyotard does bring him close to a somewhat Derridean gesture. The poem serves to prove a certain theoretical truth for Readings in his interpretation of Lyotard. First Readings moves through a series of 'ventriloquised' and partial readings which trace the possible responses to capital and labour as mapped in Blake's poem from the assumed positions of humanist Marxism (E.P. Thompson), ideology (Louis Althusser), and discourse analysis (Michel Foucault). This is done in order to criticize and then reject such readings. Readings then attempts to read 'work' and the 'work of work' in the poem as a mobile non- or anti-concept which, according to Readings's Lyotardian understanding of the text, refuses to be settled into, or mastered as, a concept from a position of power and control. It is work in Blake's text which connects art and politics. Work, says Readings, is,

> . . . a figure for an event which cannot be reduced to a concept . . .
> work is a differend, the site of struggle between the incommensurable idioms of worker and capitalist.[53]

This description of 'work' is not an attempt to provide an 'aestheticization of labour' but to offer what Readings calls a '*poetics of work*' wherein 'work is a transformative process [which] resists being made the object of a sociological description in terms of content or meaning';[54] hence Readings's rejection of the tendencies towards objectifying practices in those types of reading already named. For Readings, work, as in Blake's work of writing, is already at work in the act of writing. Blake's work is 'deconstructive' for Readings, inasmuch as Blake's use of language resists its being misunderstood as a form of representation; language in Blake is not about something one can see, but about itself '*in excess* of any conceptualization'.[55] The poem is thus not a discursive representation of work, but work itself, at work constantly.

In so far as Readings desires to read Blake's practice from a Lyotardian perspective as a figure for a radical rethinking of work which 'offers the possibility of forging a radical politics of labour',[56] this project may be said to work extremely successfully. It is certainly a project which comprehends in part what we may read Blake as writing, 'work' being one possible name, thought in this radical fashion, for 'what William Blake does with words', to use a formula which itself may suggest the avoidance of the programme. However, Readings's efforts run into trouble when he discusses London itself. Everything he has suggested concerning the radical rethinking of 'work', following his reading of Lyotard, can be suggested about Blake's own understanding of London itself as the figure beyond representation, beyond conceptualization; in short, as a figure which carries within its very contours the traces of its own excessive difference. The effort to represent London is always deconstructed by the condition of London. To stop short of this understanding is merely to position Blake as an oppositional poet of radical sensibilities who, for Readings, radicalizes 'work' but not the city. In naming the sites of London in *Jerusalem* and *Milton* Blake is not offering us an objectified view of London; he is not asking or inviting us to see the city whole. Instead he is working through a radical topography and architecture of the city's spaces, transforming them into a wall of words, as part of his own understanding of the city's potential transformative and *performative* alterity.

Let us consider Readings's words on work again, this time supplementing 'work' with *London*: London is ... 'a figure for an event which cannot be reduced to a concept ... [London] is a differend, the site of struggle between the incommensurable idioms of worker and capitalist'. Here is my understanding of Blake's London, which Readings does not or cannot comprehend. For Readings, London is a concept, a unified and oppressive site, available in his reading for thematization and conceptualization. It may be the case that in 'London' Blake is not quite able to grasp the self-transformative potential of the term 'London'; it may be that in this poem, Blake falls back partly on a dialectic structure. This would at least be to admit in part the accuracy of Readings's assessment of the capital. Yet Readings, for all his insistence on the discursive nature of the city in the poem, with its charters and marks of writing, ultimately relies on a reified version or concept of the city in order to mobilize the mobile figure of work in the text. The city, he writes, is 'itself a model of the discursive articulation of space, the grid of streets, which the poem resists'.[57] Such a statement puts the city outside the poem, as the object represented by acts of writing which are not present as such, but which are re-presented in their absence by Blake. (Blake's act of writing the charters as absent might be read as a parodic simulacrum which offers to put the official writing of the city under erasure.) What we see, and more importantly what we hear in the poem, are the sounds of the city, and the city's inhabitants, which displace and distort the city's official structures. Blake's urban sounds and cries are sounds of the other city which has no grid, no mapping. If the 'work of the poem . . . resists the dominance of the concept, and the discursivization of work as labour'[58] as Readings suggests, its work is also to resist the charting of the city. The workers are not oppressed by the city (as Readings puts it) but only a certain part of the city. Readings seems not to be aware that Blake sees 'Babylon in the opening streets of London', but also sees 'London blind & age-bent begging thro the Streets / Of Babylon' in Chapters 3 and 4 of *Jerusalem*. Inversion and displacement, difference and supplement: it is Blake's work, we can argue, to counter the partial representation of the city by presenting us with the unrepresentable city as traced through contradiction and paradox. That the poem from *Songs of Innocence and Experience* is named 'London' intimates the contention between meanings and the irreconcilable difference which the very name of the city signs. The name of the city as name of the poem indicates a textual simultaneity which cannot be resolved into a presence or truth about the city.

It is then as if in 'London' Blake rehearses in miniature the untranslatable mapping of London in his later poems, *Milton* and *Jerusalem*. The practices and processes of 'London', most immediately embodied in the catachrestic resonances of words,[59] such as 'marked' and 'charter'd', and in the serial quasi-simultaneity of sound – the crowding of sound, although seemingly simultaneous, is nevertheless spaced, thereby re-marking the spatio-temporal condition of *différance*, even as experience of the city itself must be necessarily both spatial and temporal – offers the reader an example of Blake's resistance to closure, noted by Jerome McGann in his reading of *Jerusalem*. This resistance is marked indirectly, according to McGann, through the repeated representation of 'the same topics from slightly altered perspectives'.[60]

This resistance to closure is, I would argue, generated by Blake's understanding of London, and the idea of London as composed by Blake in *Milton* and *Jerusalem* as a series of endlessly singular and iterable sites, sites which are at once singular and repeatable, repeatable as Derrida has suggested on a number of occasions, because singular.⁶¹ Thus each place-name in London utilized by Blake in his great poems of the early 1800s names its singularity and its reiterability as a part of London. Furthermore, it names London without naming it, and names it, quasi-simultaneously, as other. Even the names of areas are doubled, displaced, inverted, translated. And Blake writes London in this fashion, because London dictates its writing in this fashion. Each name, each place-name is also the improper signature of London signed as other than itself and signing itself from the imaginary topographical non-place of the other. Each of the names of London remain singular in being attached to a particular place. Yet Blake's citation of them acknowledges their catachrestic detachability, so that they figure themselves as other than themselves.

This sets the city in a series of dissonant relationships with its own spacing and placing. London therefore is always a city without a centre, without origin, without absolutely locatable place. The names of Islington, Northwood, Blackheath, Finchley, Lambeth, Hyde Park and so on figure in Blake's poetry as a quasi-transcendental series gesturing in the ghostly signatures of language towards the yet-to-come Jerusalem, and as the trace of that future possibility. If this is acknowledged it can be suggested, through the reading of the tracing of London, that the language of Blake's poetry is only *quasi-apocalyptic*: caught between the material displacements of the city and the spatio-temporal differentiation and deferral of London-as-text, which the names of London signify, Blake's writing might be said to figure the trace of the apocalypse-on-the-way-to-becoming. We should explore this hypothesis in relation to *Milton*.

What we notice, first of all, about naming the place in both *Milton* and *Jerusalem*, is the disproportionately high number of London place-names in relation to other place-names from the rest of England/Albion. This alone should signify the importance of London in Blake's later writing. The first concentrated reference in *Milton* to London occurs in 'Book the First', following Plate 6:

From Golgonooza the spiritual Four-fold London eternal
In immense labours & sorrows, ever building, ever falling,
Thro Albions four Forests which overspread the Earth
From London Stone to Blackheath east: to Hounslow west:
To Finchley North: to Norwood South: . . .

(ll. 1–5)

Loud sounds the Hammer of Los, & loud his Bellows is
    heard
Before London to Hampsteads breadths & Highgates
    heights To
Stratford & old Bow: & across to the Gardens of Kensington
On Tyburns Brook: loud groans Thames beneath the iron
    Forge . . .

(ll. 8–11)

The Surrey hills glow like the clinkers of the furnace:
    Lambeths Vale
Where Jerusalems foundations began; where they were
    laid in ruins . . .

(ll. 14–15)

When shall Jerusalem return & overspread all the Nations
Return: return to Lambeths Vale O building of human souls

(ll. 18–19)

. . . he [Los] heaves the iron cliffs in his rattling chains
From Hyde Park to the Alms-houses of Mile-end & old Bow
Here the Three Classes of Mortal Men take their fixd
    destinations
And hence they overspread the Nations of the whole Earth
    & hence
The Web of Life is woven . . .

(ll. 30–34)

Golgonooza is identified in the first verse as spiritual London, eternal London. Thus all the place-names of London which follow must be understood in their quasi-transcendental seriality as figuring both real and eternal London. Blake scholars will appreciate the ease with which we can make the connections between Golgonooza and its construction, and Blake as an inhabitant of London: Golgonooza is built by Los; Los, who figures both poetry and prophesy in Blake's visions, is, in some contexts, Blake's other. Therefore, even as Los builds Golgonooza, so Blake builds London. Within the space of thirty-four lines, though, we get sixteen references to the sites of London/Golgonooza (seventeen, if we are prepared to include the Surrey hills), with the spiritual point of transcendental desire being the Vale of Lambeth, on the south side of the River Thames, immediately opposite Westminster, the Houses of Parliament and, presumably, some of those 'Charter'd Streets'. For Blake, Lambeth was both home, between 1791–1800, the original site of Jerusalem, and the place to which Jerusalem will return, as is prophesied above (ll. 18–19). The mapping of London's topography as both real and desired, as material and quasi-transcendental also maps and marks the desired movement towards the apocalyptic city, a city already doubled in its signatures, so that it will come to be refigured as its own other, an otherness which the writing of the text figures as its own desire, the desire of the coming into being of the writing of the other, from the place of the other; a writing of London, no less, than a writing without form, without closure, without method or programme: the spiritual Four-fold London eternal.

The project without programme to which Blake envisions London holding the key is nothing short of a radical rewriting of the entire world, as the lines above confirm: from London eternal will come Albion's forests spreading across the entire earth, while the return of Jerusalem to Lambeth promises the return of Jerusalem to all Nations. The rebuilding of Jerusalem is also envisioned as the building of human souls. Blake's vision of the city is here revealed as both an architectural and spiritual ideal. The city cannot exist unless it is built of myriad souls, constructed of the spirits of the masses who give the city life. As Blake makes clear, this is a life beyond material existence. The city thus invokes a spiritual living-on, even as it is this spirit of living-on which articulates London for Blake, and which he seeks to replicate in other words, in a spectro- and cryptopoetics of the city. I use these terms because

they are strikingly relevant and apposite to my reading of Blake.
Spectrality marks and re-marks Blake's vision of London everywhere, while London is very much encrypted into Blake's
textuality. Furthermore it is seen to be the spectral city, the city
as haunting figure which 'ghost-writes' *Jerusalem*, which ghosts
and haunts the desire for an apocalyptic re-invention. Blake's
London clearly has a spiritual world and so, because of this spirit,
has being, has *Dasein*. The encrypting of spirit also speaks of the
crypt of London, the city being envisioned as tomb, sepulchre,
charnel house. Yet it is the possibility of the crypt which allows
the spirit to come forth.

As we understand, this cryptopoetics is also a cryptopolitics,
where the sites of London written dissonantly, on the way to
apocalypse, name the places of historical political, ideological and
religious dissent in London at the end of the eighteenth century,
as E.P. Thompson comments.[62] Blake's work with London involves
a simultaneous enfolding and unfolding the traces of the city
throughout his writing as the signs of this, and nowhere is this
more evident than in the constant surfacing of London in *Jerusalem*. The appearance of dissonant reiteration between this poem
and *Milton* is figured, amongst other places, in Chapter Two:

To cast Jerusalem upon the wilds to Poplar & Bow...

The Shuttles of Death sing in the sky to Islington & Pancrass
Round Marybone to Tyburns River, weaving black
   melancholy as a net,
And despair as meshes closely wove over the west of London,
Where mild Jerusalem sought to repose in death & be no more.
She fled to Lambeths mild Vale and hid herself beneath
The Surrey Hills...

There is a Grain of Sand in Lambeth that Satan cannot find
Nor can his Watch Fiends find it: tis translucent & has
   many Angles

(ll. 5, 7–12, 15–16)

Here Blake recalls the references in *Milton* to 'Lambeths Vale' as
he traces a line across London from north to west, randomly alight-
ing on place-names, the function of Lambeth, or the house of

the Lamb, altering with every gesture, but always moving and being on the way to returning to an anticipated future. The movement in the lines quoted above is eventually to the south and west. There is however no definite pattern to the movement through London, either here or anywhere else in Blake's poetry; Blake retraces his ('mental'?) steps, moving through certain districts repeatedly, while touching on others only once, even as the passages and names themselves return, marking out new threads, new meshes, as the following passages show:

> They came to Jerusalem; they walked before Albion
> In the Exchanges of London every Nation walkd
> And London walked in every Nation mutual in love &
>   harmony

> (Ch. 1, Plate 24)

> The fields from Islington to Marybone,
> To Primrose Hill and Saint Johns Wood:
>   Were builded over with pillars of gold,
> And there Jerusalems pillars stood.[63]
>   . . .
>   Pancrass & Kentish-town repose
> Among her golden pillars high:
>   Among her golden arches which
> Shine upon the starry sky.
>   . . .
>   What are those golden Builders doing
> Near mournful ever-weeping Paddington
>   . . .
>   They groan'd aloud on London Stone
> They groan'd aloud on Tyburns Brook
>   . . .
>   Jerusalem fell from Lambeth's Vale,
> Down thro Poplar & Old Bow

> (Plate 27, 'To the Jews')

I behold London: a Human awful wonder of God!
He says: Return, Albion, return! I give myself for thee:
My Streets are my, Ideas of Imagination.

Awake, Albion, awake! and let us wake up together,
My Houses are Thoughts: my Inhabitants: Affections,
The children of my thoughts, walking within my blood-vessels
. . .
So spoke London, immortal Guardian! I heard in Lambeths
    shades
In Felpham I heard and saw the visions of Albion
I write in South Molton Street, what I both see and hear
In regions of Humanity, in Londons opening streets.

(Ch. 2, Plate 34)

He [Los] came down from Highgate thro Hackney &
    Holloway towards London
Til he came to old Stratford & thence to Stepney & the Isle
Of Leuthas Dogs . . .

(Ch. 2, Plate 45)

I behold Babylon in the opening streets of London, I behold
Jerusalem in ruins wandering from house to house . . .

(Ch. 3, Plate 74)

I see London blind & age-bent begging thro the Streets
Of Babylon, led by a child, his tears run down his beard

(Ch. 4, Plate 84)

There are many other passing references; to cite them all is need-
less, for, even from these few examples we begin to comprehend
the effect of weaving and mapping the city which Blake creates,
as he crosses and recrosses London, threading London through
the textile mesh of *Jerusalem*. There is in the extract from Chapter 2, Plate 34 a revision of the 'London' text. And once again
the phrasing recalls, on occasion, lines and passages from *Milton*,
with 'Tyburns Brook', 'London Stone' and 'old Bow' figuring
vividly. The sense we have from this of London is captured in
the last line of *Milton*, cited above: 'The Web of Life is woven . . .'
(Plate 6, l. 34). Artisanal and architectural terms mark the passages, with the references to building, builders, pillars, arches.

These, with the naming of London sites, serve to build and weave (perhaps for Blake the 'male' and 'female' principles of London and the reconstruction of Jerusalem through the deconstruction of the 'charter'd streets') the text that is the city. And in *Jerusalem* Blake will even recall the four compass points of the 'spiritual Four-fold London eternal' from *Milton*, as a provisional architectural structure. 'Between Blackheath & Hounslow, between Norwood & Finchley' (Plate 42, ll. 3–4). Blackheath, Hounslow, Finchley, Norwood had been the pattern and order of naming in *Milton*, so we see even in this simple pattern a displacement, a rearrangement of the elements which serves to keep the spirit of London alive. If the structures being mapped here are architectural, then Blake's architecture of London is not monumental, not fixed in stone. London is built, unbuilt, and rebuilt constantly as a transformative textile.

What such seemingly cabalistic reiteration throughout the passages given here and elsewhere seems to suggest is that the names name a secret. The names imply a secret to London, the secret that *is* London. The names of the districts in their seemingly endless reapplication seem to hint that there is a mystery in the streets, and that the mystery is there, in the names themselves. Yet, concomitantly, in such constantly foregrounded naming, and in his need to return to names, to retrace them, to reconfigure them in new patterns of chance topography, Blake leaves the city open, undecidable, unknowable. Such a practice radicalizes the condition and experience of the city, while offering us the city as event, always awaiting the encounter with the secret to come. The names name, in the words of Derrida on the topic of names, the place of the secret. In Blake's text the names of London, the multiple-naming and naming-other of London, stand, to borrow from Derrida, '*In place of the secret*: there where nevertheless everything is said [in this case, about the city] and where what remains is nothing'.[64] All that remains is nothing because Blake's London is not a representation of the city. But all that remains to be built through Blake's verse is the secret of London, London otherwise. London is the secret, at once absolutely secret and open, as I have already said. The 'opening streets of London' announce this. Writing the city in Blake's text imposes no order, but complicates the possibility of topography through throwing open the city to all other possible mappings and, therefore, all other possibly unknowable, unlocatable configurations; which is, of course, the non-place of Jerusalem. Blake's writing of London saves the name of London from knowability, determinacy, and fixity. London is thus always safe in Blake's writings. 'London', to use a phrase of Jacques Derrida's, is the *'exemplary* secret'[65] of Blake's writings, a shibboleth to a city without gates, without walls, without closure. It is also the address of an unlocatable destination. And we know from Blake's text that the destination is not to be found, because London is always in the process of being traversed, crossed and recrossed, without any sign of a starting point or a final place of rest. At the same time, London transforms 'rhetorical versification'.[66] Blake reinvents the topography from line to line, verse to verse, and this reinvention is imposed on Blake by the condition of the city's being. It may not be going too far to suggest that it is the event of Blake's encounter with his *other* London which serves in the formal composition of a work such as *Jerusalem*, the verse of which is, in the words of Robert Essick, 'responsive to emotional tone and cadence more than a predetermined measure . . . [and] complemented by idiosyncratic punctuation that indicates vocal pauses and emphases more than logical divisions'.[67] The idiosyncracy, the emotion, the pauses and emphases are all indirectly indicative of, or at least partially interpretable as, the unpredictable figurations of the city inscribed into the form of Blake's text. The text dictates a resistance to strictly logical or formal coherence and comprehension, which in turn may be understood as a political gesture of resistance, dissonance and affirmation.

Blake's London is, in conclusion, idiosyncratically his own and yet not Blake's property, not his invention, for his imagined London is seen to come to him, unbidden. The proper name 'William Blake' becomes yet one more name for the eternal city. London *is* Blake; William Blake *is* London. This city names him over, and haunts his wandering thoughts and wondering footsteps. The spirit keeps returning, and always keeps watch in this act, to paraphrase Derrida. Blake follows a path without destination or predestination in the city. It is the double path of naming and reiteration which 'crosses the path of the entirely other. The entirely other announces itself in the most rigorous repetition. And this repetition is also the most vertiginous and the most abyssal'.[68] These are words which Jacques Derrida imagines Martin Heidegger speaking. These are also the words I imagine haunting the indeterminacy within Blake's London and London's Blake. Every time Blake names a London-place name, in effect he says 'here I am'.

But everywhere where 'I am' is named is merely a signature effect which keeps to itself, as the secret it announces, the real names of London and William Blake. What Blake then shows us is that there is no immediate access to 'London', no form of access at all, which does not in fact serve to determine our relationship to the city, where the other is always first, always ahead of identity, and always having gone ahead of our comprehension, on the way to apocalypse.

2

'Half lost in night':
envisioning London or,
Romantic poetry's Capital
snapshots

This then, is the obscure, hardly-to-be-thought-of city

Geoffrey Fletcher

INTRODUCTION

If William Blake offers us a strangely familiar, modern London, then the texts of Anna Laetitia Barbauld, Percy Bysshe Shelley, and Lord Byron offer us also a peculiarly recognisable London. Theirs is a London – and a language with which to describe London – partly separated if not wholly divorced from earlier writers, and, once again, distinctly modern. The discourse of the city to be found in the Romantic poets considered in this chapter invites us to return to the figure of London repeatedly, because the image with which we are presented is so strikingly comprehensible, even though what is not available is an uncomplicated image of the city. From Shakespeare and Jonson to Johnson, Fielding, and Richardson, we encounter a London which the writers in question feel can be depicted, given a common image to be shared by writer, reader and audience alike. Despite its crowdedness, its busy-ness (and its business), there seems to be the belief that the entire scene can be shown.

This London is a 'Rabelaisian' or carnivalesque capital city, a city at once chaotic, sprawling, excessive, bustling and grotesque. But it is still a city with a smile (albeit on occasions a vicious one), a city engendered from drink, eructation and the eruptions of belly laughs, a city of bustle and incipient chaos generated by cupidity and vanity as Pope in the *Dunciad Variorum* attests.[1] It's a city on the move and on the make, and one which is clearly visualized. Even the morality of the Restoration dramatists and Hogarth's etchings teem with visions of positive, bawdy life on a general scale, albeit at the expense of the individual. The question seems then to be one of tone and how tone can be said to alter narrative effect. There is, on the part of earlier writers such as Tobias Smollett for example (see the letters from London in Smollett's *The Expedition of Humphrey Clinker*[2]), still the effort to perceive London whole through the construction of a steady image, and thereby fix it in place, even if this effort is already being troubled by the rapid development of the city at this time. Smollett's writing of the city relies on the ability to give us a picture. Even though Smollett's characters are variously distrustful or delighted with London, there is between Matthew Bramble and Lydia Melford a shared sense of the vitality of the city, without there being a greater and more ambivalent sense of the complexity of the city text.[3] The question of visualizing London in texts of the eighteenth century is one of creating the image in its entirety, whether in words or pictures, as though such a visual image would suffice. The purpose of such a visualization is to create a backdrop or stage setting which conveys, implicitly or explicitly, a tone of moral authority and/or condemnation. If one were forced to draw on certain images in order to support one's argument, a comparison between Hogarth's London and Doré's London, between any illustration from *The Rake's Progress* (1751) or *Marriage à la Mode* (1745) and, equally, any illustration from Doré's and Jerrold's *London: A Pilgrimage* (1872) would serve the purpose.

In Plate VI of *Marriage à la Mode* the sinful Countess has just died (no doubt because she was too wicked to live, to paraphrase Oscar Wilde loosely). From the window of the room we see the Thames and the buildings of London. Here the city is merely the place where sin occurs; it serves a useful function for providing a context both for sinful activity *and* its ultimate reward. In various plates from *The Rake's Progress* such as Plate IV or Plate II of *Beer Street and Gin Lane* (in which the drunken mother drops her baby down the stairs), the city, once again a backdrop, is drawn so as to promote the overall sense of social chaos and moral condemnation. London is merely that place in which the sinful die, the poor get drunk, thieves and prostitutes abound.

Certainly, there is a sense that all of the horrors can take place only in the urban space, but, whether buildings collapse, the clouds gather, and rain or lightning strike down upon the town, all of this is only part of Hogarth's general critique of, at the local level, the depredations of the working classes and, at a global level, the excesses of Church and State, as Peter Wagner shows in his readings of Hogarth's prints.[4] As an earlier etching, Plate II of *The Four Times of the Day* (1738), shows, London is essentially a solid, merely real location; sinful, yes, and providing the location and opportunity for moral turpitude of all kinds, but unambiguously representable. London is simply for Hogarth the vehicle for the moral tenor of his texts: it serves some other purpose rather than being the subject. There is a sense in which societal representation in the mid-eighteenth century is still indebted to the images of Holbein and Breugel.

Gustave Doré, on the other hand, depicts the squalor of the poorer inhabitants of London without necessarily judging them. London provides the context for his images, as it had done for Hogarth. The principal difference, however, in an engraving such as 'Houndsditch', is that gas-lit London is now part of the fabric of misery, squalor and poverty, its windows, walls, lamps and streets, an extension of the appalling lives of its inhabitants. By the same token, the city-text can be read as seeping into the lives of those who are seen to suffer from malnutrition, disease, abuse, neglect. Doré's etchings convey a sense of mutual, reciprocal encoding between Londoner and London, between self and street. London is as much the subject as are those who exist on its streets. If for Hogarth London was merely the stage, for Doré the city has become part of the drama.

Yet this comparison does not wholly capture what we are seeking to impress upon the reader, for there is much in such a comparison which gets left out. There is much about London, about the imagining of London which neither Hogarth nor Doré succeed in capturing through images alone. Ultimately, what is omitted, elided even in the polarities – and politics – of the grotesque and the grim is something quite other than that to which representation can admit; something other than representation, the other of and within representation which may well be what Peter Stallybrass and Allon White have termed in *The Politics and Poetics of Transgression*, 'the transcodings of psychic desire'.[5] This 'transcoding' is what figures much of the ambiguity in the imagin-

ing of London as a *modern* city, and it is that which also allows,
or perhaps forces, writers to acknowledge London as the eternal
city, a city indelibly traced and haunted by a sublime alterity, a
city 'half lost in night', as Conrad puts it in *The Secret Agent*.[6]
This is a city, as I shall show in my reading of the Romantic
poets considered here, where one may wander endlessly, involved
all the while with gazing, touching, coming into contact with
and being 'contaminated' by, all that is not only the other of the
polite face of the city, but also the other of one's self, one's being.

I am not suggesting in this chapter that we read the poets in
question through a series of binary oppositions which neatly
dovetail along the vertical as well as the horizontal axes: self/
other, body/city, high/low, and so on. While such oppositions do
inform the writing and mapping of the modern city, the
structuration of such inscriptions is far more complex than such
binarisms and their use can acknowledge. The moments which
the terms in these pairings admit to are not fixed or fixable in
any secure, permanent fashion, nor can they be thought of in
this manner. For the definition of any terms such as these relies
on their own inherent and immanent instability, an instability
already traced within their own configuration within the texts in
question. The poets in question in this chapter – particularly Shelley
and Byron – rely on repetition and inversion of their city snapshots as a mode which in responding to the modernity of the
city forces the farcical or satirical onto the very idea of representation in the context of the city. This process destabilizes. It is
this instability, the undecidability which comes to figure the self,
the body, and the city itself as an undecidable city, which I read
the Romantics as acknowledging, announcing, mediating and
helping to construct, albeit even unwillingly on occasions. Narrative, continuity and representation come in for indirect critique
through the process of writing the city, as the city comes to be
written dissolving into the series of discontinuous snapshots. It
is that very quality of destabilization caught by Blake in his well-
known pun 'the marriage hearse'. What the Romantics' confrontation with the city foregrounds is certainly a troubling tension,
and, perhaps a challenge even, to what Jerome J. McGann defines
through reference to Coleridge in his influential study, *The Romantic
Ideology*, as the ideology of '"Unity of Being"' (which, arguably is
not present to any great extent in writing of the eighteenth
century).[7] McGann is alluding, of course, to Coleridge's theoreti-

cal thinking in *Table Talk*.[8] In this, Coleridge talks of reducing 'all knowledge into harmony . . . to unify the insulated fragments of truth, and therewith to frame . . . the whole truth'.[9] Coleridge's theoretical desire, if considered as one of the key ideals of Romantic thinking, comes to founder in practice when the Romantic poets come into contact with the knowledge of London. Except that William Blake's quasi-apocalyptic register seems wholly able to accommodate the city in its fragmentation, diversity and heterogeneity comfortably, without attempting to reduce it to an apparent unity of knowledge signified by its name. This is not to say that the other poets in question actively seek to homogenize and unify London. Rather, their language announces the impossibility of such a task, and consequently they look for a new language.

So, in their different, idiomatic, though occasionally related or overlapping ways, Byron, Shelley, and Barbauld partake in the vertiginous inscription of London to which Dickens, and other novelists after him, are indebted, albeit indirectly and unconsciously. It is this very oscillation from within which is missed by both Hogarth and Doré (and by writers such as Smollett or Pope), and indeed anyone, writer or artist, who insists on attempting to figure the city as a merely real city, a city to be observed, recorded and represented as though the representation were empirically verifiable. Hence my use of the phrase 'Capital snapshots' in the title of this chapter. Even as I take snapshots of Romantic poetry and their fragmentary knowledge of the urban space which the poetry figures, so I read the poets in question as producing snapshots of the city, illuminating its fragments through a fragmented knowledge thrown into sharp relief as though illuminated by artificial light.[10] Barbauld, Shelley, and Byron offer the reader snapshots of London in the full knowledge that they cannot pretend to create an image of the cityscape in its entirety. These 'snapshots' alter our understanding of London, and also our understanding of what one can say about the city and how one says it. In the hands of the Romantics and the novelists who follow, knowledge concerning how one figures London, how one *re*figures and traces instability, alterity and the sublime, undergoes what might be described as an epistemic shift, a shift which is as indelible as it is irrevocable, leaving its trace on the writing of London from the end of eighteenth century to the present day.

In this chapter then, I am going to be looking at the images of

London from Mrs Barbauld's 'Eighteen Hundred and Eleven, a Poem', 'Song for the London Volunteers', and 'West End Fair', Shelley's 'Peter Bell the Third', and Byron's *Don Juan*.[11] It is not my intention to offer thorough readings of the poems as such, but rather to concentrate on the ways in which the images of London are formed, and the ways in which the Romantic mind articulates and envisions the city.

In his magnificently celebratory, if finally pessimistic social history of London (a volume in which nineteenth-century London is given more space than the rest of the history of London put together), Roy Porter remarks of London at the end of the eighteenth century that the 'capital had become a wonder', and then asks, somewhat disingenuously it seems, 'but was it a miracle or a monster?'.[12] Porter, in posing the question unequivocally as an either/or dilemma (as though London has to be one or the other but cannot be both), does not appear to register sufficiently the ambiguity and ambivalence felt about London that is implicit in his formulation, an ambiguity and ambivalence traced in the very lines of the poets such as Wordsworth and Blake whom he quotes (although, to be fair, Porter does seem to set this question up as an Aunt Sally, only to pursue through comparison and contrast the ambiguity which the Protean city instilled in many contemporary thinkers in the period of the Enlightenment). As Blake himself can show us, that which is miraculous can be also, frequently and simultaneously, terrible and monstrous. For the Romantic poets London is, I want to suggest, most frequently both terrible and miraculous, sublime and monstrous, often in equal proportions, and at one and the same time. This is one manifestation of the spirit of London. For the Romantics 'London', as a written trace and trope, is catachrestic, always already wrested, twisted and altered from an originary sense which is no longer available. In turn, 'London' invokes catachresis in its own skewing of images and figures within the poets' writings. I am applying the idea of catachresis here in the sense given it by Jacques Derrida, who wishes to distinguish catachresis from metaphor, and it is worth giving some consideration to this distinction, if we are not to mis-recognize the figure of London as merely one more metaphor for either the miraculous or the monstrous.

In attempting a definition of the catachrestic nature of philosophy, Derrida suggests the following, provisional definition:

The term metaphor generally implies a relation to an original 'property' of meaning, a 'proper' sense to which it indirectly or equivocally refers, whereas catachresis is a violent production of meaning, an abuse which refers to no anterior or proper norm . . . . In a work such as *Glas*, or other recent ones like it, I am trying to produce new forms of catachresis, another kind of writing, a violent writing which stakes out the faults (*failles*) and deviations of language; so that the text produces a language of its own, in itself, which while continuing to work through tradition emerges at a given moment as a *monster*, a monstrous mutation without tradition or normative precedent.[13]

No anterior or proper norm. There is no anterior idea of the city to which the Romantic poets refer, or to which they have access. They respond to and thus form modern London monstrously, giving monstrous birth to its image even as they envision, articulate and inscribe it *qua* monstrous trope. London, and, by extension, the very idea of the city, by its very nature can have no original property or proper sense, for London is promethean. The Language of London is thus, inevitably, a violent language, a discourse always reshaping itself, emerging, to paraphrase Derrida, through tradition at a given moment as a monster. Is it any wonder that the Romantics find London so monstrous, in the face and in the wake of the French Revolution? Is it not perhaps the case that George III and the Prince of Wales sought to reinvent London as a wholly manageable place with the polite architecture of John Nash, as a reaction against monstrosity? And is not the catachrestic figure of London born out of one of those many 'transcodings of desire', spoken of by Stallybrass and White? Do not the poets invest the city with desire as well as fear, the desire that is at the heart of fear?

For the fear is that London will escape definition, and the desire is to name it, fix it in place, hold it in the gaze forever. And a voyeuristic gaze it is too (as are all visions), engendered as that gaze is out of the desire for presence, the presence of the city itself which is always deferred as the discourse on the city admits. Fear and desire, monstrosity and pleasure, all are inextricably intertwined. For if the city is monstrous, and if the writers are inevitably enmeshed within the snares and clews which they seek to trace, then the city is, for the Romantic poets, the figure of difference, of desire and deconstruction. These connections are speculated upon by Derrida in the conclusion of the interview already quoted:

> Deconstruction gives pleasure in that it gives desire. To deconstruct a text is to disclose how it functions as desire, as a search for presence and fulfilment which is interminably deferred. One cannot read without opening oneself to the desire of language, to the search for that which remains absent and other than oneself. Without a certain love of the text, no reading would be possible. In every reading there is a *corps-à-corps* between reader and text, an incorporation of the reader's desire into the desire of the text.[14]

'London' as catachrestic trope deconstructs stable identities – identities of the self, identities desired for the idea of the city – in Romantic poetry. In these texts London is catachrestic *because* it is marked by desire and difference. As Barbauld, Shelley, and Byron read London they open their discourses to the desire of language, the desire transformed by the figure of London into the other of identity: the identity of the poetic subject and the identity of the city.

ANNA LAETITIA BARBAULD

Anna Laetitia Barbauld's 'West End Fair' is concerned with questions of identity. This poem apparently names a geographically discernible area. It suggests in the title and subsequently a fashionable dislocation of the fairground from its more traditional Elizabethan haunts on the South Bank and amongst the Liberties. The poem thus marks historical change in London, London as a place of process, and raises the stakes of popular entertainment by turning the focus away from the traditionally lawless areas of the sixteenth and early seventeenth centuries. The fair has become gentrified, its locale naming the resort of leisured classes in the eighteenth century. It is a place determined, as the poem tells us, by 'dame Fashion' (l. 31). The text in the form of a simple narrative brings Dame Charity into contact with Dame Fashion (curiously quasi-Chaucerian allusions) through Charity's desire to 'have a play-day' (l. 6). Charity herself tells us that she 'cannot always go about/To hospitals and prisons trudging,/Or fag from morn to night/Teaching to spell and write/A barefoot rout/Swept from the streets ...' (ll. 7–12). Desire and Duty, the dualistic pair which dominate the poem, are spoken of in terms which evoke the city. The tripartite institutional structure of hospital, prison and school forms that part of the city which Charity serves and yet would escape from for a single day. So that which provides the solution is a spatial and topographical one: the West End, which is itself defined exclusively by the fair held in this location (this is at least the way it appears at first reading). But the play-day is no innocent one and Charity, 'being rather apt to tire' (l. 40), meets with the substances of the West End fair, the 'whiskey, chariot, coach, and chair' (l. 43), and the 'flowers and sweets' (l. 48). The range of terms serves to suggest other possible, equivocal narratives.

This poem, first printed on Barbauld's death in 1825, but possibly written from the evidence of Barbauld's letters as early as 1805, is a response not to the West End of London itself but to a West End Fair held in Hampstead, the fashionable North London suburb where Mrs Barbauld lived, and also the home of John Keats. The poem is clearly critical of the 'fashion' amongst 'Society Ladies' in London for establishing charitable enterprises, only to drop their worthy causes soon afterwards. It toys with this curious desire, mapping the desire, 'transcoding' it, through the reference and allusion to locale. This enfolding of identity and place, of habit, fashion, and social activity produces for the reader a strangely dense configuration of London and a selection of its inhabitants at a clearly discernible historical and cultural moment. In doing so it plays out the instability implicit within a particular carnivalesque London identity, resonant with the traces of class and society, as well as geographical location. (Arguably it is the acknowledgement of the instability and the extent to which that is foregrounded which distinguishes Barbauld from writers of the eighteenth century.)

'Song for the London Volunteers' is a response to the fears of a threatened French invasion of England and the formation of companies of home guard. Yet what is particularly of interest here is the focus of the text on London, in a manner which, like 'West End Fair', relies on the construction of a particular aspect of London, its commercial and civic life. This is immediately seen in the first line, with the invocation of the 'golden Streets of Commerce' (l. 1) which are transformed catachrestically into the 'blaze of Arms' (l. 2). The suggestion here is of the interrelation between commerce and the military, capitalism and warfare. London is the focus, and specifically the City of London, the commercial hub of the country and of empire. London sets the example to the rest of the country. It is from the City that the rest of the country should take its lead.

The City is pieced together from a range of familiar figures and images which today, after a century of reading Dickens and Trollope (and even Galsworthy), we somehow feel we already know. There is the desk (l. 5), the counter (l. 5), the 'civic feasts and halls' (l. 6). These synecdochic figures indicate in a particularly abrupt form the various social strata of City life, and it is from the locations intimated by these figures that '[t]he Londoners come pouring' (l.7). Interestingly, 'Londoners' for Barbauld are not those who live in London in this poem, but those who work in the City and thereby define the City's Being. Indeed the City has no Being unless it is in the endless event of its inhabitants' occupations.

But this is not all of the City, for we are presented with the equally familiar sights – and sites – of the 'hurry of the traffick/ And buzz of the crowded 'Change' (ll. 11–12). These lines develop the idea that the life of the City *is* the City. 'Buzz' picks up Barbauld's earlier 'human hive' (l. 3), and the image we have is of the City as beehive, composed of its various hierarchies and orders, constructed out of the numerous and differentiated tasks which come to figure the City and which are in turn figured by the fragmented images already mentioned. The 'hive', as figure for the many levels of the City, is closer in the violence of its image to Derrida's definition of catachresis than to being purely or simply a metaphor, and for very good reason: what is clearly noticeable here from the first three stanzas alone is that, in this image of the City of London in the process of being transmogrified by responding to a call to arms, there is no one mastering image, no single, original figure. Unless of course it is figured in that catachrestic proper name, the name of 'London' itself, a name which, you should notice, is never named in the poem but only in the title. However, amongst the images of the hive with its confusing noise, the elements of the City, and the projected details of imagined future battle, no one single image takes precedence. There is no original sense, only a violent production of meaning with no anterior presence. While the remaining stanzas focus on the imagined time of warfare and defence of the country, these opening verses offer us a startlingly monstrous image of the City of London driven by commercial desire (a desire which Barbauld attempts to erase by finding more altruistic purpose in the energies of the City's commercial inhabitants).

We begin to see from these two short poems some of the ways in which complex configurations of London come into being. We also witness the violence which language undergoes in an effort to respond to the spirit and phenomena of the Capital. We can furthermore understand how writing about London is not simply a matter of describing location, activity or architecture; nor is it a question of perceiving London and interpreting its empirical data, as though such an approach could begin to account for 'the nature of the city's being', for want of a better phrase. Even in these two relatively simple, straightforward texts London is already being figured in quite drastic images and from interwoven traces which exceed mere representation or imitation.

Romanticism, understood in this study as perhaps the discourse *par excellence* of excess and desire, is perfectly suited and situated therefore to explore the possibilities of mapping and tracing the forces which articulate the city. What Romantic poetry's visions of London provide are what Paul Virilio calls, with reference to photography (to return to the figure of my subtitle), *phatic images*, 'targeted image[s] that [force] you to look and [which hold] your attention'.[15] If we recall Marc Augé's definition of the non-place quoted in the Introduction to this book, above, we will see a resemblance between the power of the phatic image and the power of the non-place, both of which share that 'power of attraction' described by Augé. It is this power of attraction which attracts the attention of the Romantic poet, who registers in the verbal snapshot the phatic image of the city's non-places. Paraphrasing and borrowing from the same passage by Virilio on the effects of illumination in photography, the Romantic poets single out 'specific areas, the context mostly disappearing into a blur'. Virilio's flashgun-snapshot language seems ideal at this point to suggest the particular focus drawn on the city of London by the Romantics. Barbauld, Byron, and Shelley blur the edges, while drawing into sharp relief some aspect of the self's mediation of London's images, in the projection of images which go beyond the real, beyond the purely imitative or mimetic, beyond simple representation, so that what you come to see you also come to feel, to sense, but with that imperfect and often violent comprehension of the image left on the retina of a subject having just been caught in the flash of artificially illuminated photography (as opposed, say, to the attempt to draw or paint the image of the city more fully in texts of the eighteenth century).

Barbauld's poetic retina retains a startling image of London in her 'Eighteen Hundred and Eleven', a prophetic, perhaps even apocalyptic vision of a future Britain, a decayed and decadent island, the stop-off spot for American tourists. 'Eighteen Hundred and Eleven' begins to map London as a sublime city, if by sublime we mean that which is excessive, conceived, in Frances Ferguson's words, as 'a mark of one's inability to control all the elements involved in producing a word or sentence, much less an artistic object'.[16] If 'London' cannot be reduced to a 'Unity of Being' so much desired by Coleridge, still less can it be controlled within words or treated as an artistic object. London resists absolute knowledge because it is marked everywhere by excess and movement, fragmentation and heterogeneity. Barbauld's 'Eighteen Hundred and Eleven' seeks to encounter the city's condition in a positive manner. Once again, as in the 'Song of the London Volunteers', commerce is seen to have been central to the power of Britain, but now the 'Midas dream is o'er' (l. 61), and Britain is left in the grip of 'Enfeebling Luxury and ghastly Want' (l. 64; the capitalization of the oppositions recalling the personification of Charity and Fashion in 'West End Fair').

Barbauld continues by pointing out the influence of Britain over the rest of the world, and the world's indebtedness to Britain's cultural and spiritual past, as well as its 'stores of knowledge' (l. 87). The first reference to London is an indirect one, '"Old Father Thames"' being named as the theme for future American poets.[17] However, against this hopeful vision, comes the prospect of a cultural night-time, named 'Night, Gothic night' (l. 121) in which England will be known only by 'gray ruin and . . . mouldering stone' (l. 124). The vision of decay as being of a specifically architectural nature is important at this point, coming as it does amidst the prophecy of cultural decay, for it suggests structures falling into ruin as well as discourses; in short, Barbauld's vision suggests the possibility of a 'concrete' location.

Barbauld uses the poem as a travel-guide to future England, mentioning along the way 'natural' locations and details such as the Rivers Isis, Cam and Avon (ll. 133, 135, 141), with their indirect though obvious allusions to Oxford and Cambridge Universities and Shakespeare. Also part of the guided tour are the names of the good and the great, such as Isaac Newton, Thomas Clarkson, William Jones and William Cowper (ll. 138, 143, 144, 146). Amongst these also are two brief references to Skiddaw, a mountain in the Lake District (l. 154), and Edinburgh, named poetically as Dun Edin, which, as a city, is noted only in passing for a natural feature, the long-extinct volcano known as Arthur's Seat, and referred to as the 'classic brow' of the city (l. 155). Britain thus far is composed of natural features, much praised discourses and ideologies, and famous Britons, in Barbauld's whistle-stop tour, with the brief exceptions, already mentioned, of commerce, the Thames, and the decaying stonework. All of which, I would argue, tend to direct the reader, however obliquely towards an idea of London as a specific, though highly fragmented location. It is possible to suggest that we are being led towards the capital as a location which gives a name to the conceptual and ideological climax of the text. The poem reaches this climax in its ninth stanza in envisioning future ruin and dilapidation, culturally, spiritually and commercially, in London. Here Barbauld asks whether the ambiguity of response ('mingled feelings', l. 157) engendered by seeing the rest of Britain can be pursued upon seeing the vision of London, with its 'faded glories' (l. 158).

Barbauld's envisioning of London is an important, though troubled, one, and certainly one worth giving over to careful consideration:

> The mighty city, which by every road,
> In floods of people poured itself abroad;
> Ungirt by walls, irregularly great,
> No jealous drawbridge, and no closing gate;
> Whose merchants (such the state which commerce brings)
> Sent forth their mandates to dependent kings;

> (ll. 159–64)

It is important to note here how Barbauld registers the different and differing, heterogeneous levels of the city, without seeking to reduce them to a unity of being. Instead she provides us with a taxonomy of the city without hierarchization, compiling snapshots and fragments to produce a sense of London, a vision of the city which does not rely on slavish imitation of real features. She constructs a London at once cosmopolitan and multicultural (and not threatening, as in Wordsworth's *Prelude*; see the next chapter, below), the streets brought to life by

> . . . the turban'd Moslem, bearded Jew,
> And woolly Afric, . . . the brown Hindu;

(ll. 165–6)

The city, you will notice from the first quotation, has no defined limits. It is not a place of (en)closure. Barbauld observes the absence of wall, gate or drawbridge, and marks the city with a fluid movement, where roads give way to 'floods of people'. The city is generous, multiform and irregular in form. Its commercial power is such that it inverts conventional political structures, so that merchants have higher social status than 'dependent kings'. The fluidity of the city is remarked again, as the streets, like the roads before them, are traced in the following manner:

> Where through each vein spontaneous plenty flowed

(l. 167)

What is immediately noticeable here is that the fluid figure has transformed from a flood, suggesting water, into a vein, so that the streets are now the veins of a huge, continually mobile body. In this heterogeneous taxonomy no figure is given precedence. Each gives way to the next group, each catachrestic gesture, each monstrous and miraculous snapshot of London marked formally by Barbauld's use of the semicolon, that mark in writing which is at the limit between absolute monumentality, absolute solidity, and continuous flow. The semicolon marks a margin, a momentary hiatus, as we are left to ponder the vision Barbauld presents, before being moved on, almost with a feeling of relentless energy. It is as though Barbauld is close to acknowledging the sublime nature of the city, even as she attempts to record its disseminative excesses. Her use of semicolon traces the point at which the snapshot must be left to work its own magic, when no more can be said, because the city has already escaped description.

As a counterpoint to London-past and London-present entwined together in these lines, Barbauld projects the wandering of visitors to a future London:

> Pensive and thoughtful shall the wanderers greet
> Each splendid square, and still, untrodden street;
> Or of some crumbling turret, mined by time,
> The broken stairs with perilous step shall climb,
> Thence stretch their view the wide horizon round,
> By scattered hamlets trace its ancient bound,
> And choked no more with fleets, fair Thames survey
> Through reeds and sedge pursue his idle way.

(ll. 169–76)

What is of particular interest here, I think, is the way in which Barbauld's discourse alters to accommodate the projected London, a London without life, without Being. London becomes monumental, architectural in a traditional, conventional sense (for more on this distinction, see the chapter on Dickens, below), marked out by squares and streets. The alliteration and minor plosive effects within the line – Each splendid square, and still, untrodden street – serve to re-enforce the monumentality, the fixedness of the vision. Upon closer inspection the architectural details – the broken stairs – are revealed as already decayed. These stairs suggest a disinterred skeleton, housed within the sepulchral buildings of a dead city. The snapshot gives way to the still life, the intensity of the rapidly executed image to be displaced in the passage above by the panoramic view, which affords a moribund vista of unconnected suburban villages. Furthermore, the banks of the Thames have been reclaimed by nature.[18]

The monumentalization of London is deathly, and continues in the lines which follow in a more direct manner, as Barbauld's tourists tread

> The hallowed mansions of the silent dead

(l. 178)

This is developed further in the 'long aisle and vaulted dome', the 'chill sepulchral marbles . . . [w]here all above is still, as all beneath'; there is the 'antique shrine' and 'sculptured urn' (ll. 179, 181–2, 183, 184). In Barbauld's vision of London, architecture imposes death upon the city; if there is no life flowing through the city's streets, then all architecture becomes both monumental *and* sepulchral.[19] And, almost as if this killing vision is too much to bear, too great a weight of architectural imposition, Barbauld invokes an anonymous tour guide whose mind echoes with the voices, words and spirits of Johnson, Garrick, Chatham, Fox, Nelson and others (ll. 185–204). It is only the presence of such spirits which keeps alive the spirit of London, in the face of its future 'fallen' counterpart (l. 211). Thus Barbauld offers us a momentary binary figure of London-past/present/London future, which comes to be refigured through the spirit/body dualism, a dualism which in turn works in Barbauld's text by inverting relationships suggested by such pairings. Spirit and the past have vitality, while the future offers only a dead corporeality and materiality, to which 'Spirit' (l. 215) returns, haunting dead London, typified in the text by allusion to that imperial tomb of past civilizations and cultures in central London, the British Museum (l. 210). The image of the monumental dead London haunted by its spectral other may be read as a suggestion that *real* London is more than merely buildings, streets and squares (as discussed in another context in the Introduction to *Writing London*).

However, even this Spirit invoked by Barbauld is rendered ambiguously, as the poet shows its work of inspiring and then abandoning cultures (ll. 215 ff.). In this inevitable historical process, London is located as one more momentarily inspired location which will come to have its time, which having lived will die. Barbauld thus utilizes the very nature of the city itself, its vitality, its forms, architectures, topography, its cultural and geographical/political-historical location to unfold through the fragments and ruins of words the city's sublime condition. And as if to acknowledge the painful paradox of the cultural entropy which lies at the very heart of the city's transient vitality, Barbauld, in showing the work of the 'Spirit' on diverse cultures throughout history, returns to the image of London one last time, before prophesying the renaissance of 'Genius' on the American continent:

London exults: – on London Art bestows
Her summer ices and her winter rose;

(ll. 305–6)

. . .

Crime walks thy streets, Fraud earns her unblest bread,
O'er want and woe thy gorgeous robe is spread,
And angel charities in vain oppose:
With grandeur's growth the mass of misery grows.

(ll. 317–20)

Barbauld's final vision of London is, for those of us who were
chilled rather than thrilled by London life in the 1980s, ominously
prescient. The brief snapshots of Artificial London with its paradoxically inverted images give way all too easily to a vision of a
city infested with misery, crime and poverty, all, Barbauld seems
to be telling us, the inevitable by-products of the excesses of
commerce and its concomitant desires. This is named in the text's
singling out of fraud as the crime worthy of particular attention.
And we are left with one last snapshot, one brief appalling image
which, in 1812, pointed its readers towards the 'mass of misery'
to be observed by Engels and Mayhew, a possible spirit of London-
yet-to-come in the Victorian age, where London for the vast
majority of the working class was nothing less than a Hell. Once
again, Barbauld can only figure fragments of the city in her writing,
acknowledging the consumption of the miraculous spirit by the
monstrous future.

SHELLEY

Percy Bysshe Shelley also saw London as a vision of Hell in his
anti-Wordsworthian satire *Peter Bell the Third*.[20] Like Barbauld,
Shelley was deeply critical of both the British Government of
this period and of George III. Again, like Barbauld, Shelley utilizes a vision of 'London-in-ruins' to represent 'a crowded metropolis instantly emptied', to borrow Steven Goldsmith's words.[21]
Indeed this is the image Shelley gives us of London in his letter
prefixed to the poem, in which he imagines a future time

when London shall be an habitation of bitterns; when St. Pauls
and Westminster Abbey shall stand, shapeless and nameless
ruins, in the midst of an unpeopled marsh; when the piers of
Waterloo Bridge shall become the nuclei of islets of reeds and
osiers, and cast the jagged shadows of their broken arches on

the solitary stream, [and] some transatlantic commentator will
be weighing in the scales of some new and now unimagined
system of criticism. . . .[22]

Once more there is the noticeable coincidental similarity in vision
between Shelley's future London reclaimed by nature and Mrs
Barbauld's own future London, enclosed by 'reeds and sedge'.
Also close to Mrs Barbauld's imagined vision is Shelley's reference to a transatlantic commentator, who recalls for us Barbauld's
references to America and the visitors to ruined London. But this
future is not the subject of the poem itself, even if 'London-ruined'
is apparently much desired by Shelley, or at least his alter ego,
Miching Mallecho. This future is marginalized in the dedication
by Shelley who, in the poem, chooses to present his reader with
a wholly other London.

Shelley's is an apocalyptic image of London in this poem which
typifies his thinking on political issues of the time, issues which
come to inform the writing – and the delay in publication – of
Prometheus Unbound.[23] But Shelley's satire, with which I am immediately concerned, is more than a merely polemical poem, the points
being scored through the double-critique of Wordsworth and the
dominant ideologies of Tory England (from Shelley's perspective
at least, the former might be said to be the name *par excellence*
for the latter). *Peter Bell the Third* is also a poem concerned with,
in the words of a recent critical appraisal, 'the role the psyche
comes to play in social life, and the importance of social power
in the life of the psyche'.[24] This concern is cogently addressed in
the response to, and representation of, London. London in turn,
in all its dark refractions, is seen to engender the life of the mind.

London is introduced in Part Three of *Peter Bell the Third*, the
part entitled 'Hell', which begins:

I
Hell is a city much like London –
    A populous and a smoky city;
There are all sorts of people undone
And there is little or no fun done
    Small justice shown and still less pity.

II

There is a Castles, And a Canning,
   A Cobbett, and A Castlereagh;
All sorts of caitiff corpses planning
All sorts of cozening for trepanning
   Corpses less corrupt than they.

III

There is a * * *, who has lost
   His wits, or sold them, none knows which
He walks about a double ghost
And though as thin as Fraud almost –
   Ever grows more grim and rich.

IV

There is a Chancery Court; a King;
   A manufacturing mob; a set
Of thieves who by themselves are sent
Similar thieves who represent;
   An Army and a public debt.

(ll. 1–20)

The opening verses of Part Three set the tone for Shelley's London,
a London recognizably similar to that of Barbauld's more negative comments in its heterogeneous taxonomy, its fragmented
representation and its description of the ills of the capital. Like
Barbauld, Shelley employs – and deploys – the names of the famous,
the common, and the institutionalized crimes of the day. Chancery,
the 'manufacturing mob' and the cheats of government introduce
London to us as the institutions and agents which join together to
provide an image of a particular aspect of the city. Unlike Barbauld,
who at least sees the cultural side of London life as distinct from
the commercial and the criminal, Shelley envisions this smoky,
crepuscular demiworld in a range of terms which seem always to
connect to commerce and politics, and the entwined (self-)interest
of the two. This is not to say, though, that Shelley orders his images;
if anything, his are given an even more rapid display than those of
Mrs Barbauld, as Shelley whirls us past his snapshots, until even
grammar and syntax begin to break down in the sixth verse, where
single words are strung together in an impressionistic blur:

German soldiers – camps – confusion –
Tumults – lotteries – rage – delusion –
Gin – suicide – and methodism;

(ll. 174–6)

This is a world where no term supersedes the other, and where
gin, lotteries and suicide are as much a part of the capital as is
the public debt (how depressingly familiar). What Shelley does
reveal to us about the constructedness of London, however, despite
his wildly catachrestic stream which always threatens to escape
him, is that 'modern' London, the London which is much more
than either the images of Hogarth and Doré can convey, is as
much if not more than a location, a site, constructed out of
concepts, practices and habits, ideologies, as it is composed by
the sum of its people and its buildings. Chancery is as much a
place as it is the representative name of a group of legal discourses. What Shelley's verses also show us in their frequently
fragile grasp on linguistic representation (as shown in verses VI
[above] and IX), is that, to write of London, one must acknowledge that one must write at the very limits of knowability. Furthermore, one must write at that limit, whilst acknowledging that
there is much in and about the modern city which exceeds and
escapes inscription or articulation. Shelley's city is a more immediately monstrous city than the London of Barbauld, but it is
still a sublime location nonetheless.

Shelley's achievement here is to secularize Hell through the
images of London, rather than to turn London into a recognizably Christian place of punishment for sin. He dissolves all social
polarities by showing the contamination and interconnectedness
between apparently opposite spheres. Bishops, lawyers, judges,
robbers, 'Rhymesters' are all yoked together (IX, ll. 187–91). The
twenty-three verses which make up Part Three of *Peter Bell the
Third* do not coalesce into a coherent narrative of London life,
even though London – or a certain version of the city – is
envisioned with a rapidity of description which is itself '[t]hrusting,
toiling, wailing, moiling,/Frowning, preaching – such a riot' (ll.
197–8). Shelley's self-performing cacophony of words, figures and
images constantly implodes as a taxonomy of meals given for
political and hegemonic purposes supplant the chaotic images of
city life (vs XII–XIV). These dinners, breakfasts, teas and balls

are all part of London for Shelley, and he can do no more than offer the act of naming them, as one is left in mute stupefaction in the face of such turmoil. Finally, we are returned to the image of the 'smoky city' of the first verse, in verses XXI and XXIII:

XXI
...when day begins to thicken,
None knows a pigeon from a crow, –

(ll. 250–51)

XXIII
All are damned – they breathe an air,
Thick, infected, joy-dispelling:

(ll. 257–8)

This is Conrad's London 'half lost in night'; it is Dickens's smog-enmeshed and mud-encrusted, law-and-commerce corrupted capital of *Bleak House*, which Shelley, for want of description, can only annotate. In this twilight world, types of birds become indistinguishable, and there is the obvious sense in the last verse of Part Three that infection is both bodily and moral, physical and mental. Steven Goldsmith argues that *Peter Bell the Third* is perhaps Shelley's least sublime poem.[25] There is a certain truth in this, and yet the sublime in its most excessive and monstrous forms dominates the writing of the city for Shelley, who we witness at the double limit of narration and knowledge.

Yet, while we see the ways in which the city is imagined in Shelley's writing, it has yet to be shown how, in the text in question, there is a working through of 'the role the psyche comes to play in social life, and the importance of social power in the life of the psyche', as this equation has relevance to *Peter Bell the Third* and, indeed, Peter Bell. 'London', Shelley's London, it should now be realized, has no existence as such outside the poem; nor is it, in the words of Nicholas Abraham (from an essay on psychoanalytic aesthetics), either 'a copy [or] an expression of something else apart from itself. The affect is pure fiction'.[26] This can be seen in Part Four of the poem:

I

Lo, Peter in Hell's Grosvenor Square,
A footman in the Devil's service . . .

II

But Peter, though now damned, was not
What Peter was before damnation.

III

All things that Peter saw and felt
    Had a peculiar aspect to him;
And when they came within the belt
Of his own nature, seemed to melt,
    Like cloud to cloud, into him.

IV

And so the outward world uniting
To that within him . . .

IX

Yet his was individual mind,
    And new created all he saw
In a new manner, and refined
Those new creations, and combined
    Them, by a master-spirit's law.

Here we find Peter located in this other London, in a specific,
nameable location, the name of which – Grosvenor Square – carries
with it associations of power, wealth, governmental and commercial
intercourse and interdependence. Yet, what is readable here is
the construction of the subject through the fragmentary traces of
the city which are mapped by Part Three of *Peter Bell the Third*.
Verse II of Part Four describes in passing the fundamental division
in subjectivity of Peter. This division we can suggest is exempli-
fied by the division between text and agent, between *Peter Bell*
and Peter Bell, where the text comes to map what a recent study
of Byron has described as 'mental topography',[27] most graphi-
cally remarked in the fragmented and fragmentary anarchy of
the mapping of London. The text as discourse before the subject
serves to construct the subject. Similarly, the text as the psychic
mechanism of the subject also produces the subject *from within*,
functioning as it does through the London section at times like

the desiring id, and at times like the unconscious in the production of dream images. This is confirmed by the verses quoted
above from Part Four: following the textual division of the subject, we read in verses III, IV, and IX of the curiously immaterial
nature of all that Peter saw in London, it being possible that
'London' is the subject of phenomenological projection. That which
Peter envisions melts into him, like 'cloud to cloud'. The sense
here is that Peter's mind is no more a material location than is
London, despite the concomitant naming of subject and place
('Peter Bell'; 'Grosvenor Square'). In anticipation of Derrida's early
arguments *contra* Saussure, what *Peter Bell* reveals is that there is
not some anterior or ultimate signified to which the signifiers,
the proper names point. As the melting clouds figure so perti-
nently images function as signifiers as do words and names.

Shelley takes the deconstruction of the division between subject
and object, inside and outside, mind and world, further, in the
following lines of verse IV: 'And so the outward world uniting/
To that within him . . .', all of which recalls, once again, Derrida's
own deconstruction of 'internal/external' binarisms, positions and
polarities, through his use of the figure of the hymen in a number
of texts. Yet, in order to present a fully phenomenological subjectivity, Shelley must make us aware that the movement of world
and mind is not a one-way street, and to this end describes in
verse IX how Peter's mind is fundamentally separate from other
minds, and that he actively partakes in the creation of the capital, even as the images of the capital impress themselves upon
his mind (ll. 303–7). London may shape you, but the city is what
you make it. This fragmentary vision of London, composed from
the unordered snapshots of Peter's psyche, offers a double topography: of the city and the psyche.

In part, Shelley's construction of subjectivity as a metropolitan, urban, divided subjectivity, a subjectivity in itself protean
and indeterminate but always on the way to becoming, – *just
like London itself* – enacts by chance, unconsciously, the failure of
representation at the close of the eighteenth century to hold
together disparate discourses and bodies of knowledge, a failure
mapped by Michel Foucault in *The Order of Things*, and discussed
with reference to Byron by Andrew Elfenbein.[28] As Elfenbein points
out, Foucault suggests that earlier knowledge had relied on taxonomic systems which were supplanted by 'transcendental terms
that designated a prior reality'.[29] Certainly 'London' is in effect a
transcendental term in the Foucauldian sense, and it is against

this sense that Shelley may be read as struggling. Certainly what we see in Part Three of the poem is the absolute breakdown of the usefulness of taxonomy for classification of the city. In *The Order of Things*, Foucault makes the following comment:

> Through literature, the being of language shines once more on the frontiers of Western culture . . . from the nineteenth century, literature began to bring language back to light once more in its own being.[30]

There is, I would argue, a certain struggle with the being of language, a certain uneasy and even monstrous rebirth, at work in the representation of London, in *Peter Bell the Third* particularly, but in Romantic images of London in general, as these discourses work between what Foucault calls 'the limits of the world', the 'writing of things', and the 'being of language'.[31] It is precisely because of this struggle with language and with the break between culturally and historically determined forms of knowledge and representation as they come to be embodied and embedded in the Romantic figuring of London, that I have begun with the Romantic poets.

BYRON

Which brings us to Byron, and to his 'representation' (which word hereafter should be thought of as being placed *sous rature*) of London in Canto XI of *Don Juan* (1823).[32] Written just twelve years after Barbauld's poem, three years after *Peter Bell the Third*, and only thirteen years before *Sketches by Boz* reconfigures the entire literary landscape of London, *Don Juan* offers us the possible shape of things to come, in terms of the literary imagining of London,[33] while still being sufficiently recognizable as having those elements which belong to the Romantic discourse on the city.

Byron has disdain for description because, as he puts it, any fool can do it; the poet is rendered a mere travel guide by such activity, and, Byron assures us, there are already more than enough such tour operators (Canto V, vs. LII). So, London must not be described, but rather imagined and engendered through Juan's senses at the close of Canto X (LXXX–LXXXIII), and throughout Canto XI. Byron's hero thus first approaches London 'half lost in night', as the sun goes down. Sunset is named as the time, twice

(Canto X, LXXXI; Canto XI, VIII). Modern London, that is to say London of the nineteenth and twentieth centuries, must be only dimly seen, all the better to be sensed. In Juan's entrance to London there is a possible pun on Byron's part, a moment of catachrestic reinvention of Juan and the city:

LXXX
Juan was now *borne,*
Just as the day began to wane and darken,
    O'er the high hill, which looks with pride or scorn
Toward the great city.

(Canto X; emphasis added)

This being the beginning of Juan's life in London, it is perhaps significant that he is brought into the city by carriage, with 'borne' carrying in it the homophonic suggestion of birth also. The carriage is important because it allows speedier access and, concomitantly, more fleeting impressions of the city's images to both the reader and the Don. And if there is a hint of Shelley's Hell in the crepuscular moment (which hint is to be picked up in the metaphor for London used in LXXXI, the 'Devil's drawing-room'), there is also the anticipation of a later remark by Boz, who will write: 'But the streets of London, to be beheld in the very height of their glory, should be seen on a dark, dull, murky winter's night'.[34]

The next three verses impress upon the reader the first visions of London in the evening, a city where 'streets ferment in full activity' (Canto XI, VIII). They also reveal to us Juan's response towards the close of Canto X, which is distinguished from the apparently empirical data:

LXXXI
The sun went down, the smoke rose up, as from
    A half-unquench'd volcano, o'er a space
Which well beseem'd the 'Devil's drawing-room,'
    As some have qualified that wondrous place:
But Juan felt, though not approaching *home,*
    As one who, though he were not of the race,
Revered the soil, of those true sons the mother,
Who butcher'd half the earth, and bullied t'other.

LXXXII

A mighty mass of brick, and smoke, and shipping,
    Dirty and dusky, but as wide as eye
Could reach, with here and there a sail just skipping
    In sight, then lost amidst the forestry
Of masts; a wilderness of steeples peeping
    On tiptoe through their sea-coal canopy;
A huge, dun cupola, like a foolscap crown
On a fool's head – and there is London Town.

LXXXIII

But Juan saw not this: each wreath of smoke
    Appear'd to him but as the magic vapour
Of some alchymic furnace, from when broke
    The wealth of worlds (a wealth of tax and paper):
The gloomy clouds, which o'er it as a yoke
    Are bow'd, and put the sun out like a taper,
Were nothing but the natural atmosphere,
    Extremely wholesome, though but rarely clear.

(Canto X)

The juxtaposition of volcanoes, the image of the Devil's drawing-room and the phrase 'wondrous place' speak of both the monstrous and the miraculous, the catachrestic and sublime nature of London. London is not composed as a stable image, as these figures show. But the name 'London' does not bring to rest the seething activity of Byron's London. The name can neither calm nor gather together the activity of the streets, the endless movement and sound of creaking wheels, the 'bee-like, bubbling, busy hum' (Canto XI, VIII). London as a name does not provide unity of being; nor is it constant within itself, for it is just one amongst a range of non-hierarchized figures in the poem. It may be the great city, but what is the great city other than a range of heterogeneous elements, without order, a mixture of the material and the immaterial brought together, and reimagined in the mind's eye? We see this in the yoking together of 'brick, and smoke, and shipping'. Like the later Dickensian taxonomies, lists such as these do not build a particular image, no one figure having precedence over any of the others. Indeed such lists, connecting Shelley, Byron, and Dickens affirm the absence of order and resist all ordering, denying that such an improbable idea could exist.

The structuring of London is thus typical of much of *Don Juan*'s process of fictive performance, where, in the words of Nicola J. Watson, 'even the most apparently stable figures . . . are destabilized by their . . . mutation'.[35] London is already destabilized, always already a mutation without an original or stable identity, the authenticity of Byron's construct being in the fact that there is *no* original, *no* true image from which he has departed. London just erupts, and such is the confusion of this 'eruption', that the metaphor of the volcano above is itself skewed by being 'half-*un*quenched', rather than being merely 'half-quenched' (there seems a strangeness about this figure which I can only dimly apprehend and not explain). Such figures – and the writing of London in general in this text – support Jerome J. McGann's assertion that 'displacements and illusions are [Byron's works'] central preoccupations and resorts'.[36] We witness the immediacy of displacement in the momentary appearance and disappearance of the sail, while figures of wilderness and forestry obscure the city as a whole, even while they comprise the arbitrarily gathered details – the masts and steeples – which serve to impress 'London' on the mind's eye.

But, as we are told, Don Juan sees none of this. Instead he sees the smoke which he translates in alchemical terms, reinventing the city as an unreal world. As in *Peter Bell the Third*, clouds are an important part of what the city is, just as mud, fog, and papers will become for Dickens. London in these verses is an atmosphere, a magical composite of hastily transposing details, a rag-and-bone shop of the heart, though not quite foul. It is very much Juan's heart that is captured, the city being the vision of all that he desires, its very bricks, smoke, steeples, clouds mapping out the transcoding of that desire. And so he can do nothing but give 'way to't, since he could not overcome it' (Canto XI, IX).

Byron conducts the reader along with Juan's 'chariot' as it passes through the suburbs, which, Byron archly informs us, 'make us wish ourselves in town at once' (Canto XI, XX). London, though it has no visible limits or walls, clearly is demarcated by the psyche according to certain vague parameters defined by questions of taste. The carriage passes swiftly on (although not swiftly enough for Byron's taste apparently), where the hinterlands and nether regions of London are defined paradoxically and even oxymoronically. Places such as Arnos Grove are revealed as having no trees.

Mount Pleasant has nothing which pleases, and certainly no mountain (Canto XI, XXI). Byron undoes the illusions on which such places depend; their names are shown to be empty signifiers, simulacra of suburban dishonesty. He continues his scathing critique of the suburban areas and their middle-class inhabitants, reducing their rented houses to little boxes, while mocking the pretentious naming of such ordinary dwellings. There is nothing here to inform us of the nature of London, unless we are given to understand London by what the suburbs are not.

The speed and movement of the city return in the next verse (XXII), as a variety of images and noises gather in a 'whirl' of 'confusion'. Once again, unordered taxonomy takes over from description, as we witness the 'mails fast flying off like a delusion', followed by barbers' blocks, wigs, the windows of shops reflecting and refracting the light of street lamps. Taxonomy of this kind, so beloved of Dickens, is not description, precisely because it is composed of snapshots and not narrative. There are no causal or logical links; no item, no detail is ever frozen in place by the attempted telling or showing of every detail of which it is composed. Instead, the city is performed through the chance viewing of its random elements which jumble together. This in turn means that, through the resistance to description, the city's random elements appear as a host of signifiers without a final signified (except, that is to say, 'London' which is no signified at all, but merely one more signifier of all the clouds, bricks, lamps, coaches, wheels, voices, and so on). London is thus affirmed through the text's resistance to description. True to his word, Byron refrains from attempting to provide a narrative of London life, once again on grounds of taste: 'I could say more, but do not choose to encroach/Upon the Guide-book's privilege' (XXIII). This 'nicety' on Byron's part is of course no mere pose; it is instead, I would argue, an acknowledgement on the poet's part of the limits of narrative in the face of the sublime, monstrous city

The sublime condition of the city is touched upon in verse XXIV (Canto XI),

> That's rather fine, the gentle sound of Thamis –
>   Who vindicates a moment too, his stream –
> Though hardly heard through multifarious 'damme's.'
>   The lamps of Westminster's more regular gleam,

> The breadth of pavement, and yon shrine where fame is
>   A spectral resident – whose pallid beam
> In shape of moonshine hovers o'er the pile –
> Make this a sacred part of Albion's isle.

A quality which is addressed again in verse XXVI:

> The line of lights, too, up to Charing Cross,
>   Pall Mall, and so forth, have a corruscation
> Like gold as in comparison to dross,
>   Matched with the Continent's illumination ...

The sublime is here intimated by the material display of the lamps which adorn both the city and the text. Certainly this is not the sublime as described by Edmund Burke, who imagined that the sublime would excite terror rather than the breathless excitement which seems the appropriate and corollary emotional response to Byron's London. Yet the speed and movement in Byron's delivery of night-time London is not altogether reassuring, given the chaos of London generally. This chaos will be echoed later in the lines: 'Then glare the lamps, then whirl the wheels, then roar/ Through streets and square fast flashing chariots hurl'd/Like harness'd meteors' (LXVII). Here we are witness to the Urban sublime in all its mobility and breathtaking confusion of images. The idea of illumination is itself carried by that forceful figure of the 'harness'd meteor', a figure which, though controlled, threatens to break free from control. London is made all the more unreal for the splendour of its artificial illumination; the combined whirl and roar enhance and emphasize the sense of barely controllable power which London holds. Byron utilizes this throughout his writing of the city. He uses the illumination to pick out random scenes along the streets which Don Juan's carriage passes, until the Don reaches his hotel (XXVII-XXIX). Thus, the further into London one goes, the less real it is, visited by the spectres and chimeras of the fashionable *demi-monde*. Byron's night-time world, perhaps partly an underworld, becomes indistinct as a whole, although images are left. The reader is left with a topographical memory where the edges of the images are blurred by the brightness of the artificial light, and the specific scenes to which our attention has been directed by the chance illumination. To recall

Paul Virilio's words again, context has mostly disappeared in a blur. London is thus produced as a sublime figure or conception because, as Byron's dismissals of description announce, the power of the city is such that it cannot be contained by narrative or even rational discourse.

London then challenges the very language of visual perception, and the poetics of that perception, where description is not only barely adequate but also wholly inappropriate. London challenges by confronting the subject with plenitude and excess in whatever the subject chooses to see, wherever the subject cannot help but look. In doing so the city exposes to view whatever the subject desires, so that the subject produces the city as the other of identity. At the same time, London gestures towards its own sublimity, towards that sublimity envisioned by Blake, by the immanence of the infinite which the city's countless, whirling images, figures, objects, tropes, concepts intimate, all suggesting that which cannot be put into words or experienced as such. Each poem discussed here announces the illimitability of the eternal city, capturing both the terror and wonder that are simultaneously readable through a mode which might best be described as satiric parable: the writer can only write indirectly because experience is not expressible, even though the attempt is made through allusion; the satirical allows for the projection of laughter as the aporetic register of the city's otherness. The sensory overload that is the teeming life of the capital defies narrative powers and the power of the psyche to comprehend, so that the mind is forced to find ways of articulating London, changing and mutating its non-fixable features in an effort to come to terms with the city's monstrous nature. Yet because language is all the poet – or novelist – has to work with, new articulations, new discourses appropriate to the condition of the city must be wrested out of old material. The city imposes a new poetics, a new rhetoric, on discourse wherein the sight of the subject, the act of vision which the subject directs, envisions and simultaneously cites the sights of the city in terms dependent on vision and sensation, rather than narration and explanation. Paul Virilio wonders whether 'seeing is in fact foreseeing'.[37] In the case of Barbauld, Shelley, and Byron the proposition might be rephrased: is sightseeing in fact foreseeing? The answer would seem to be 'yes' (as it is also for Blake), for what the poets foresee is the London of the next one hundred years, stretching out across the century into infinity itself. What they call into being is a spirit which was already there, already at work in their words with the terrible face of the other, perhaps even an angel.

3

Citephobia • the Anxiety of representation or, fear and loathing in London: Thomas De Quincey, Friedrich Engels, and William Wordsworth

There emerges from here a radical shift in our understanding and interpretation. . . . These can no longer be associated with a stable epistemological point of view depending upon the presumptions of a transcendental, unique and homogeneous truth . . .

Iain Chambers

Fear, revulsion, and horror were the emotions which the big city crowd aroused in those who first observed it.

Walter Benjamin

INTRODUCTION

I suggested towards the conclusion of Chapter 2 that the word 'representation' should hereafter be placed under erasure, at least when used in relation to the city text and the writing of the urban space, given that certain city texts in their appreciation of alterity and aporia signal the exhaustion of the idea of representation, conventionally understood. What the first two chapters make manifestly apparent about the identity of London in nineteenth-century writing is that the city's representation is always unstable.

We take this as something of a critical truism, but it is important nonetheless to understand – or try to comprehend – the instability in all its newness, as it first came to be contemplated. Our critical understanding of the history of the city's representations is founded on a certain 'stability' of the city's unstable identity; instability itself becomes a familiar and recognizable simulation of the city itself. The premise of writing the city, of writing about the city as modern, and accommodating one's discourse to that act of inscription involves a recognition and acknowledgement of the destabilizing nature of what one is caught up in describing. Criticism can only follow in the wake of acts of writing which are themselves marked by the signs of destabilization. Certainly, as Jeremy Tambling argues with regard to Dickens's and Baudelaire's 'modernist' constructions of London and Paris, 'nineteenth-century bourgeois reality is destabilized, seen as phantasma'.[1]

This is not merely a response to the modern city as the urban sublime, even though the idea of the sublime needs to be taken into account at this stage. If we accept the destabilizing nature of the modern city on the writers of the nineteenth century and their modes of production, then there is a case, at least with regard to urban and metropolitan influence on the act of writing, that the modernist aesthetic begins to take shape much earlier than is conventionally assumed. However, this destabilization and the concomitant resistance to aesthetic unification is not always engaged with in as exhilarating and open a fashion as in the writing of Blake, Shelley, Byron, Barbauld and, as the next chapter shows, in the novels of Dickens. As I state in my Introduction, this study of nineteenth-century representations of London is principally concerned with acknowledging the constant registration of mutability, states of upheaval and change, and the positive or, at least, ambiguous, challenge which that presents to imaginative writing. There is, on the other hand, another story to be told, a story where the flâneur becomes explicitly the voyeur and where obsession and fascination mingle with fear and loathing. The modern city promotes these ambivalent responses on the part of the individual as part of a broader class-based anxiety, described by Anthony Vidler. Vidler connects the response to the city's architectural and topographical spaces as being the manifestation of the *unheimlich*, the uncanny, and sees this, quite correctly, as the 'outgrowth of the Burkean sublime'.[2] He continues to point out that the response is also generated by class formation in relation to the urban space: 'At the heart of the anxiety ... was a fundamental insecurity: that of a newly established class, not quite at home in its home. The uncanny, in this sense, might be characterized as the quintessential bourgeois kind of fear'.[3] As I shall go on to suggest in this chapter, this not being at home in the city was a mark on being which endured, at least for the first half of the century.

This chapter is thus concerned with the anxieties belonging to the phobia which London generates in certain writers. Taking a range of texts across the period considered in this study as exemplary manifestations of this phobia, I argue that some of the most familiar 'versions' of London are those which indulge a phobic drive, a compulsion, on the part of various authors to express – to bring out of the closet – the heart of darkness which is, for them at least, the modern capital. These anxieties manifest themselves in more or less related ways, the reading of which dictates the use of the term 'phobia' as a definition for shared concerns. I will therefore be looking at the ways in which Thomas De Quincey (in *Confessions of an English Opium-Eater*), Friedrich Engels (in *The Conditions of the Working Class in England*), and William Wordsworth (in Book VII of *The Prelude*: 'Residence in London') display the anxious symptoms of their shared phobia.

I wish to begin, though, with the term 'phobia' itself. Any work of literary analysis drawing on such an obviously clinical term has to justify its use of the term in relation to the texts in question. While this is not a purely psychoanalytic reading of the four authors, nonetheless it is necessary to situate this reading theoretically, given the use of terms such as 'phobia', 'symptom' and 'anxiety'.

READING SYMPTOMATICALLY

The discourse on anxiety and phobia undergoes a significant revision in Sigmund Freud's writings. This is not the place to go into the minutiae of the revisions, but we can at least outline the principal change as a means of offering an introduction to the symptomatic reading of the texts in question. Freud's first discussion of anxiety was in 1895, when working with Breuer, and the theory of anxiety discussed there is presented fully in Freud's 1914 lecture, 'Anxiety'.[4] The ideas concerning the manifestation of anxieties as a result of libidinal repressions are reiterated and given further airing in Freud's 1932 lectures, specifically the lecture 'Anxiety and Instinctual Life'.[5] By 1926, however, Freud had already revised his earlier notions, particularly with regard to the problem of the relationship between anxiety and the libido. Significantly, in 'Inhibitions, Symptoms and Anxiety',[6] Freud rejects what he had seen earlier as the primarily libidinal or sexual cause of anxieties. He goes so far as to that: '[a]nxiety never arises from repressed libido'.[7] In this later discussion, Freud now suggests that anxieties are the product of the ego: 'the anxiety felt in phobias is an ego anxiety and arises in the ego, ... it does not proceed out of repression but, on the contrary sets repression in motion'.[8] Later, Freud will make the seemingly obvious point that anxiety is always anxiety or fear of something; the ego, subject or identity which fears or is anxious, is expectant.[9] Here Freud points out also that there exist different levels of anxiety, diagnosable as either 'normal' or 'neurotic' anxiety.[10]

With regard to the texts in question in this chapter, Freud's revisions and observations put in place some important observations which can be turned upon the act of reading the city. First, I wish to state that I am not reading the texts as symptomatic of some phobic or neurotic condition on the part of the respective authors. What I am suggesting is that the four writers provide us with texts which are marked by and share common anxieties which become apparent in the writing, walking, mapping, and construction of the city. In each case, it can be suggested that the text foregrounds a heightened reaction to the effect the city has upon that which each text seeks to position in relation to the places which it records: the construction of identity. Freud's move away from a specifically sexualized source for the production of anxiety, to an understanding of the subject's persistent registration of a range of signifiers which do not merely reflect the self's anxiety but which serve in large part to generate and perpetuate that anxiety, allows for the possibility of this reading.

There is in each text an act of writing the city, remembering the city which allows the generation of a fear of the city at the expense of the idealized desire of a unified identity pursued in each text. The concomitant over-reaction in the face of the multiple, mobile and fragmentary phenomena of the city serves to point to the fragmentation of identity, whether that identity is positioned as a fiction entitled the flâneur, the author, or the narrator.

Once again such fragmentation and the resulting anxiety is well known from the relationship between individual protagonists and the cities they inhabit, as in the examples of Stephen Dedalus or Leopold Bloom and Dublin, or Clarissa Dalloway and London. However, what is of startling interest in the texts of Wordsworth, De Quincey, and Engels is that the 'I' of the subject is not mediated by an anonymous narrator or narratorial voice, but speaks instead directly of the experience of encountering, and responding to, the city of London.

Freud's theorizations concerning the indefiniteness about the source of the anxiety for the subject[11] come to have a particular cogency in this understanding of the texts at hand; for in each case, the city assumes an indefinite and vague threat to the stability of the identity, which the identity seeks to survive through the act of writing. This quality has already been noted by Raymond Williams. There is, writes Williams, 'a failure of identity in the crowd of others which worked back to a loss of identity in the self, and then, in these ways, a loss of society itself, its overcoming and replacement by a procession of images'.[12] No immediate danger presents itself as such to the writers in question. There are no anarchists or terrorists, no criminals or murderers, no 'perverse' or 'monstrous' individuals who are to be encountered in other fictions of the city. There is not even the specific threat of institutions such as the law courts or government offices, such as we encounter in Dickens, Collins or Trollope. There is merely the city, with its crowds, its poor, its liminal and marginal figures, its lights, and anonymous masses, its locomotion, all of which give rise to the crises of identity and a range of anxious responses. What makes the texts particularly open to a quasi-psychoanalytic reading is the repetition in each writer's representation of the Capital, described by Celeste Langan in her study of Wordsworth as the ' . . . endless seriality that the capital city sets in motion', the city being a place where endless walking leads to potentially unending inscription.[13] This 'endless seriality' is found immediately in photographs of the Victorian docklands, which show ' . . . the vast array of warehouses endlessly repeating their recessed bays and giant hoists down the East End quaysides'.[14] Thus it is the city itself, the materiality, the reality and the reiterated immensity of the city, which generates both the writing and the fear. Significantly, Freud points out that all perceived threats seem to have something of a 'realistic basis'.[15] At the same time, though,

'the external (real) danger must also have managed to become
internalized if it is to be significant for the ego'.[16] The 'internal-
ization' is found to be installed in the remarking of the city as
threatening other to the sense of identity, which comes about in
the very act of writing (about) the city and one's place in the
metropolis. The anxiety which therefore leads to the phobic writing
of the texts is rooted in the perceived – anticipated – loss of self,
the erasure of identity or loss of control over identity which is
the cost of imagining the city.

IMAGINING THE CITY

A number of recent critical works on Victorian representations
of the city have dealt extensively with the double acts of walking and seeing the streets and the life of London.[17] The flâneur
and the observer achieve a dominance in the imaginary life of
the nineteenth century and in subsequent revisions and
reinventions of that life. Certainly, the development and increasing
sophistication in optical technology during the Victorian period
meant that, amongst other things, the middle classes could 'see'
for the first time areas of London other than their own, but in
the safety of their own homes. Paintings and photographs were
obviously of importance. But, as Jonathan Crary points out, the
development of the stereoscope conflated the real with the optical
in a disconcertingly powerful fashion.[18] You could actually feel
as though you were 'there' in the streets, the 'real' apparently
brought home in a quite uncanny fashion by the three-dimen-
sional projections. And to a certain extent, *The Prelude*, *Confessions*, and *Conditions* all rely for their effect on the accretion brought
about by an insistent repetition of a range of visual images.

One direct access to visual phenomena was through the act of
walking the streets. We have already seen William Blake walking
the streets, apparently coming directly in contact with that which
he will later remember for the purposes of writing. Thus the
perambulatory figure's powers of movement and observation are
powerful, even dominant sources of mapping nineteenth-century
London, as I have suggested already. Yet it is important to
acknowledge (as in the chapter on Blake) that the walker of the
streets (to recall De Quincey's phrase, of which more below) is
as much a construct, as a form of unified identity, as are the

scenes he supposedly sees and recounts through writing. The stroller is a fiction of the nineteenth-century writer's creation as much as, if not more so than, his (and, occasionally, her) alter ego. Walking and seeing are modes of production which imply a unity of perspective against which the texts in question work through the tropes of the city. The flâneur implies a single body, with a single pair of eyes. Indeed the feet of the flâneur – whether that wanderer be Blake or Boz, Lucy Snowe in *Villette*, Henry James or Joseph Conrad – become both the eyes and the pen in acts of tracing, writing, mapping the city.

As M. Christine Boyer points out in her study of city spaces, of architectures and topographies, making visible meant making safe (at least for the purposes of middle-class psychic reassurance): 'The great legacy of nineteenth-century London improvement schemes . . . lies in mapping the topography of invisible fields . . . . These fields focused on sanitation and circulation problems.'[19] Boyer illustrates this point by examining the etchings of Doré which serve to make invisible London visible, thereby making it knowable, and therefore safe; incomprehensibility is what causes anxiety, horror being never quite so horrific once you know what the problem is. Similarly, photographic records sought to make unknown London more knowable, reduce it to a safe narrative form, and containing its shadowy, marginal figures at the margins.[20] Criticism which focuses on the visible at the expense of other forms and tropes may have a concomitant tendency to make safe, to domesticate, the *unheimlich*.

Furthermore, while the visual with its imagined unity provides a dominant and convincing mode of apparently unified production in the act of putting together the image of the city, – a photograph always implies that its viewer, its reader, provides the eyes which produce the scene, as does realist discourse – to accord such visions uncritical hegemonic dominance is to sideline the importance of phenomenological and psychic acts or processes of production, while also reproducing the containment and control of the first visual acts. The imagination and memory function to produce their own images, their own architecture, in acts of fictive or creative city building. Thus the double emphasis on walking and visual creation in criticism can tend to suppress, at least implicitly, the psychic process in favour of a more mimetic, and even, on occasions, empirically oriented, aesthetic.

This is not to deny the importance of either the visual or those studies to which I allude (and in some cases, draw on, both above and below). My concern, however, is with the *ways* in which the rhetoric of the city comes to be shaped as a form of architecture in writing (or what I call below, in the chapter on Dickens, 'architexture'), whereby the architecture and topography of the city, when reinscribed through acts of inscription, reveal themselves, as determining the shape of the writing, and as acknowledging what Japanese architect Kojin Karatani calls 'the self-differential differential system as formal precedent'.[21] We are not implying that there is a definable 'formal precedent', a single shape or structure of the city, which the literary text then reproduces in its own words. The city is a self-deferring, self-differentiating space or event which enacts what Iain Chambers calls (in recalling Michel de Certeau) 'the flux of the imaginary, the slippage of the metaphor, "the drift across the page . . . the wandering eyes"'.[22] In its insistent, endlessly iterable, acts of difference, the city imposes on writing its own shapes which, in turn, proscribe the desire to enunciate a unified self. And as the city dictates its own writing, so anxieties are produced in the face of this other writing of the city. The city 'can be the locus for an act of self-recognition' in the words of Carol Bernstein;[23] but it can also be the place which makes impossible any such act, hence the fragmentation of self.

Thus I choose in this chapter to discuss the shared phobia, the *citephobia*, which seems to arise as a response to the perception of the city not being civil, not creating but, rather, dismissing a sense of *civitas*, of 'civil' identity or community, in which the 'I' of writing can locate itself. Furthermore, this *citephobia* does not find its sources, either primarily or specifically, in acts of scopophilia. None of the texts are organized exclusively in visual terms. In the case of each of the writers, the visual serves merely as a means of bringing into focus other concerns, other issues, which are not necessarily logically connected: in Engels's case, this is the sense of moral outrage and disbelief in the face of the alienating and oppressive effects of capitalism in a metropolitan setting; with Wordsworth, the anxiety comes about as the ability of the city to hinder and defer 'the growth of a poet's mind'; De Quincey's London becomes the location-as-premise for the condition of becoming-addicted; all such writing produces anxiety out of the communication of the possibility of isolation as the preface to loss of control and imminent chaos, with the city assuming a role which is the very antithesis of acts of civilization.

PERPETUAL SLIDING: DE QUINCEY, NOT AT HOME WITH HOMELESSNESS

Architecture has been intimately linked to the notion of the uncanny since the end of the eighteenth century. At one level, the house has provided a site for endless representations of haunting, doubling, dismembering, and other terrors in literature and art. At another level, the labyrinthine spaces of the modern city have been construed as the sources of modern anxiety, from revolution and epidemic to phobia and alienation.[24]

Anthony Vidler's introductory remarks serve as a useful introduction to Thomas De Quincey's representation of London, the more so because De Quincey's two primary concerns are with the space of the deserted house and the streets of London through, and bordering, Soho. The first scene, that played out in the house in Greek Street, offers the internal site of uncanny experience, only to be reiterated externally in the streets of central London. Both spaces are filled with anxiety, and connected by the memory of young women. The representation of young, desirable women and, specifically, the image of the prostitute, is a common image, 'almost synonymous', as Mary Jacobus puts it, in her discussion of De Quincey and Wordsworth, 'with late eighteenth-century representations of the city'.[25] Certainly this is true, but, as I shall go on to argue below, the function of the female figure comes to serve a different purpose in the modern city of the nineteenth-century imagination. For now, though, we can say that female images are used in an effort at self-definition on the part of De Quincey, a homeless person, one amongst many, walking William Blake's streets, though not, he assures us, as a street-walker.[26]

De Quincey's London is what Vidler describes as a '. . . fully developed spatial uncanny . . . [a] space of endless repetition';[27] there is, furthermore, noticeable in De Quincey's writing, '[t]he perpetual sliding between the homely and the unhomely, the imperceptible sliding of coziness into dread'.[28] We see this perpetual sliding as part of the endless repetition itself, in the disappearance of the young nameless girl from the house in Greek Street, and the eventual disappearance of the young prostitute Ann, whose location becomes the source of unending anxiety for De Quincey. Both women, and their association with knowable, familiar locales, slide away from De Quincey's younger self, causing him to feel

anxious. This perpetual, reiterated sliding is, itself, the condition
out of which anxiety arises, as Freud informs us, anxiety being
'a combination of certain feelings in the pleasure–unpleasure
series'.[29] De Quincey becomes anxious at the loss of an other,
but perpetuates his anxiety by searching for the lost one, the
always already absent and deferred other, among the streets and
infinite crowds. Writing further perpetuates the condition of
anxiety. The city offers identification with the other only to swallow
up such recognition, in movement and anonymity. Entering the
streets to look for Ann, and finding himself in the 'great Mediterranean of Oxford-street',[30] De Quincey forgets whether he ever
knew Ann's surname, or whether indeed she told him at all. In
a clearly Freudian scenario he has thus lost 'the surest means of
tracing her hereafter'.[31]

The anxiety caused by the loss of Ann is, in itself, merely symptomatic of the larger effect of London on De Quincey. For London
is a city of losses, disappearances, obscured identities, dreariness
and dream-like states. It is the place of anxiety and anguish, of
both body and mind. Personal relationships are unsustainable in
a location peopled by anonymous attorneys, Jewish moneylend-
ers, unfulfilled desires and addictions. Of the texts considered in
this chapter, *Confessions* is the most purely symptomatic London
text, haunted relentlessly by the figure of the desiring self
constantly in search of a knowable other as the means by which
to define the limits of personal identity. Ann and the ten-year-
old from the unoccupied house serve to repeat each other's
functions, functions which define the frustrated, anxious subject
who searches for a mirrored stability for self-identity in the image
of the other. The functions of the females are defined by the city
as belonging to a decentring psychic mechanism, wherein the
ego cannot locate itself and the movements of which are endless, repeatable, and circular. De Quincey's writing merely perpetuates the operation of the mechanisms of the Capital, the act
of writing fuelling the city's engine, while the folds of the text
trace the lineaments of the machinery.

John Barrell notes such connections between individuals and
crowds, and the effect on the individual of the 'developing modern
metropolis' in his study of De Quincey.[32] De Quincey's search
through myriad faces in search of Ann conveys what Barrell calls
'the sense of the sheer terrifying numberlessness of the world's
[in this case, London's] population'.[33] As Freud points to the pain–

pleasure association at the root of anxiety, and as Vidler, in his discussion of the *unheimlich* with reference to De Quincey's residence in London, talks of the movement from coziness to dread, so Barrell identifies the other side of De Quincey's fascination with the proletarian masses who pass through the 'dreamy lamplight' of Oxford Street,[34] which manifests itself as a 'fearful suspicion, a paranoia'.[35] De Quincey is never at home with his presence in London, even at the remove afforded by memory and confession. What we can observe about London as a modern metropolis is a connection between the city and the Oriental Other discussed by Barrell. Certainly the two come together for De Quincey in London, in that the habitual taking of the 'drug of the Orient', opium, is always connected with the Saturday night pleasures afforded by the city at the heart of empire, such as going to the opera or observing the proletariat.[36] Interestingly though, Barrell doesn't go as far as he might. Barrell makes connections between De Quincey's response to the poor of London and the unknowable (unknowable, that is, to the Englishman, because vast) populations of India and China, size being the source of anxiety for De Quincey. Yet while the rough analogy here is indisputable, India and China, the 'sources' of opium, are, obviously, countries. For De Quincey countries are knowable and available to the mind, as possessions of empire, maps and territory reconstructed so as to belong to England, and made over as British. The modern, catachrestic city in all its mutability is not. What is singularly terrifying for De Quincey, as for the other writers under consideration here, is that London is a city with monstrous, sublime and seemingly infinite – and therefore unknowable – proportions.[37] The city has become an unknown country, terrifyingly foreign through its vastness and not a place in which one could feel at home.

If De Quincey turns to the female image as a locatable knowable referent it is certainly to give him a sense of (gendered, and therefore defined) self; to this end the city serves, in the words of Elizabeth Grosz, as 'one of the crucial factors in the social production of (sexed) corporeality'.[38] But the figure of the woman, like the opium found in the city, is merely one more addictive trace offered by London and serving as a metonymic figure or signature for the Capital, which fuels simultaneously both desire and anxiety. Thus the city, to quote Grosz again, '. . . always leaves its traces on the subject's corporeality'.[39] In De Quincey's case, not only are the traces left on – and in – the body, but also on and in the body of the text. London generates that fear which in turn shapes the writing as a compulsive, repetitive form, marked by loss and absence. Ann, half forgotten, is merely the image and signature of a desired point of reference which, in being drawn from the conventional tropes of the city's representation in eighteenth-century art (tropes which, however illicit and 'distasteful', still serve to make the subject feel at home), is employed by De Quincey as a way of bringing home the uncontrollable, fearful foreignness of London. 'Ann', as a familiar form of the uncanny within the aesthetic imagination, is the writer's device by which he hopes to dominate the waywardness of the city. This breaks down, however, because the city dictates the erasure of this familiar image.

What we see in De Quincey's representation of the city and the city's effects is a shift in aesthetic comprehension. Whereas the prostitute had been a conventional figure for representing the city in the arts in the previous century, now the modern city determines the representation of identity. It is precisely as a result of this realization – albeit not fully consciously – that De Quincey's anxiety and *citephobia* comes into being, even as his ideal being is registered as being fragmented. The modern city is now 'one particular ingredient in the social constitution of the body', writes Elizabeth Grosz; 'the form, structure, and norms of the city seep into and affect all the other elements that go into the constitution of corporeality'.[40] There is little corporeality as such for De Quincey which does not vanish to be replaced by the signifiers of an absence dictated by the city; but if we substitute 'subject' and 'subjectivity' for 'body' and 'corporeality' we comprehend the significance of Grosz's observations to De Quincey's narrative in relation to *Confessions'* depiction of London.

The absent, deferred female as the other of the denied unity of specular selfhood is one (highly powerful) figure for the relationship between the insufficiently formed ego in relation to the symbolic matrix of the city. We may suggest that, in learning how to write of the modern city, writing must pass through, or attempt to traverse something akin to Lacan's mirror stage. Knowing how to find oneself in the city requires knowing how to see oneself reflected in the city. But if the city is composed of myriad, heterogeneous images and figures, all of which are transitory, then the ability to fix the self becomes all the harder, caught as it is in a fixation with the transient, ephemeral other, which is misrecognized as a possible image or reflection for the self.

Thus, this 'I' of the *Confessions* is involved in what Lacan terms *méconnaissance*, a constant act of knowledge and memory bound up intimately with a failure to recognize how one's subjectivity is constituted. The 'I' of the narrative returns again and again to the streets in search of its other, as the development of the 'I' in relation to the city is experienced in this narrative as what Lacan calls 'a temporal dialectic that decisively projects the formation of the individual into history'.[41] The history in question is the history of London as a profoundly textual formation, a rhizomic configuration without centre, in which the subject loses itself. And this development is described in *Confessions* specifically in relation to the maturation of the subject as a subject-of-the-city, a subject whose identity, an identity fraught with anxiety and anticipation of the possible (desired) re-sighting of the other amongst the sites of London, is, again in Lacan's words, 'caught up in the lure of spatial identification, [and] the succession of phantasies ... [extending] from a fragmented body-image'.[42] London offers the possibility of spatial identification and yet denies identification in any sense of totality or completeness.

De Quincey's narrative self is spread, then, across the city, fragmented by it, divided between his moaning voice, which comes to him as another's voice in a dream,[43] and his sleeping, haunted self. Being in London means to suffer continually,[44] a suffering which emerges from the impossibility of giving one's identity a fixed location or a sense of well-being resulting from a unified sense of subjectivity. At one point, the act of writing plays out the fragmentation of the self: 'It was strange to me to find my own self, *materialiter* considered ... accused, or at least suspected, of counterfeiting my own self, *formaliter* considered.'[45] The possibility of subjectivity is a possibility traced by false identity, a condition made stranger by the writer's conceit of finding himself in the possible act of counterfeiting himself. When we do encounter the few corporeal references, the body of the writer is on the verge of disappearing due to hunger, or collapsing because of faintness.[46] Writing always writes of the body in a precarious condition in the city. Elsewhere De Quincey attempts to re-member himself corporeally in relation to the other, quite literally it would seem. In seeing his body at all De Quincey recalls it synedochically, and connected to one of the two significant females. He recalls his arms around the body of his first female companion;[47] later, in remembering the last time he sees Ann, he recalls a 'brotherly' kiss, and Ann, in a reversal – a mirrored inversion – putting 'her arms about my neck'.[48] In this opium-memory, this dream of the self lost in London, the body of the dreamer is only recalled as fragments and always in touch with the body of the other.

In attempting to recall his movement through and his memory of London, De Quincey must admit of a further fragmentation, further loss. One part of the town through which he used to walk has, at the time of writing, 'now all disappeared' and 'I can no longer retrace its ancient boundaries; Swallow-street, I think it was called'.[49] Topographical disappearance and absence are connected with the inability of the walking, writing, remembering self. Here, 'retrace' does not only refer to the possibility of walking once again the same streets but also to acts of naming and writing, as the subsequent clause shows. The name of the street is uncertainly recalled, along with the impossibility of marking out, mapping, the 'ancient boundaries' which gave identity to the lost city location. In another place, the older De Quincey recalls his other, younger self as having already forgotten completely the names of his father's friends who lived in London.[50] The city is connected to this lack of memory, as, 'never having seen London before, except once for a few hours, I knew not the address of even those few'.[51] Proper names and addresses are all erased in the city, unless they serve as ironic indicators of precisely what is at stake in the city, and how fragile is the grasp on identity, and what that grasp can mean, within the metropolis. De Quincey makes the mistake of believing that memory and knowledge of the city and its inhabitants is a result of seeing the city. His identity would be assured if only he had seen more of London, had spent longer there, and could identify its places and people within it. Again, we understand the subject's act of *méconnaissance* and the frustration of agency which this entails.

The city thus causes loss and is composed of loss and misunderstanding, even to the extent that De Quincey is at a loss to remember Ann's surname.[52] So complex is this loss that the writer cannot recall whether Ann had ever told him her surname, 'the surest means of *tracing* her hereafter',[53] or whether he had in fact forgotten it. The fragmentation of identity in the city disturbs once again memory and inscription, so that for De Quincey, the narrator and the other narrated character within his own narration, a fragmented double, the anxiety of identity is always a double one. Whether in relation to street-name or surname, whether to place or person, the city-subject's acts of writing are always traced by loss, mystery and the penumbra of half-identities. The truly frustrating thing for De Quincey here is that the loss of Ann, the loss of her presence and surname are related to a precise memory of a precise location: Great Titchfield Street.[54] This is the last time De Quincey sees Ann, before leaving London. It may be suggested that, in this case, location displaces identity, the street name writing itself as a palimpsest for the absent name. Significantly, De Quincey recalls that his 'final anxieties' before leaving the city, are connected to this moment.[55]

Only on his return to London, does De Quincey understand what losses, what erasures, the city holds. Returning to Great Titchfield Street (which is misnamed Titchfield Street in this second citation),[56] the writer recalls putting 'into activity every means of *tracing* her'[57] in his power during his final hours in the city. The act of tracing once more conjures walking, articulation and writing, in a manner which both holds out the hope of finding the other, and dooms that struggle to the infinite reiteration wherein the subject fades away under the palimpsest of the trace. And it is in connection with this frustrated effort that London is described in the following manner:

> If she lived, doubtless we must have been sometimes in search of each other, at the very same moment, through the mighty labyrinths of London; perhaps, even within a few feet of each other – a barrier no wider in a London street, often amounting in the end to a separation for eternity! . . . I may say that on my different visits to London, I have looked into many, many myriads of female faces, in the hope of meeting her . . . .[58]

This passage, more than any other, makes clear the effect which London can have. The figures of the labyrinth and eternity suggest the double abyss of endless space and unending time, spaces beyond mapping and temporality which cannot be registered. Identity is dissolved through the very figure of London. It is significant that De Quincey refers to Oxford Street as being composed of 'never-ending terraces' and echoing to 'innumerable groans'.[59] Despite the precision of reference, the effect of the city is to invoke a discourse hinting at endlessness, both in architectural and human terms. Architecture, location and human suffering are inextricably linked in the mind of the writer, in relation to his perception and his perambulations, which are marked by 'anguish'.[60] Identity in London is traced in writing through recollection of its being 'oppressed by anxieties' and the 'youthful ejaculation of anguish'.[61] And is this not the very source of all anxiety for writers such as De Quincey? The immensity of the city, that which affords the subject the possibility of 'losing oneself', as the phrase has it, brings about anxiety and anguish rather than pleasurable loss, because London figures the self as an identity always on the edge of an abyss.

Indeed (and in conclusion to this section of the chapter), we see in *Confessions* that it is London which, because of its threatening, engulfing aspect, causes De Quincey to turn to opium, as a means of controlling his loss of identity, in the face of loss which he cannot control: 'It was a Sunday afternoon, wet and cheerless: and a duller spectacle this earth of ours has not to show than a rainy Sunday in London'.[62] The threat here, with its echoes of Wordsworth, is altogether of a more banal kind, and, as Avital Ronell has suggested in her study of *Madame Bovary*, there is always a connection between '[l]iving boredom' and the accession of the subject to 'a domestic drug administration'.[63] This descriptive sentence may be read as one of the most ordinary, one of the dullest, in the entire text, and suggests the erasure of identity through a complete absence of stimulation, which is precisely what the writer craves.

As a result, De Quincey visits a druggist's shop on Oxford Street, the proprietor of which appears to the author to have exactly the same dull, stupid qualities as the city.[64] Here we see the city erasing identity by imprinting itself in all its banality onto the individual. But what is chiefly curious about this connection between the city, boredom and addiction is the singularity of the event (as though boredom were the real problem in and of the city). On seeking out the druggist on another occasion, after having become addicted, it is noted by De Quincey that the shopkeeper had appeared to have vanished from Oxford Street, to have 'evanesced, or evaporated', rather than having been 'removed in any bodily fashion'.[65] Once again, the self encounters the other only to have the other – to whom the self has become addicted, whether the addiction be to sexual beings or opiates – vanish. Once more, London consumes, leaving absence, desire and anxiety in the trace of writing as the signs of its topography, and as its imprint on the anxious self. The city traces itself in the veins of the text as the signature of addiction and anxiety. Sex and drugs are folded into the traces of London as the signifiers of the self evanescing, the subject writing himself into his own oblivion. London, properly understood, is not just a reality, but of the order of a discourse wherein the subject searches out the symptoms of his selfhood. But the labyrinthine structure is such that the subject is always already lost within such a discourse, never at home, and always moved on, always being moved on, by what he misconstrues as the signs of his self-identification.

ENGELS, WITHOUT THE BEGINNING OF AN END OR, ANXIETY AND CAPITALISM

A town, such as London, where a man may wander for hours together without reaching the beginning of the end, without meeting the slightest hint which could lead to the inference that there is open country within reach, is a strange thing.[66]

So Friedrich Engels begins Chapter 2 of his *The Condition of the Working Class in England*. London, although not a manufacturing town strictly speaking, is Engels's primary concern in the chapter on 'The Great Towns', the city from which the lexicon of poverty, squalor, oppression and incomprehensibility is taken. Engels's attitude towards the great centres of commerce and industry is well known, and it is neither my intention nor my purpose to cover that ground once again. What I am interested in is the rhetoric produced by the 'Impression Produced by London', as Engels puts it in his List of Contents.[67] Although Engels writes a generation after De Quincey's and Wordsworth's initial responses, the register of anxiety is still markedly present and leads, in Engels's case at least, to the opening of an aporia in the logic of anti-capitalist discourse. In this aporia there can be read, in the place of logic, the imposition of a moral opposition to the effects of capitalism as the language which tries to re-place, resituate the anxious individual – in this example Friedrich Engels himself – who feels himself engulfed in the monstrous city. This aporia is however constituted by the very contours of capitalism itself.

This opening sentence is highly instructive. It twists and turns hesitantly through its various clauses, as it searches its way gropingly towards a definitive comment as a mark of the impression left on language by the city. Forcing it a little (but only just a little), we can read the following: A town is a strange thing. This indeed is the substance of Engels's chapter on the 'Great Towns'. But the sentence is caught in thrall to the 'marvel of England's greatness',[68] and so replicates in the act of writing the confusion felt by the 'man who may wander for hours together'. The inability to reach even the beginning of an end is doubled by the admission of the inaccessibility of 'meeting' – notice the chance element in the choice of word, the random event or encounter of the lost wanderer – 'the slightest hint which could lead to' an 'inference'. Walking and interpretation take on precariously unstable, unpredictable qualities for the subject who can no longer trust to signifying systems, such systems already being in the process of breaking down as a result of urban immensity. As a result of which the subject cannot find himself, cannot map either his movements or his responses, in anything resembling an adequate form. So the sentence peters out inadequately in a hint of the sublime, in the face of the erasure of subjective certainty. A strange thing, indeed. Such language is found throughout the eight-page impression of the capital. There are 'countless ships', 'endless lines of vehicles', 'hundreds of steamers', 'the thousand vessels',[69] various references to crowds and crowding,[70] 'hundreds of thousands of all classes ... [in] opposing streams', 'nameless misery',[71] 'the immense tangle of streets ... hundreds and thousands of alleys and courts'.[72] The immensity and profusion, the endlessness and unlimited reiteration refuses to give itself to description, and Engels's descriptive powers are forced to record the unrecordability of the city, as each figure mimics and reiterates every other in a monstrous metonymy of the capital.

Against the abyss, and as the measure of the certainty of the subject's identity, Engels seeks to oppose a numerical order, which here breaks down, over and over again, into the vagueness of hundreds, thousands, hundreds and thousands, and the absolute loss of identity which is nameless and countless (a modernist discourse of indeterminacy which anticipates the description of the jungle by Conrad in *Heart of Darkness*). In an attempt to battle isolation, anxiety and the self-erasure which the very act of writing installs in its efforts to get to grips with the city's

representation, Engels will increasingly rely on numbers, mathematical formulae, statistics, and finally case histories of individuals,
as a means by which to secure his comprehension in the face of
the anxiety which the city produces. The other key rhetorical
device relied on is a rhetoric of proximity, by which the author
insists on the intimate relationship between wealth and poverty,
legitimate and illegitimate;[73] but paradoxically these numerico-
mathematic and proximal devices only serve to erase discrete and
formalizable identities further. In Engels's heated anti-urban fervour,
it is the very rhetoric of impression which reveals the level of anxiety
in the writing subject through a constant reminder of the event
of deconstruction that haunts every line and passage. We shall
return to the specifics of the passage through the city in relation
to the desire for numerical construction and its failure to represent
London in a moment, but for now it is necessary for a brief return
to Freud as a way of understanding further to what extent Engels's
language – and subjectivity – is charged by anxiety.

Anxiety, as has already been made clear, arises out of the subject's
attempts to reconstruct and control through the imaginary (in
the form of the text) the perceived symbolic order of the city
(not the city as real, but the city as interpreted as composed of
the signifiers of the symbolic order in the mind of the subject).
Identity relies on the ability to stage a series of repetitions which
confirm for itself the stability of its own condition. The city should
be the Freudian *Darstellung* or Lacanian *mise en scène* onto or into
which a stable identity is projected, in which it finds or mis-knows
itself. This is the function served by nature in Wordsworthian
projections of the self (as I shall mention again, below). However, the city's reiterations are reiterations of the unnameable,
the unsayable, as the phrases from Engels above make plain. The
very first sentence forestalls all possibility of what can be known.
The *mise en scène* is, therefore, always already replaced, *displaced*,
by the *mise en abime* into which the subject threatens to hurl himself in the act of enunciation. This occurs because none of the
images, figures, representations or tropes which compose London
have any precedence or priority over any other. There is no central or grounding figure; London is a system of writing without
ordering principal, without a transcendental signified to calm and
order the subject's perception.

The act of writing the city is an act of realizing the decentring
and dispersal of the subject. In the face of such a disfiguring

figure as London, the subject cannot but lose face in the city. Every time the city is written the act of writing maps the unmappable topography of the decentred subject. As Engels's first sentence implies, London is everywhere, an endless topography and anti-architecture without hierarchy. The subject can never be the sum of the city's signifiers, and to be in the city, to find oneself in the city, as Engels does in his opening sentence, is to lose one's self, and to give one's self up to the other, to random chance, undecidability and multiplicity. The idea of unrestrained multiplication teases at Engels's rhetoric, and is at the heart of his anxiety, appearing twice in different forms on the first page.[74] That very figure of mathematical increase which carries in it the promise of a precise manipulation of numbers on the part of the subject, becomes the very figure which challenges such control, promising endless replication. Multiplication is, we might say, another provisional signature for deconstruction. Indeed it is the act of multiplication which occurs between what Freud describes as 'the generation of anxiety and the formation of symptoms':

> In an analysis of realistic anxiety we brought it down to the state of increased sensory attention ... our attention was drawn to a highly significant relation between the generation of anxiety and the formation of symptoms – namely that these two represent and replace each other. For instance, an agoraphobic patient may start his illness with an attack of anxiety in the street. This would be repeated every time he went into the street again. He will now develop the symptom of agoraphobia.[75]

Let's connect this to an earlier passage of Freud's on situation phobias and those types of anxieties which are connected to phobias:

> [anxiety] ... is bound psychically and attached to particular objects or situations.[76]

The situation and 'object' which serves to generate the subject's anxiety is London, and the interrelation and attachment between the anxiety and the phobia is of a mathematical and multiplicatory order, so that the more one encounters that which aggravates one's phobia, the greater, and more pronounced incrementally will be one's anxiety, to the extent that anxiety overwhelms and stands in the place of the subject. Engels's writing acts out and stages the multiplicatory condition described by Freud in trying to write about what is most feared, and what Engels is most obsessed by: the city. This is seen in the first sentence of Chapter 2 of *The Condition of the Working Class in England* where the language of that sentence is marked from the outset by the phobia which induces the anxiety, which increases the phobia, which heightens the anxiety, which . . . (you get my point).

We see this immediately in Engels's text, in the second sentence of the chapter:

> This colossal centralization, this heaping together of two and a half millions of human beings at one point has multiplied the power of this two and a half millions a hundredfold; has raised London to the commercial capital of the world, created the giant docks and assembled the thousand vessels that continually cover the Thames.[77]

The nearly unimaginable prospect of 'two and a half millions' is an astounding number; the population at the turn of the century had been 1,000,000; by 1881 that figure would have more than quadrupled. In terms of population the next largest cities could only muster one-tenth that number at the very most. Indeed, London's population in the mid-century was larger than that of some European countries, such as Norway, Greece, and Switzerland. Even Australia's population was not so large.[78]

But historical detail aside, what we notice in Engels's writing is an attempt to multiply the sense of the city beyond mere numerical detail, so that, in the act of numbering, and thereby defining, numbers fly out of control and the one possible means of defining the city is rendered insufficient. Engels's incremental calculation reproduces rhetorically the incalculable effect of the city on the subject. In this act is to be found the very fear which counting might have promised to quell and keep under control. The image of the size of the docks and the fluid continuity of vessels which consume the Thames works curiously to swallow up the subject who attempts to take the city in, in a single observation. What such anxiety is marked by, and what is peculiar to Engels's text in a particularly concentrated way, is the expression of what Immanuel Kant describes in the *Critique of Judgment* as the mathematical sublime.[79] This arises out of 'sheer cognitive exhaustion' and can be accounted for in Neil Hertz's words, as 'the fear of losing count or being reduced to nothing but counting – this and this and this – with no hope of bringing a long series or a vast scattering under some sort of conceptual unity'.[80] Engels's attempt to describe London, and to inform his reader of all the horrors which that city holds, becomes nothing less than a documentary expression of the Kantian mathematical sublime, where the 'vast scattering' and the overcrowded proximity of the city, can only be attested to by numbers. The irony is that, as I have suggested, the numbers are what Engels seems to hope will bring everything together, providing a mathematical unity for a city the proper name of which only suggests chaos and the abyss, and which reduces the subject to nothing other than a subject who counts.

The ineffectual and self-defeating act of counting has already been seen in the first paragraph and first pages of 'The Great Towns'. It is instructive to follow Engels over the following pages as his writing struggles to come to terms with the condition of the city. Moving from the figures already noted which suggest multiplicity and countlessness with its promise of infinity – that absolutely unknowable number at the heart of all mathematical precision; mathematics dreams its own erasure – Engels resorts to statistics as his writing becomes traced with its own exhaustion in the face of the innumerable crowds, the countless streets and the hundreds and thousands of London life. Statistics promise certainty. They offer the counterbalance to the amorphous powers of urban multiplication. Numbers in the form of statistics name for Engels what he cannot name himself. We read, for instance, of the '5,366 working-men's families in 5,294 "dwellings" (if they deserve the name!), men, women, and children thrown together without distinction of age or sex, 26,830 persons all told'.[81] These figures for the working inhabitants of the parishes of St John and St Margaret are drawn, we are told, from the *Journal of the Statistical Society*.[82] This is backed up with statistical evidence concerning the inhabitants of the Parish of St George, in Hanover Square. Rents in Drury Lane are listed, as are other rents, as Engels subdivides houses into floors and apartments, registering the rents as he goes. All of this is calculated into a total gathered from families in Westminster, which, we are assured, amounts to £40,000 per year, as a final and irrefutable statistic with which to end the paragraph.

I am not challenging the veracity of these figures, nor am I seeking to make anything less of the horror, depredation, squalor and misery which Engels must have seen in London. But it is important to understand how, and to what extent London, as a location within which rich, poor and all other finely graded social and economically determined classes live, has an effect on the writer. What is chiefly of interest here is the fact that, in the face of urban monstrosity, a monstrosity produced specifically by the enormity of the capital city in conjunction with the economic practices which take place in that city, Engels can only resort to economic and quasi-economic modes of representation. The discourse of economics is itself a displaced rhetoric which speaks indirectly of the real, material hardships caused by capitalist modes of production in cities other than London. The capital is thus written as an indirect movement of forces occurring outside itself, although Engels is unable to articulate the discursive and displaced relationships which he feels so painfully. Engels can only feebly, angrily, interject 'himself' through the ironic suspension on quotation marks of the word 'dwellings' and the accompanying parenthetical aside, which hints at the limits to which one can go in naming – or being unable to name – the constructions of the city. Sidelined, Engels locates himself, and finds himself, in a city which marginalizes his role as informed observer. The city imposes on him an economic mode of expression which erases identity. And yet this mode is *the only possible expression* of urban impression on the subject. Culminating in a sum total of rents, Engels does not – perhaps cannot – make clear the rhetorical irony of the proximity which he reveals between the £40,000 and the location of Westminster.[83]

Yet Engels's expression of the mathematical sublime which is his response to London does not end here. As if figures were in themselves insufficient, as if citing a printed source indirectly could not substantiate his moral indignation and the concomitant anxiety in the face of such excess and poverty, Engels compels 'us' to hear 'Mr G. Alston, preacher of St Philip's, Bethnal Green, on the condition of the Parish', who is then quoted at some length.[84] Alston gives similar numbers and calculations to those already provided by Engels, while also taking the reader inside a typical dwelling. This is stock description of the time of course, which relies on anthropological comparison between the inhabitants of Bethnal Green and the 'savages of Australia or the South Sea

Isles';[85] it is the kind of description which can only make the
East End of London knowable – and inscribable – through a
discourse of liberal-Christian ethnography, an ethnography which
is also a topography. But, in the context of Engels's own writing,
what we have is an act of research which, in seeking to give
proof to the previously cited statistics, serves instead as a kind
of grim palimpsest which only helps to erase Engels further from
the scene into a more generalized voice of moral dismay and
increased anxiety. There seems also, following on from Engels's
earlier use of words such as 'wander' and 'roaming' and the
subsequent phrase 'stray thither',[86] a strange, typically Victorian
rhetorical conflation. The conflation also partakes of a form of
elision, whereby discrete knowable identities become confused,
blurred, commingled as a sign of the effect of the city on the
subject, so that there is the resonance or ghost in the concerned
social observer of the bourgeois flâneur, addressing a bourgeois
audience and leading them into those areas of London which
are geographically 'out of bounds', so to speak.

Furthermore, Engels removes himself from the scene in allowing the voice of Alston to take 'us' deeper into the heart of darkness. This is not the last instance of numerical and mathematical
urban mapping. However, after this Engels's tack changes, and
the reader is given over to a series of three case histories of particular individuals and the conditions of their existence.[87] It is as if
the very fact of mass poverty becomes unmanageable rhetorically for Engels. Faceless masses do not excite the emotions of
the liberal bourgeois subject as positively as do the mishaps of a
single sufferer. Engels's writing acknowledges that the very
immensity of London which he had been trying to convey with
all its related ill effects, might well work against him. Yet, despite
the examples of Ann Galway, the two boys brought before the
magistrate, and Theresa Bishop, Engels cannot help but return
to numbers, to provide the reader with the number of London
homeless.[88] In the face of these 50,000 Engels can only sketch the
briefest description of a day until he is forced to desist from writing:
'our language, grown more humane than our deeds, refuses to
record'.[89] As with the earlier example of Alston, Engels silences
himself in favour of the more authoritative and impersonal voice
of the 'London *Times*'.[90] As he had done when invoking Alston,
Engels employs the phrase 'Let us hear'.[91] This command which
is not a command, which has the gesture of liberal inclusion

marked across it, has a couple of functions. It hides Engels in a form of faceless crowd, signed 'us'.

This suggests that Engels's anxiety is a shared anxiety. His writing aims to convey his personal anxiety, an anxiety which cannot find true voice in his own writing, as an anxiety which mere representation and statistical support can generate. The other function is to remove the textuality of the citation. In both cases we are invited / commanded to hear, as though we had first Mr Alston, and then the nameless correspondent for the *Times* present. Voice here is clearly used to the ends described by Derrida in *Of Grammatology*. As a 'proof' of presence – the presence of the respective authors, the presence of the subjects of poverty – and truth. Engels's attempt to obscure himself is part of the rhetoric of presence. In obscuring himself, he seeks to open the way for a more authoritative voice and experience to tell with greater clarity and emotive power, the condition of the poor in London. But what we read are repeated textual effects, devices which seek to impose presence in moments when presence is placed under erasure, the act of citation being the acknowledgement of writing over the guarantee of voice. London generates this textuality and the inversion of the 'metaphysics of presence' because its scenes, its events are endlessly iterable.

This is the all too awful 'truth' of the city, where identity and subjectivity can be erased through the direct and indirect force of economics and the logic of exchange. And as if to assert this, despite himself, Engels concludes his writing about London by resorting to a final statistical inventory of the number of homeless for whom beds are provided in two examples.[92] The numbers grow, the last statistic being 96,141, the 'portions of bread distributed'.[93] There is the slightest hint of New Testament narrative in this last detail. But what we have, as the attempted antidote to the nameless, material horrors of the city, is mathematics as melodrama, a discourse of the numbers of others as a result of realizing that no language is yet available with which to represent a certain part of London life. If we take Marx's famous dictum from the eleventh thesis on Feuerbach as a point of departure – "Die Philosophen haben die Welt nur verschieden *interpretiert*, es kommt drauf an sie su *verändern* [Philosophers have only *interpreted* the world in various ways, the point is to *change* it]"[94] – we see how far Engels's writing has to go. Marx's comment suggests that even reading the world is insufficient; Engels's statistics, statistics which are borrowed, which are not his strictly speaking, but are merely grafted onto his writing to cover for his silence, his anxiety, his erasure, do not even begin to read. They are open to interpretation, and to the possibility of change as a result of interpretation. But for change there must be agency, and Engels shows none, only moral recoil and anxiety at the ever growing number of poor, homeless, ill and criminal.

For Friedrich Engels's response to London produces a writing which is wholly ideological in its orientation, despite its efforts to provide the bases for a critique of the effects of capitalist ideology. The deployment of statistics as the driving force of Engels's narrative of the city produces an ideologically overdetermined structure for the writing which can only ever move between ever increasing figures in an incremental spiral. Such a display of numeracy hints at the ways in which economics govern even representation; and this is what Engels is most anxious about perhaps: that his inscriptions and representations amount to no more than a strange parody of the system they seek to open up for criticism, for interpretation and then change. The anxiety of the subject is the anxiety of the subject-under-capitalism, a capitalist-subject riven by the contradictions of capitalist ideology as that ideology finds itself encrypted in the city's manifestations. There is already a crisis of identity at work in Engels's narrative, a crisis which is all too familiar to Marxist commentators in the 1990s as that crisis of identity where the critical voice is subsumed within the system. Fear of losing count and fear of being reduced to nothing but the act of counting is not only the apprehension of one manifestation of the sublime; it is the ultimate anxiety of the capitalist subject. Engels is caught in this fear, and so misrecognizes 'London' as the source of that crisis, and not merely one more product. He also confuses the social machine with the economic one. The statistics he employs are not signifiers of the city or the city-affect, but codes (in the sense used by Deleuze and Guattari in *Anti-Oedipus*)[95] drawn from Victorian capitalist flows by which the subject is subsumed. Engels's text is thus constitutive of the capitalist machinery of the nineteenth century, as well as being a product of it, reproducing both the (il)logic of its representations, and revealing to us its limits.

WORDSWORTH: THE 'MONSTROUS ANT-HILL' AND THE SELF

'Twas at least two years
Before this season when I first
  beheld
That mighty place, a transient
  visitant,
And now it pleased me my
  abode to fix
Single in the wide waste.
 	
(1805: 72–6)
	Three years had flown
	Since I had felt in heart and
	  soul the shock
	Of the huge town's first
	  presence, and had paced
	Her endless streets, a
	  transient visitant:
	Now fixed amid that
	  concourse of mankind
	Where Pleasure whirls about
	  incessantly,
	And life and labour seem but
	  one, I filled
	An idler's place;

$$(1850: 65–72)[96]$$

London exercises Wordsworth's imagination and anxiety a good deal. The changes to Book VII of *The Prelude* between 1805 and 1850 offer some interesting insights into the ways in which London never lets go of the poet's imagination, troubling or disturbing his sense of identity for nearly half a century. Wordsworth's constant worrying at his relationship to the city belies the admiration expressed in the earlier poem 'Composed upon Westminster Bridge, September 3, 1802', in which 'This City now doth, like a garment, wear / The beauty of the morning . . . / Ne'er saw I, never felt, a calm so deep'[97]. If Wordsworth's personification of London as a sleeping beauty does suggest a calm unrivalled in the countryside at this moment, it is also a vision which will never come again to the poet, and one which he will strive to disavow.

The two passages above resonate with small but, nevertheless, notable changes. There is the memory's uncertainty about the passage of time; there is the shift away from vision and empirical observation ('beheld') to phenomenological response ('. . . felt in heart and soul the shock'); the fixity of 'place' gives way to the more suggestively spectral 'presence'; and the 'transient visitant' is all the more transient, all the less identifiable, as, in 1850, he is now moved along endless streets, caught in the incessant whirl of pleasure, unable to distinguish life from labour, as though the city invoked some immense Sartrean moment of *mauvais foi* as the condition of Being for the populace (the poet included). In 1805 at least, the writer had been able to identify himself by pointing to his isolation, 'fixing' his singularity, in the 'waste' of the modern urban city. However, even this poor sense of self becomes swallowed up in the subsequent revision, the term 'concourse' being the signature of the city's abyss.

The etymology of the word is significant in the context of writing the city, in the twin contexts of writing and the city. *Webster's Ninth New Collegiate Dictionary* informs us of the joint origins of the word, perhaps an illegitimate relationship, between Latin and Celtic tongues. In Latin there is *currere*, meaning to run (out of which has come 'concur'), and *concurrere*, meaning to run together, out of which comes 'concourse', being the 'act or process of coming together and merging', 'a meeting produced by voluntary or spontaneous coming together', 'an open space where roads or paths meet' or 'an open space or hall where crowds gather'. Celtic kinship to the Latin is signalled by the Old Irish and Middle Welsh *carr*, meaning vehicle, from which comes the present-day 'car'. Language as a vehicle for meaning is that which the poet attempts to bring under control. The act of writing the city brings or runs together those images, those memories and figures which threaten the stability of any identity which might emerge out of poetic consideration of the urban space or concourse. In writing of the merging of humanity in the city, the poet writes himself out of sight in his revisions, blending in with the crowd. The act of poetic concourse, the running together of figures and images, is also, through merging and concurrence, significantly, an act of erasure. 'Concourse' is thus a significant term for Wordsworth, given the ways in which its various meanings oscillate and jostle one another within the crowded space of the verse, much as 'Mankind' impresses itself on the mind as jostling in the city (and once again in the memory). The various meanings bring together, in an altogether felicitous fashion which the poet could not have imagined, the writerly, the topographical, the architectural and the spatial, in a flow of words which will not admit of a sustainable single identity. And the fear of the absolute absence of single identity is announced most succinctly by the figure of the 'monstrous ant-hill on the plain' (1850: 149), the city transformed into a spatial-architectural irregular structure. Seemingly organic, without discernibly differentiated inhabitants, the city worries the writer intent on definition.

In this final section of this chapter I want to trace some of the ways in which, in *The Prelude*, the urban scene of writing counters and frustrates the desire to produce a definition of the self on the part of the writer. This frustration is, yet again, the source of anxiety and *citephobia*. The effect of London on Wordsworth is already much-charted critical territory, and I shall allude to, and draw on, some of the arguments and analyses in a moment. After looking at certain critical discussions of Book VII, I will turn once more to the construction of the city and the problems such a place holds for Wordsworth. However, while the poem is certainly to be taken at various levels as 'concerned with definitions of the self', as Philip Cox has suggested in his recent *Gender, Genre and the Romantic Poets*,[98] I am not attempting (to paraphrase Cox) to read one episode or book from *The Prelude* as a '"paradigm" of the poem in its entirety'.[99] The nature of London demands an altogether different approach and response. Its singular heterogeneity dictates this. Certainly, an analogous relationship may be suggested as a reading of apparent similarities between the ways in which London is represented and the 'variety of conflicting generic signals',[100] or, in the words of Alan Liu, the 'patterns of generic turbulence'.[101] This is not an analogy I wish to extend, however, assuming a simple corollary to exist. The problem which the city presents is a problem of comprehension, and a concomitant failure of comprehension. Nature is clearly Wordsworth's paradigm, and, equally clearly, the city cannot be thought of as natural. Not being 'of Nature' in Wordsworth's understanding, the city cannot be incorporated into a vision of the natural. Therefore, signification and representation break down: hence, anxiety and phobia.

Furthermore, while this reading is focused on the city, the self and anxiety/phobia as the f(r)ictional product of the two, I do not wish to pursue this in terms of narcissistic or Oedipal relations, as have other critics. Oedipal and narcissistic frameworks are employed by Philip Cox in his reading of the 'boy of Winander' episode, which draws on Harold Bloom's use of Freud and Julia Kristeva's work on narcissism in relation to the formation of the self. Cox's reading centres on the specifically 'gendered' construction of identity, which emerges as the expression of '. . . generic confusion . . . associated . . . with an equally disconcerting ontological doubt'.[102] Book VII certainly can be read as an expression of disconcerting ontological doubt, which the acts of revision aim to suppress. As I shall suggest, though, it is the condition of London, understood as aesthetically unclassifiable and phenomenologically unorderable, which generates and reproduces the anxiety and phobia manifested in the act of writing about the city itself. But, for now, I want to rehearse some of the critical assessments concerning Book VII's representation of London.

A number of critics have already commented, either at length or in passing, and from a variety of perspectives, on William Wordsworth's encounter with the city, its representation in *The Prelude*, and the effect of the city on his writing. Antony Easthope points out sweepingly that 'for Wordsworth the world's greatest city of the time is a void without meaning or value' in Book VII.[103] Geoffrey Hartman contends that Wordsworth believes that 'imagination is dulled rather than delighted by' the city.[104] Refining this point further with regard to the fairs and festivals of the book, Hartman suggests that the existence of these entertainments 'shows the imaginative impulse asserting itself blindly, yet being reduced to superstition and torpor by too quick or crude a satisfaction'.[105] Hartman's interpretation describes an initial 'one-way-street' movement between the city and the imagination, where the imagination seems a somewhat passive receptacle for the impressions made on it by London. Where the imagination does respond, its reaction is altogether too hasty, too coarse, as though these responses were themselves dictated by the condition of the city. The problem is that Wordsworth is unable to locate himself in the city; his response is uncertain because he is not capable of interpreting what he sees or hears. It is this uncertainty and the force of its shock which the 1850 revision of the quotation above indicates.

Hartman's focus on the crude theatricalities and cheap entertainments which occupy much of Book VII and Wordsworth's memory of London is shared by other critics, such as Mary Jacobus, Carol Bernstein and Neil Hertz. In *Romanticism, Writing, and Sexual Difference*, Mary Jacobus reads the entire book as theatrical (in terms of both content and form), offering an alternative to Hartman's perceived dullness and torpor. She suggests that Book VII is '. . . demonic not only in its imagery . . . but in its *exuberant* parody of Pandemonium, itself already parodic of Creation'.[106] Pointing out the literary antecedent of *The Prelude* as eighteenth-century city poetry, which Jacobus argues Wordsworth attempts to banish while simultaneously appropriating,[107] it is suggested that '[t]he self-transcending natural legibility of the Alps is usurped by urban illegibility, a system of signs where "differences . . . have no law, no meaning, and no end –" (vii. 704–5)'[108] (1805: 703–4 / 1850: 727–8). It is not that the urban is truly illegible. As Wordsworth's emphasis on difference suggests, the city's meanings are multiple and mobile, the writer and observer becoming anxious in the face of a text which he does not know how to read. Theatricality proffers a form of shallow textuality, beyond which there is no discernible anterior meaning; it thus promotes the play of difference typical of the city which appalls Wordsworth, through the constant recycling of imitations and simulacra.

Neil Hertz also announces theatricality as the figure for the city's representation in his reading of the Bartholomew Fair episode (1850: 718–21), in which there occurs the 'sometimes *exhilarating*, sometimes baffling proliferation, not merely of sights and sounds, objects and people, but of consciously chosen and exhibited modes of representation'.[109] Once again we see in the interpretation the perceived expenditure of excessive energy which is everywhere in the city, and which proves so problematic for Wordsworth. This is an energy which is transferred into the writing of the city (against Wordsworth's wishes), as the quotation from Mary Jacobus shows, with its emphasis on the parody of Pandemonium. Jacobus's constantly doubling parodic figure enacts the endless dissimulation and displacement which, for Wordsworth, is part of the condition of the city, the chief cause of anxiety over the (dis)location of the self. What Jacobus's choice of the word 'exuberant' makes clear – as does Hertz's 'exhilarating' – is that Wordsworth himself becomes involved in a kind of carnivalesque activity, a relentless effort to inscribe and thereby control the energies of the city in terms of theatricality, which lead inevitably to the exhaustion of self picked up on by Hartman. And, as I have suggested elsewhere in this chapter, it is out of such restless phobic activity, such constant obsession and reaction, that anxiety about the self is generated. Paradoxically, it is the 'differences / That have no law, no meaning, and no end' which produce and reduce the city to 'one identity' (1805: 703) composed of 'self-destroying, transitory things' (1805: 739). There is an irony here in that this 'one identity' is that which Wordsworth constructs as his response to, and remembered version of, a city in which he cannot find his own identity.

Thus, throughout Book VII Wordsworth concentrates on what

Carol Bernstein calls '[t]he urban carnival of objects and signs'.[110] The carnival of the city interrupts narrative for Wordsworth, and narrative for the poet in *The Prelude* means narrative of the self. In recognizing the city, Wordsworth must address it directly on its and not his terms, for this is what the city imposes upon the imagination.[111] The nature of the city is that 'the site of an encounter takes precedence over the encounter itself'.[112] Neil Hertz echoes these points. Talking of the 1850 passage which begins with the image of the 'monstrous ant-hill' (1850: 149–67), Hertz makes some important distinctions about the act of writing the city as being atypical of Wordsworth's narrative and descriptive acts: 'These lines, so full of detail, are not exactly narrative; they conjure more than they describe. And what they summon up is a different order of experience from what we think of as characteristically Wordsworthian.'[113] Wordsworth is already writing himself out of his act of writing the city. He is already effacing his identity because there is nothing in the city which fulfils the writer's desire to find a single, stable object or identity in which he can find a reflection of his own subjectivity.

Hertz continues by noting about the ant-hill passage that, instead of producing or reproducing the usual 'Wordsworthian modes of experience – *seeing and gazing*, listening, remembering, feeling [they] . . . present a plethora of prefabricated items . . . that are intended to be legible, not merely *visible*, and mix these in with sights and sounds . . . in rapid appositional sequence until everything comes to seem like reading matter'.[114] I have emphasized Hertz's attention to the ways in which the passage is involved with much more than merely seeing: seeing, the mode of perception and representation central to Wordsworth's representation of memory and experience, is insufficient to any comprehension of the city, something which recent critics of the city have forgotten. The reading produced only by seeing, rather than interpreting or translating will always be insufficient, an act of *méconnaissance*. All that Hertz says here has direct implications for what he calls the 'Wordsworthian modes of experience', those modes which we assume serve to construct an identity and reproduce the self to itself as a proof or guarantee of its own self-presence and unity. Wordsworth sees, gazes at, remembers, listens to, and feels London.

However, if the city is a complex text – or a 'scene of writing' as Bernstein calls it[115] – composed of prefabricated phenomena, items, signs, traces to the extent that Wordsworth's experience is 'mediated by the semiotic intentions of others',[116] then the self is forced to recognize the limits of its control and, in Carol Bernstein's words, 'its inability to "grasp" the other'.[117] The desire to grasp the other carries in it the possible confirmation for oneself that one's identity is in place. The inability of the self is forced upon one's identity in the face of the city, in the face of its numerous textual relations, the inference being that the self might be merely another textual trace, open to (mis)interpretation. If the self, as expressed through the memory of experience, is open to and mediated by, not only the semiotic intentions of others, but also the myriad significances given to the self by the urban space, then the meaning of selfhood or identity can never be pinned down or controlled; it is always subject to endlessly shifting contexts within which it merely finds itself inserted as a figure open to interpretation. As Jacobus asks about the theatrical city, drawing out Wordsworth's anxiety over identity expressed in lines 366–74, 'how are we to recognise the difference between the Maid of Buttermere and a Sadler's Wells prostitute, between a Romantic woman and a painted theatrical whore?'.[118] Jacobus continues: '... the fallen or painted woman becomes an emblem of representation allowing Wordsworth to cling to the (here perilously sustained) fiction of a self that is not the subject of, or in, representation'.[119]

For Wordsworth, then, everything in the city is false, every identity marked by indeterminacy and belonging to 'the carnival world of the city'.[120] Mary Jacobus describes London as '... the theatrical underworld of *The Prelude*, that mingled threat to and seduction of the imagination',[121] while Carol Bernstein suggests that the city 'contains an underworld of representation' which Wordsworth reads as a 'chaos of signs', and in which he refuses to immerse himself,[122] as Jacobus's point about the fallen or painted woman has just made plain. This refusal of immersion always leaves the writer 'outside' the city, an observer of a world where all images are inauthentic, and in which every inhabitant is one of a countless number of potentially infinite 'grotesque copies'.[123] I would suggest that all of London is produced in Book VII as an endless series of grotesque copies for which there are no originals. The images of London written by Wordsworth are only copies of each other; simulations without substance, they are constructed by differences.

The movement of difference is acknowledged by Wordsworth,

not only when he states that ' . . . things that are, are not' (1805: 642), but also in the lines, 'There is no end' (1805: 576), and the interjection ' – things that are / Today, tomorrow will be –' (1805: 581–2). Such comments unveil Wordsworth's concern for the self in the face of infinite deferral, the play of difference, and what Celeste Langan describes, with reference to London society, as 'an excess of mobility and paucity of purpose'.[124] It is such a duality, a duality akin to exuberance and torpor, which leads Langan to conclude that 'London paralyzes Wordsworth's imagination'.[125] Perhaps it is Wordsworth's imagination – his poetic ego – which paralyses his own imagination, because the certainty of that imagination requires the solidity and certainty of an other identity as proof of his own. Wordsworth's imagination cannot adapt to the play that London offers. True enough, this play is relentless, perceived by the poet through sights, sounds and feelings as something akin to an amplified and distorted urban susseration, which tells of the fragmentation of self.

We read, for example, the collapse of a possible unified surface or identity in lines such as ' . . . the quick dance / Of colours, lights and forms; the Babel din; / The endless stream of men, and moaning things' (1805: 156–8). The details of the city are unorderable and crowd upon perception with an immediacy which is spread across the senses of the subject, identity being the place where the city writes itself, rather than being a unified location prior to encounter with London. The 'Babel din' (which becomes the 'deafening din' in 1850) evokes the multivocal nature of the city. The immediate impression of this line is that the city inflicts itself on the subject and contaminates subjectivity, breaking down the discrete limits of the self through the multiple and near-simultaneous dissonance set up in sight and hearing. The confusions of colour and the complex textuality of light reverberate elsewhere, in advertisements which assault the sight (1805: 211) and in the trimmings of the theatre, with its ' . . . lustres, lights, / The carving and the guilding, paint and glare' (1805: 440–1), all of which is illusory, leaving its mark on the city's inhabitants who are 'falsely gay' (1805: 396); at the same time, crowds, noise and seemingly pointless flow, converge time and again in 'the bustle and the eagerness' (1805: 161) of the 'crowded Strand' (1805: 169), the continuing roar (1805: 184), the 'vendor's scream' (1805: 198), and the 'ten thousand others' (1805: 567); London is a place of 'random sights' (1805: 233), and the constant catalogue of moving objects, confused with sounds (1805: 160–70), which will later be parodied and reinvented, reiterated as part of the seriality of the text, in the description of St Bartholomew's Fair (1805: 666–94).

The narrating subject is incapable of giving a structure to any of these catalogues of chaos, other than to name them London. And the city is comprised of vast numbers of people, as much as places and events, as some of the quotations already show. We also read that 'foolishness and madness' is on 'parade' (1805: 588) among the 'many-headed mass / Of the spectators' (1805: 466–7), the image of which is reiterated in 'That huge fermenting mass of human-kind' (1850: 621), and which, later still, becomes the fairground crowd, 'Monstrous in colour, motion, shape, sight, sound! . . . alive / With heads' (1805: 661, 663–4). Once more we see the perception of sensory overload which threatens to engulf the self. It is, in fact, the teeming life of the city which seems so troublesome, because the poet can barely keep up with what he encounters, even years after the event, as his memory struggles to recreate the scene. The confusion and multiplicity which attend London worry at the medium of language itself, which for Wordsworth has always been a medium for the contemplative consideration of fixed scenes, single events, objects which suggest unity, centre, origin.

And there is also the image of cosmopolitan confusion which displaces the knowable self, as representatives of different nations impress themselves on Wordsworth's vision, implying that London, though the capital, is not even to be thought of as the location of discernible, separable national identity; London seems to exist as the concourse of the others of the nation (1805: 229–43). London as capital is erased by this other London, the London of the other. The singular absence from this passage, with its Jews, Turks, Russians, Italians and other identities, is the Englishman. Wordsworth is implicitly excluded from the scene he observes, his identity invisible. As the city imposes its images for confused recitation, so the subject, compelled by the motion which writes the city as always already a palimpsest of itself barely caught in the act of constant reinvention, catalogues the urban movements, vanishing in the act of writing the city, caught up in the anxiety over this confrontation with the unfolding difference and alterity.

Wordsworth's language of vision, vision being the supposed guarantor of presence, is caught out in its inadequacy as it is pushed to the limits of description by the constantly circulating traces of the city. Wordsworth relies on the possibility of presence but observes only difference: difference from his self, his desired identity, and the difference of the city, difference within itself. For, to paraphrase Derrida, difference is not, it is not a present being.[126] And the idea of a present being is what Wordsworth desires most. The city is never constantly present, never constant as a stable entity or identity, and the act of writing (about) the city only serves to reproduce through inscription the 'truth' of the trace: *différance*, not itself, we might say. Writing the city, even in Wordsworth's case, demonstrates that, as another signature for *différance*, London (using Derrida's words out of their context, but with their purpose very much in mind) 'differs from, and defers itself; which doubtless means that it is woven of differences . . . but without any chance that . . . [it] might "exist", might be present, be "itself" somewhere'.[127] Writing the city only ever maps the event of the city after the event of the city. There is always the delay, the deferral, the spacing and ungovernable, unpredictable topography, which Wordsworth's writing enacts, even though Wordsworth's imagination can only dimly grasp what occurs. In *The Prelude* the difference of the city is misunderstood, being taken instead as false figures, illusory simulations.

Elsewhere there are the false images and metonymic simulacra which compose and announce the nature of the city for Wordsworth, even as they mark the destabilization of identity: there are the 'glittering chariots' (1805: 162), the 'dazzling wares' (1805: 173), 'shop after shop, with symbols, blazoned names' (1805: 174); there is the 'masquerade' (1805: 214), the 'spectacles /Within doors' (1805: 245–6) and the 'shifting pantomimic scene' (1805: 282), which names the material surface of the city with its constant dissemination of signifiers without even the hint of a transcendental signified on which the exhausted, frenzied, anxious self might come to rest. There cannot even be certainty about material surfaces, as these dissolve into 'less distinguishable shapes' (1805: 228). Wordsworth cannot be certain about people with whom he has had chance encounters; a face has a hazy familiarity in 1805, 'perhaps already met elsewhere' (1805: 218). The uncertainty here is brought about by the city's 'confusion', but the lack of certainty is also on the part of the narrator's memory. As an effort to fix memory, the line is rewritten, so that in 1850 the face becomes 'one encountered here and everywhere' (1850: 202). The revision serves to emphasize how the city imprints itself on the faces of all its inhabitants, marking them for the narrator with anonymity, similarity and a lack of single identity.

This also suggests that the narrating subject is also erased as a distinct identity within the city. Like places, events, streets, London's inhabitants lack particularity and therefore personal, knowable subjectivity. Like theatrical events, like the life and flow of the streets; like the courts, the church and Parliament, the capital's occupants are, to borrow a phrase of Derrida's 'always shadows and virtualities which are elusive, unactualizable, and nonexistent in the first place'. Every act of writing the city only forces upon the writer the realization that London 'cannot have an absolute subject or an absolute center'.[128] The city is informed by the condition of *bricolage*. Writing the city, in order to be true to the condition of the city must be an act of *bricolage*, writing without 'reference to a *center*, to a *subject*, to a privileged *reference*'.[129] Wordsworth, with his lists, his multiple and confused observations and perceptions with all their random, unorderable sensory responses, writes the city-as-*bricolage*, and thus understands the city unconsciously. London is not a subject properly speaking; it is not a privileged reference, merely a location within which unanticipatable events occur. Despite his desire to control the condition of London, and despite all his efforts, Wordsworth conveys the sense of the city, even as he fears what the implication of that might be for him.

The city thus forces on Wordsworth a sense of anxiety because the nature of the city breaks across and threatens to suspend the possibility of what Forest Pyle describes as Wordsworth's 'poetic act[s] of preservation and celebration' or 'enshrinement', where 'the poetic act of revisitation both preserves and celebrates the spirit'.[130] Enshrinement is 'the mode by which imagination is figured in *The Prelude*'.[131] 'Enshrinement' is a useful term here, for it echoes with conventional classical architectural-structural resonances, implying solidity, unity, presence. Significantly, for the purposes of this present study, Pyle never discusses Book VII in his consideration of 'enshrinement'; significant because, by its very nature, London is signally resistant to any act of enshrinement on the part of the poet. London does not serve the poet's imagination in any manner, but is compelling in its resistance to that greater project. Pyle's critical reading must perforce remain silent about Book VII not because of any fault

in the reading of enshrinement, but because Wordsworth is unable
to enshrine the capital, unable to bring to order its signs; unable
also to find a reflection or mediation of his self in the capital.

What the capital thus maps out for the reader is what Slavoj
Žižek describes as 'the structural deadlock of desire'.[132] In a passage
which defines the movement of desire and its structural function, Žižek provides us with a model for comprehending how
the articulation of Book VII comes to be, and how Wordsworth's
desire for an ideal self is always frustrated by the mistakenly
identified 'object' London.[133] Žižek continues:

> When . . . every empirical object becomes available, [the] absence
> of the prohibition necessarily gives rise to anxiety: what becomes
> visible via this saturation is that the ultimate point of prohibi-
> tion was simply to mask the inherent impossibility of the
> Thing . . . .

In Book VII, London is anticipated as the possible source for what
Žižek calls elsewhere in this passage the 'primordially lost Thing',
this being for Wordsworth, I would argue, the transcendental or
ideal self. The city, however, only serves to re-enforce an awareness of the impossibility of access to such an ideal self. At the
same time, all the material, available objects – which belong to
London, are found in London, but which are not 'London' –
announce to Wordsworth the inaccessibility and unknowability
of London as a totality, and thus the inaccessibility and unknowability of a transcendental and supposedly true (constant, unified) identity. As a chance grouping of events and random,
unorderable signifiers London 'saturates' Wordsworth's self, and
Wordsworth's writing, exposing his desire as an always already
frustrated desire, giving rise, as Žižek puts it, to anxiety.

If London is nothing other than its materiality, and its range
of significations, it is also, as I have already suggested, a strangely
immaterial place, spectral without being spiritual, for the poet.
To make a point already made, but to which we must always
return in our attempt to understand Wordsworth's relation to
London: the city is composed of streets, crowds, theatres, church,
courts, government, fairs, prostitutes, recycled faces, painted faces,
'false' women, 'grave follies . . . public shows' (1805: 543), and
'spectacle' (1805: 653). None of these has any precedence or position
over the others, even though Wordsworth tries to promote the

Fair as a model of the city itself, as part of his continuous effort to link performance to civic immorality and irresponsibility as a means of producing a meaning for London. All – even individuals – are 'entertainments' (1805: 516), the staged events of the capital without any discernible purpose or higher function, other than being signifiers of one another, palimpsests of palimpsests, which give no access to 'London'. Even the blind beggar is merely the carrier of one more text, amongst a range of unorderable texts, written on shops, posters, pavements, signs (1805: 176–7, 209, 210, 222, 611–22).

Everything, even the people, are part of a script, a code, waiting to be read but which remains to Wordsworth unreadable:

> How often in the overflowing streets
> Have I gone forwards with the crowd, and said
> Unto myself 'The face of everyone
> That passes by me is a mystery!'
> Thus have I looked, nor ceased to look, oppressed
> By thoughts of what and whither, when and how . . .

> (1805: 594–9)

The image is of 'I' being swallowed up, made anonymous and carried along unresisting by excess, ineluctable movement and overwhelming mass, what is elsewhere described as a swarm and an 'undistinguishable world' (1805: 698–9). Faces are unreadable, unknowable. And, of course, if everyone is marked by this condition which the city writes onto so many faces, then so must 'I' be similarly marked and erased. The terrible possibility is written into the verse in its own constant flow, its lack of end-stopping and its single, solitary comma in the second line, the only punctuation in four lines. This brief, mute caesural pause seems itself a signifier of anxious subjectivity, the pause being given only to draw breath in the headlong rush, so as to be able to give voice to the impression of unreadability. Even sight becomes an ambiguous sense, because unending sight leads to oppressive questioning thoughts, unanswerable reflections on the condition of the city. When there is the possibility of interpretation, this remains tentative:

> Words follow words, sense seems to follow sense –
> .... till the strain
> ....
> Grows tedious even in a young man's ear

>   (1805: 539, 540, 542)

Profusion leads first to uncertainty ('seems') and then weariness, if not exhaustion. The senses are attacked everywhere in London, and the subject is unsure how to respond. The tedium of endless rhetoric and discourse infects and enervates the subject.

Sound serves the same function as visual image in London, constructing illusion and promoting distrust and anxiety. The city's sounds and sights belong to that order of 'things' which are not to be accepted at face value because they 'ape / The absolute presence of reality' (1805: 248–9). Wordsworth does not comprehend that absolute presence is not available, and every act of writing on his part only defers and mediates what he desires most. In seeing and hearing the city composed of texts, of it being a scene of writing and a textual construction, he is not aware that his attempt to write the city adds to, or reveals, the city's being. His anxiety in the face of the city is an anxiety about representation. He begins the writing of the city in 1805 by asking about the task he sets himself: 'Shall I give way, / Copying the impression of the memory, / ... / ... shall I, as the mood / Inclines me, here describe ... / Some portion of that motley imagery, / A vivid pleasure of my youth ...' (1805: 145–6, 148–51). Anxiety is traced here, haunting the questioning mode concerned with the ability to inscribe and the possibility of giving one's self up to the act, while also being inextricably linked to pleasure. The first two lines announce that all Wordsworth has to say on the subject of the city is already palimpsestic in its nature, origin and reality at a remove. Furthermore, the quotation illuminates a remark of Freud's, quoted earlier, about anxiety arising out of 'a combination of certain feelings in the pleasure-unpleasure series'. Vivid pleasure is wrapped up in the anxiety concerning the individual's ability to remember and control the scene.

I have said above that the city was both material and immaterial, a series or seriality of material conditions perceived as immaterial. Wordsworth's writing is always implicated in the anxiety of the subject because London forces upon one the recognition of its material / immaterial condition, and the fact that, like every act of writing about the city caught up in the reconfiguration of its condition and being, it 'alludes continuously beyond itself to something that can never really be possessed'.[134] Wordsworth's self-questioning manifests what Freud describes as 'expectant anxiety',[135] which, later in 'Residence in London', is addressed in phrases, comments and expressions concerned with the need to assert control. Indeed, in 1850 these questions are replaced with the command, 'Rise up, thou monstrous ant-hill on the plain / Of a too busy world' (1850: 149–50), in which the poet seeks to conjure the city, as Neil Hertz suggests (already quoted, above). Wordsworth's act of conjuring is also clearly an attempt to control the uncontrollable.

Yet, as the phrase 'too busy world' implies, control is already giving way; the act of conjuration is marked by the imminence of chaos, echoed further on when we read of an 'unmanageable sight' (1805: 708). Wordsworth's desire for control is marked by the typical paradox of all desire: which is (as is well known, after Lacan) that desire can only function by the loss of what it most desires, in order that the function of desire might be perpetuated. Wordsworth seems to desire control, but words such as 'unmanageable' tell us of his inability. Finally, he can only respond by attempting to create a distance between himself and the city, protecting his identity by placing it at a remove from the excitements and anxieties stirred up in even the copy of an 'impression of the memory'. He states near the end of the book that, throughout his stay in London, 'The spirit of nature was upon me here' (1805: 735). In the revised version the line is changed slightly: 'The Spirit of Nature was upon me here' (1850: 766), while in the lines immediately before these, London has been changed from a 'vast receptacle' (1805: 734) to a 'vast domain' (1850: 765). What is readable here perhaps, in the act of capitalization, is a fear of the power of the city and the extent to which its unruliness might still have the ability to return, like some figure for the repressed which Wordsworth cannot acknowledge. The invocation of the spirit of nature is intended to protect, to ward off the monstrosity of the unnatural city. But the insistence on capitalization suggests a certain anxiety brought on by the memory of the city concerning the efficacy of this spirit to keep Wordsworth separate from London, to maintain him outside the subject of the city. The change to the description of London also hints at a desired separation and distance. 'Receptacle' is the more appropriate word as a tentative meaning for London, for what it is and how it might be conceived. Having its root in the Latin source for 'receive', meaning 'to take', there is the implication that the space of the city will take the subject into it, obscuring the subject's identity as that identity is accommodated into the larger, unknowable identity. 'Domain', on the other hand, offers a precise, supposedly discernible definition relating to the proper, to private property. Less metaphorical, 'domain' hints at bound-aries, limits to London; also implicit in this term is knowability: the city can be defined, delimited in the strictest sense of that word, which recalls the marking out of boundaries and the mapping, the identifying, of lands. The promise of topo-*graphy*, of writing and mapping, signifies the fear of the metaphor with its perpetual slipperiness, and the implications that has for the subject. London thus contained (supposedly), *known* and made knowable in a single act of revision; apparently kept in check, it is unable to spill out uncontrollably into Wordsworth's efforts to construct the poetic image of the self. The limits of Book VII are the limits of London for Wordsworth. Yet the gesture of rewrit-ing introduces in a moment of attempted closure the spectre of anxiety.

Of this enormous Babel of a place I can give you no account in writing.

Thomas Carlyle

'Where will London end'?
'Goodness knows'

Conversation between
a journalist and a bystander, 1870

The writings of De Quincey, Engels and Wordsworth are not unique in registering fear, anxiety, loathing, incomprehension, bafflement and that sense of the unspeakable about which one is nevertheless compelled to comment, as Thomas Carlyle's remark above shows (even as it seems to link the comments of Mary Barton's father and Henry James, quoted in the Introduction).

Such is anxiety and its associated phobias. Desiring escape from such feelings, we are doomed to seek it out. The very lack of uniqueness is itself a sign of the erasure of the self about which the authors in the chapter are concerned in different fashions, and of which their writing is symptomatic. Roy Porter's extensive history of the city of London records many documentary sources, letters and other examples of Victorian prose, all of which are marked by similar anxieties and shared phobic responses.[136] Anxiety and fear are as widespread as the city itself in the nineteenth century. And is this not precisely the point here? Despite the idiomatic singularity of De Quincey's *Confessions*, Wordsworth's seemingly endless re-writes of *The Prelude*, and Engels's documentary, all are, finally, typical symptoms of a shared condition, a common response to London, which lasts as long as the century itself. When, in the same letter as cited above, Carlyle describes the London fog as 'fluid ink', he catches in that metaphor the textual process of the city, its constant coming into being, a being which is always being written and not yet having dried on the page.[137] Writing about the city re-traces and re-marks the symptoms which produced the sense of anxiety and phobia when the city was initially encountered. In writing this down the symptoms double and re-double themselves as the manifest content of the writing itself. The city spreads itself and engulfs the subject which 'signs itself over to the signifier'[138] in the act of writing. The subject becomes subject to the multiple, multipliable inscriptions of the city. Writing of the subject in Lacanian discourse, Samuel Weber suggests that '[l]eft to its "own" devices – that is, to the metonymic movement of the signifier – the subject would become a hopeless drifter'.[139] Isn't that exactly what – *who* – De Quincey, Engels, and even Wordsworth are? Left to their own devices, they drift through the city, drawn by the hope that something will ground them, decide their identity. But London, and the act of writing London, is generated by that very metonymic movement in all its relentless circulation and flow, which marks the subject not as some fictive flâneur (the excuse of identity or the narrative insertion of the fictive subject; *méconnaissance* in the agency of vision), but as the drifter, the homeless, lost individual, whose identity is swallowed up in the search for some sign of order.

The city as a range of symptoms thus replaces the now displaced anxiety of self so that phobia acts as a compulsive and continual re-staging of the perceived erasure of discrete identity. As all writers of nineteenth-century London acknowledge in one way or another, to a greater or lesser extent, to write about the identity of the modern city is to write about a destabilized and destabilizing identity, which in turn serves to dispel all possible notions of any identity as singular and absolute. The city's identity is polymorphous and, as such, bears in its own disseminating being the possible 'threat' of losing oneself. Writing the city therefore becomes a paradoxically reiterative act of self-erasure and symptomatic perpetuation. The phobic text is inscribed in every moment and every movement of its grammar, syntax and rhetoric with the condition of its becoming phobic. And the symptoms are addictive.

4

Dickensian architextures or, the city and the ineffable

The reader must not expect to know where I live. At present, it is true, my abode may be a question of little or no import to anybody; . . . I live in a venerable suburb of London, in an old house which in bygone days was a famous resort for merry roysterers and peerless ladies, long since departed. It is a silent, shady place, with a paved courtyard so full of echoes, that sometimes I am tempted to believe that faint responses to the noises of old times linger there yet, and that these ghosts of sound haunt my footsteps as I pace it up and down . . . . Its worm-eaten doors, and low ceilings crossed with clumsy beams; its walls of wainscot, dark stairs and gaping closets; its small chambers, communicating with each other by winding passages or narrow steps; its many nooks, scarce larger than its corner-cupboards; its very dust and dullness . . .

(*MHC*, pp. 5–6)[1]

. . . this alien city . . .

Peter Ackroyd

INTRODUCTION

'*The most distinctive cities,*' writes Paul Virilio, '*bear within them the capacity of being nowhere*'.[2] If this is true of London, where, then, do we imagine the city to be in the writing of Charles Dickens, whose writing of the city covers so much that, like the city of London itself, it seems virtually endless, infinite? What is this city? What are its buildings like? What can we say about it, what do we think we know about it, what do we understand about it? If anything? Naming the city implies and even imposes both recogniz-able location and architecture: location *as* architecture. To imag-ine the act of writing about that city one would also have to imagine the possibility of the recognizable imposition; unless, on the other hand, we were to understand the unknowability, the unlocatability of a city such as London, a city which is distinc-tive because nowhere. This would leave the writer of the unknow-able, ineffable city with the possibility of imagining endless acts of writing, which by their unendingness imply both an unfinished quality and a virtual reality in the most radical sense. As Jarndyce says to Esther Summerson, 'nothing ever ends' (*BH*, p. 146), and this is certainly true of London. But whether we accept the idea of imposition, or whether we imagine the endless configuration, as possible figures for the city of London, before reading Dick-ens on London, a certain idea conjured by this proper name comes to find itself installed. A structure is put in place, conceptually, geographically, figuratively, especially when associated with another proper name, such as that of Charles Dickens.

Much criticism has been written about Dickens's London,[3] and the various biographies have also had their share in the discus-sion of Dickens's London. Indeed, the very phrase, 'Dickens's London' seems to deliver itself as a hieratic title, already armed with defensive and bullying quotation marks, marking off the subject of the city as one of which we can no longer speak; a subject which is, because of the volumes already spoken and written, ineffable. But if we can return to Dickens's London, shed-ding or erasing the quotation marks, even partially, it may be possible to witness Dickens as already writing the ineffable city, writing of a city which cannot be constructed simply and unproblematically, which cannot be expressed through words, a city which is unpronounceable, beyond description or expression; except, that is, through descriptions which speak of the unspeak-ability, informing us of the ineffable condition of the capital's architexture.

So, a proposition, from which to begin: the reading of 'Dickens's London', which this essay gestures towards, is built around an understanding of the novels and the city that they map as *events*. The term 'event' is drawn, in the particular sense that I am employing it, from its use in recent strands of architectural dis-course. This is neither the origin nor the entire history of the use of 'event' in this context however. The architectural situation

or context neither exhausts nor monumentalizes the construction of this particular definition, drawing the term itself from
the language of the Situationists and the moment of 1968.[4] Before
turning to readings of Dickens's texts which will first offer an
understanding of Dickens's acts of writing the city in terms of
the event, and also a consideration of the mapping of the city
and its buildings and sites in certain of Dickens's novels, a brief
definition of the 'event' in architecture.

ARCHITECTURE AND/AS EVENT

Architectural thinking, according to Bernard Tschumi, has relied
in its classical and conventional stages on an implicit and reassuring received wisdom concerning what he calls the 'hierarchical cause-and-effect relationship between function and form'.[5]
Without going into lengthy analogy at this moment, it is possible to see how literary criticism relies upon similar relationships,
especially in the case of the nineteenth-century novel and its
interpretation. Contrary to such hierarchical relationships, the
architectural – and, by implication, textual – event offers a
'combination of spaces . . . and movements without any hierarchy
or precedence amongst these concepts'.[6]

For Tschumi and other architects and architectural theorists,
the 'event' takes place as part of an ongoing, active definition,
definition-as-translation, of a situation, space or, let us say, architectural narrative. In novels such as *Bleak House* or *David Copperfield*,
the architecture of the city imposes itself on the minds of the
novels' narrators, shaping and determining their thinking and
memory in often unexpected ways. Character is 'translated' by
the event of the city, which is also, often and concomitantly, the
event of narration. The event is that which takes place, the taking
place or encounter between the subject and the other, in this
case the city. Dickens's writing also partakes therefore of such a
process through the development of the narrative of the city as
event, whilst formally constructing the narrative – and thus the
image of the city – from series of reiterated tropes, figures of
speech, repeated syntactical structures, all of which, in certain
ways, rely on negation or the impossibility of being able to describe
a scene in full.[7] For Dickens, London is where the knowable is
constantly displaced, as *différance* takes place.

Some of the rhetorical gestures just mentioned can be seen in *Our Mutual Friend* when the city is deplored for its Spring evenings:

> ... the city which Mr Podsnap so explanatorily called London, Londres, London is at its worst ... a black shrill city ... a gritty city ... a hopeless city, with no rent in the leaden canopy of its sky; such a beleaguered city ....
>
> (*OMF*, pp. 144–5)

Despite the weary irony at Mr Podsnap's expense, an irony which reveals the inability to describe London through the paucity of Podsnap's own bilingual definition, Dickens is equally frustrated in his writing of the city. He resorts to repetition with an adverbial variation, the interminable description imitating the interminability of London in the springtime. The one break in the pattern comes when Dickens points to the absence of a break in the sky. This passage typifies the Dickensian architexture (or one aspect of it), with its combination of repetition, the failure of definition, the inclusion of negation and the collapse between form and content. The text fails to describe London with any sense of completeness, but becomes exactly what it fails to describe. In its movement this passage serves to introduce a sense or idea of the event, but the idea requires further elucidation.

To borrow from Tschumi once again, the architectural event involves the 'combination of heterogeneous and incompatible terms' and the 'questioning of multiple, fragmented, dislocated terrains'.[8] The passage from *Master Humphrey's Clock* which serves as an epigraph to this chapter illustrates this definition, with its sense of spatiotemporal movement, its refusal to identify a single, frozen site or location, and its serial, fragmented detail which refuses to coalesce into an architectural whole. To go further, such an event is what Jacques Derrida has defined as 'the emergence of a disparate multiplicity'.[9] Again, to refer to the passage – in both senses of that word, both literary and architectural – from and through *Master Humphrey's Clock*, the emergence of which Derrida speaks occurs through echoes, beams, stairways, passages, communications (between rooms and between the past and the present), lighting, nooks and dust. As this one extract demonstrates so eloquently, the 'event' goes beyond singularity and the invocation of a static monolith, whether that monolith be a building such as a house, a monument or the very idea of the 'book' as a complete, discrete, and self-defining object, in which a narrative or textile weave is transformed and solidified through a process of reading. What the emergence of the concept of the event has done is to call into question and to 'open up', in Tschumi's words, 'that which in our history or tradition, is understood to be fixed, essential, monumental'.[10]

Elsewhere Dickens disrupts the fixed, and with that the identity of domestic stability, with images of the house in transition, mobile and unceasingly changing, as in the image of Dombey's house up for auction, when we are told that there occur '[c]haotic combinations of furniture' (*DS*, p. 928), items appearing in inappropriate places or put to improper use. The use of the present tense suggests unending movement and transference, and we can tell from previous descriptions of the house – after Mrs Dombey's funeral (*DS*, pp. 74–5); during the renovation of the house, with the obscuring 'labyrinth of scaffolding' alive with builders and details of domestic architectural construction (*DS*, pp. 482–3) – that the domestic, architectural form is always in process. Never finished, the domestic architecture is a space of writing, of invention and revision. Dickens's texts can be read as calling into question and opening up the fixed, essential, and monumental. This is so particularly in his later novels, such as *Bleak House, Little Dorrit, David Copperfield*, and *Our Mutual Friend*, where the event of the city, or the buildings composing that city, are frequently opposed, or used to subvert, forms of oppressive, monumental structure, in the forms of institutions, authorities, practices, discourses. In many of these cases, some of which I shall consider in the latter part of this chapter, the act of writing the city often affirms the city as event which itself resists containment, mastery and monumentalization.

Before we rush too headlong into a wholly celebratory reading of Dickens which draws from Tschumi's theory of the event, we should recall a *caveat* against the seduction of such an idea. Derrida cautions that we question the possibility of imagining an architecture of the event, if only because architecture and the event cannot be spoken of, at least in the singular, without recalling both the classical and conventional and the desire in Western tradition for such fetishes. Events are so radically other, in their calling to mind space, movement, fluidity and the constant flux between non-fixed places, to the notion of architecture in its classical sense, and all that is implied in the imminent history of such a term,[11] that the idea of an architecture of events can often only be considered either through what cannot be said and what is left unspoken, or through metonymic or metaphorical traces.

Take, for example, certain passages in *Our Mutual Friend*. Dickens has no adequate positive language with which to describe Holloway, the home of Reginald Wilfer. He therefore names it alliteratively as a 'suburban Sahara', composed of a catalogue of tiles, bricks, bones, carpets, rubbish, dogs, and dust (*OMF*, p. 33). The initial image of the desert as a figure for Holloway destroys any possible locatable referent. London is described by what it is not, by a term wholly inappropriate yet strikingly apposite. Furthermore, the lexicon of items following does nothing to add to or to concretize the image of the desert. The figure is not given credence or authority, but immediately displaced by a series of domestic details, refuse, animals and skeletal remains. These, we are asked to understand, figure Holloway. They retain their disparate atomization. They do not speak directly of London. They do not have a hierarchy, there is no fixed, essential or monumental image. Each term substitutes itself for every other in the serial itemization of a North London suburb. Yet together they supposedly figure the city whilst not speaking of it directly.

We can read Dickens as having an understanding of this problematic condition through his narratives of the city. Although Mr Micawber's language is a source of mockery and humour, like that of Mr Podsnap, when Micawber describes London twice as the 'modern Babylon' (*DC*, pp. 211, 592), do we not have a sense that this phrase comes closest to Dickens's own understanding of the city and the problems involved in imagining and writing about the Capital? Dickens comprehends the city in terms of its spaces as having texture, and being of a frequently chaotic textual nature, rather than being a series of fixed sites which are unproblematically defined and presented. 'Babylon' is of course a virtual cliché in the nineteenth century for speaking of London's unspeakability. To name London Babylon is to admit to the city being composed of multiple, disparate voices and strands of writing, and to recall the undecidable as the texture of the city.

And this texture, this *textual* quality which constructs the writing of London, is indicated through lists of seemingly random elements. Take for example, the point in *Bleak House* – a novel obsessed with textuality, as is *David Copperfield*, albeit in a much more light-hearted manner – when Esther first sees Krook's shop front, a passage like that from *Master Humphrey's Clock* in which nothing provides a key, nothing promises order, and all is seen in motion:

> Slipping us out at a little side gate, the old lady stopped most unexpectedly in a narrow back street, part of some courts and lanes immediately outside the wall of the Inn .... She had stopped at a shop, over which was written, KROOK, RAG AND BOTTLE WAREHOUSE. Also, in long thin letters, KROOK, DEALER IN MARINE STORES. In one part of the window was a picture of a red paper mill, at which a cart was unloading a quantity of sacks of old rags. In another, was the inscription, BONES BOUGHT. In another, KITCHEN STUFF BOUGHT. In another, OLD IRON BOUGHT. In another, WASTE PAPER BOUGHT. In another, LADIES' AND GENTLEMEN'S WARD-ROBES BOUGHT. Everything seemed to be bought, and nothing to be sold there. In all parts of the window, were quantities of dirty bottles: blacking bottles, medicine bottles, ginger-beer and soda-water bottles, pickle bottles, wine bottles, ink bottles: I am reminded by mentioning the latter, that the shop had, in several particulars, the air of being in a legal neighbourhood, and of being, as it were, a dirty hanger-on and disowned relation of the law. There were a great many ink bottles. There was a little tottering bench of shabby old volumes, some outside the door, labelled 'Law Books, all at *9d.*' Some of the inscriptions I have enumerated were written in law-hand, like the papers I had seen in Kenge and Carboy's office, and the letters I had so long received from the firm. Among them was one, in the same writing, having nothing to do with the business of the shop, but announcing that a respectable man aged forty-five wanted engrossing or copying to execute with neatness and dispatch .... There were several second-hand bags, blue and red, hanging up. A little way within the shop-door, lay heaps of old crackled parchment scrolls, and discoloured and dog's-eared law papers. I could have fancied that all the rusty keys, of which there must have been hundreds huddled together as old iron, had once belonged to doors of rooms or strong chests in lawyers' offices. The litter of rags tumbled partly into and partly out of a one-legged wooden scale, hanging without any counterpoise from a beam, might have been counsellors' bands and gowns torn up. One had only to fancy ... that yonder

bones in a corner, piled together and picked very clean, were the bones of clients, to make the picture complete.

As it was still foggy and dark, and as the shop was blinded besides by the wall of Lincoln's Inn, intercepting the light within a couple of yards, we should not have seen so much but for a lighted lantern that an old man in spectacles and a hairy cap was carrying about in the shop.

(*BH*, pp. 98–9)

In describing the contents of the window, Esther's narrative becomes the window, the window becoming the narrative. The contents are so numerous that to describe the contents is in fact to describe the composition of the window itself, to provide the reader with an architextural approximation of the window itself in the form of the chance narrative, as the eye takes in by accident, the multiple and heterogeneous elements. Esther's narrative is shaped as an event according to her chance encounter with the front of Krook's shop. Architecture assumes textual form which cannot be wholly governed. Esther appears in the process of seeking to impose order and taxonomy on the window, by grouping its miscellaneous bric-a-brac: bottles, volumes of books, papers, bags, more papers, keys, rags, and bones. These, she imagines, have to do with the legal trade, but this is only a narrative of her own fancy, a narrative which Richard tries to support through interpreting the skeletal piles. However, as the types of bottles attest, there is no absolutely justifiable order which can be composed or constructed. The various phenomena have merely random, uncontrollable relationships, marked by ambiguity, as in the case of the rags which are simultaneously 'partly into' and 'partly out of' a scale, and shown only by chance, as the last sentence reveals, because of the accidental movements of a lamp carried by Krook inside the shop. Thus the perceived architecture of the window is opened up to the architexture of the event of encountering the window and its contents. Textual randomness confronts the desire for order on the part of the subject.

Hence my use of the term 'architexture' in the title of this chapter, which suggests, among many other things, the desire to shake the solidity of the monumental, which desire is always present in Dickens. The history of meaning which the term 'architecture' puts into place and into operation every time it is used is so overdetermined that, like the phrase, 'Dickens's London', it cannot be evoked or announced without there being a certain return to particular understandings, a certain monumentalization. Architexture, on the other hand, speaks of architecture without speaking it, privileging the narrative over the monumental, movement over the static, and informing us through the possible homology of structural resemblances between architecture and narrative, form and content. This is most immediately apparent in the phrase 'winding passages' in the excerpt from *Master Humphrey's Clock*, with its self-conscious reference to Dickens's own prose and to the details of the house. It is also apparent in the cataloguing of Holloway. We read the text listing the items as a substitute for description. The items comprise the list which simultaneously serve to imagine the particular area of London, whilst also constructing the text itself. Dickens builds his narratives out of such lists, the repeated presence of which mark the text as architextural event.

DISPARATE MULTIPLICITIES

In writing London, Dickens clearly opens up the fixed, essential and monumental to a questioning and destabilization, involving techniques which require the understanding of disparate multiplicity. He does so, furthermore, in an effort to be faithful to the ineffable labyrinth that is the modern city of London. While the novelist may well be 'very particular about street names', as Peter Ackroyd puts it,[12] this strategy does nothing to counter the immanence of the urban abyss which Dickens conjures. In Ackroyd's words again, the city 'both is and is not the same'.[13] Dickens happily substitutes, displaces, confuses and reduplicates elements which speak about London. His language registers the endlessly signifying processes of iterability and *différance* which is the city, and which mark the city as being structured like the unconscious (or like a language) whilst also revealing that the city is not to be spoken of directly or seen whole.

In *Oliver Twist*, a novel in which all of the neighbourhoods are, 'but for their names, mutually indistinguishable',[14] the Artful Dodger objects to entering London with Oliver until night; so, although Dickens names the streets around Islington, neither we nor Oliver can see the place (*OT*, pp. 99–103). The street names hover, like disembodied spectres in the chimerical text.[15] All we are told is that the streets are the dirtiest, most wretched streets, narrow, muddy and filled with filthy odours (*OT*, p. 103). Any possible structural identification is lost, obscured in ephemera and effluvia. Mud, fog, rain all serve similar obfuscating and metonymic purposes through an open series of endless substitutions in *Bleak House*, while, in *Our Mutual Friend*, vessels appear to be 'ashore', houses 'afloat', the ceiling of a room is not the ceiling at all but the floor of the room above (seen from below), lacking the plastering necessary to conform the architectural convention of defining a ceiling (*OMF*, p. 21). Roof, walls and floor are comprehensible only in the process of decomposition (*OMF*, p. 21). Stairs are little better than ladders because of 'inappropriate' construction (*OMF*, p. 21), while a building is described as having a forehead, marked by a 'rotten wart of wood' (*OMF*, p. 21). How this can be seen is literally not clear, however, because, as we are told, '*the whole was very indistinctly seen in the obscurity of the night*' (*OMF*, p. 21; my emphasis).[16] While we can see details with poetic licence (as was clearly the case with street names from *Oliver Twist*), the architectural entirety is resisted, hidden, erased. Indeed the entire architectural meaning is brought into question, deconstructed as it is into a series of ambiguously architectural details (this being the case whether Dickens writes of a building, a street or an area). The eye is moved from piece to piece, but the gaze is ultimately refused an overall meaning, a monumental, organized presence on which it can fix.

Once again the scene of the event is clearly one which questions meaning and the possibility of its assertion. Dickens writes the city-event at every level, making fixed and essential meanings ambiguous, whether describing a single building, building materials, a street, structures such as Chancery or the Circumlocution Office, the streets of *Our Mutual Friend*, a district of London, or what can appear to be the movement of the entire city at any given moment. Even fog is not a fixed element, not some essential or originary source of architectonic or structuring ability, capable as it is of being smeared by the 'light of kilnfires' in *Our Mutual Friend* (*OMF*, p. 33).

This all points in a certain direction. While Dickens is obviously an urban, rather than a rural writer, as Terry Eagleton has suggested[17] – and there is very much a sense for Dickens that to be urban means being part of London, as opposed to just any city – there is nonetheless an ambiguous, even ambivalent relationship between the writer and what is written. I raise this point because it is necessary to understand the continuous presence of this tension throughout Dickens's novels. Against this tension Dickens plays off the writing of the city as a writing which, if hinting at the ineffable, reassures to a certain extent through the comfort (to some) of endless seriality and reiteration. There is not a shift between early and mature form, argued for by Terry Eagleton. Eagleton suggests that the 'anarchic, decentred, fragmentary forms of the early novels' come to be replaced by the 'unified structures of the mature fiction',[18] which forms and structures parallel the developments in capitalist modes of production, ideological state apparatuses and juridico-bureaucratic networks. In his Althusserian impersonation – he do the theorists in different voices – Eagleton argues that the later novels 'mime . . . a set of [systematic] conflicts and non-relations'.[19] Appealing as they are, such contentions are only partly accurate in their assessment, and for a very good reason: whilst recognizing, in the words of Allon White, a 'certain homology between sentence structure and plot structure',[20] analyses such as Eagleton's do not take the recognition far enough. Such analyses do not comprehend the strategic use of the fragmentary situation of the city as a non-hierarchical counterbalance to the monolithic imposition upon the urban narrative of the juridic, capitalist, bureaucratic, ideological architectures. The counterbalance which is the city's constant *taking place*, its unfolding of its otherness, effects an aporetic opening between oppressive systems and that which does take place. The fulcrum becomes in effect a lever.

One striking instance of the deployment of the city against an imposing structure (in this case the power of the Law), and the attendant ambiguity which such a scene uneasily articulates, comes with the scene of Oliver Twist's arrest. In Chapter 11, Oliver is arrested for having allegedly stolen a pocket handkerchief. The movement and events of the scene are notable in their precipitous violence, a violence of structure which acknowledges the force with which the Law is enforced, as Dickens works deconstructively between issues of justice and the Law.[21] We are told:

> The offence had been committed within the district, and in the immediate neighbourhood of, a very notorious police office. The crowd had only the satisfaction of accompanying Oliver through two or three streets, and down a place called Mutton

> Hill, where he was led beneath a low archway, and up a dirty
> Court . . . by the back way. It was a small paved yard . . . [Oliver
> entered] . . . through a door . . . which led into a stone cell. . . .
> The cell was in shape and size something like an area cellar,
> only not so light. It was most intolerably dirty.
>
> (*OT*, p. 118)

The passages down which Oliver is hurried also compose the
passage in writing which hurries the subject to that place where
he will be brought before the Law. Yet, where exactly is that
place, the place of the Law? Can we even talk about the place of
the Law? This seems unlikely, precisely because of the precipita-
tion that marks the passage, and which the passage marks. Dickens
talks of the 'district' and the 'immediate neighbourhood'; both
are very domestic, urban descriptions rather than being specific
names for the place of the Law. The Law is gestured towards
but not indicated outright, such a si(gh)ting being impossible.
And Oliver's passage is described, indistinctly, as being through
'two or three streets'. Mutton Hill is named, but this gives us no
real sense of place. Furthermore, Oliver's access to the Law is
very indirect, being through low archways, dirty courts and back
passages. The overall sense is not one of precision but of the
labyrinthine nature of the city, and of its indescribability. Given
this, and the way in which Oliver is admitted to the unknown
place of the Law, there is available to us a sense that the ineffability of place undoes or, at the very least, troubles, the structure
and site within which the Law is supposed to operate.

There is something curiously illegal about Oliver's taking, and
we read, I believe, that the Law is for Dickens illicit in its force
and violence, both of which have little to do with justice. The
Law is made to appear fragile and improperly situated by its
being precariously placed in an unspeakable landscape. Even when
Oliver is taken to the cell and placed in it, the details given are
brief. They are the dirty court and a small paved yard. The cell
itself is described as being 'in shape and size something like an
area cellar, only not so light. It was most intolerably dirty'. 'Something like' is hardly the most precise of analogical phrases,[22] and
this itself is negated by the fact that the cell is 'not so light' as an
area cellar. None of the descriptive phrases used by Dickens invoke
the Law; they belong instead to the taxonomy of working-class
slum housing familiar from Engels and Mayhew, the details being

general enough to invoke a sense of any slum dwelling in London at the time of the novel.[23] This of course can be read as suggesting that all the poor are in a metaphorical jail. But Dickens's use of an architectural lexicon descriptive of poverty does nothing to uphold the sense that Oliver is either in the presence or the place of the Law. The play between cell and cellar is vertiginously ambiguous, while the Law is further reduced in power through the use of the term 'court' in its architectural and domestic, rather than judicial sense. When the Law does come to be represented in the shape of Mr Fang, its power is immediately unsettled by Fang's lack of power over proceedings, by Mr Brownlow's worrying interjections, and by the arrival of justice in the court of Law in the shape of the bookseller.

What we are witness to in Chapter 11 – what in fact we are required to bear witness to – is a certain oscillation of architextural structures between the siting and citation of the city, and the place of the Law (which is precisely the aporetic experience of the event). The structure being described, to borrow from Derrida on justice and the law, is one in which 'law (*droit*) is essentially deconstructible, whether because it is *founded, constructed* on interpretable or transformable textual strata ... or because its ultimate *foundation* is by definition unfounded'.[24] Derrida's language uses specifically architectural terms in order to demonstrate the Law's structure and the possibility of deconstruction. He continues: '... it is the deconstructible structure of law (*droit*) ... that also insures the possibility of deconstruction. Justice in itself ... is not deconstructible .... Deconstruction is justice'.[25] Dickens performs in the passage above the very deconstructibility of Law described by Derrida as imaginable. And he does so furthermore through the use of London's mobile structures which serve to produce justice for Oliver. Architexture *is* a condition of justice, its very possibility.

DISORGANIZING SYSTEMS

It can be seen then in this performance that, in all its immanence and ineffability, the architexture of the fluid, mobile, abyssal city is ranged against – and through – the solid architecture of whichever power structure is Dickens's target. Certainly, there is a 'certain homology'; but that homology is not necessarily between, say, sentence structure and Circumlocution Office, or syntax and

Chancery, even though there may very well be such elements available to our reading. The homology is more complex as we can see from the opening pages of *Bleak House*. In Mark Wigley's words (talking of Derrida's writing, though what he says is equally applicable to Dickens):

> ... the text, in a kind of strategic transference, assumes the form of what it describes ... it begins to shape itself according to the *spatial logic* ... in order to articulate the somewhat uneasy relationship between a certain kind of thinking and a certain kind of space.[26] (emphasis added)

At the beginning of *Bleak House* Dickens's architextures assume the spatial logic of the city, rather than the ideological logic of 'repressive institutional spaces'.[27] The form being assumed is not that of Chancery or the Circumlocution Office, but the streets, the houses, the fog, the weather in general, the aleatory movements of the city's inhabitants, whose wanderings constitute 'London' at any given instance, yet which constitutions are always changing. The uneasy relationship belongs to an effort to shape thinking and writing in a manner faithful to the condition of London itself. The opening of *Bleak House* is worth quoting at length:

> London. Michaelmas term lately over, and the Lord Chancellor sitting in Lincoln's Inn Hall. Implacable November weather. As much mud in the streets, as if the waters had but newly retired from the face of the earth, and it would not be wonderful to meet a Megalosaurus, forty feet long or so, wading like an elephantine lizard up Holborn Hill. Smoke lowering down from chimney-pots, making a soft black drizzle with flakes of soot in it as big as full-grown snowflakes – gone into mourning, one might imagine, for the death of the sun. Dogs, undistinguishable in mire. Horses, scarcely better; splashed to their very blinkers. Foot passengers, jostling one another's umbrellas, in a general infection of ill temper, and losing their foot-hold at street-corners, where tens of thousands of other foot passengers have been slipping and sliding since the day broke (if this day ever broke), adding new deposits to the crust upon crust of mud, sticking at those points tenaciously to the pavement, and accumulating at compound interest.

Fog everywhere. Fog up the river, where it flows among green aits and meadows; fog down the river, where it rolls defiled among the tiers of shipping, and the waterside pollutions of a great (and dirty) city. Fog on the Essex Marshes, fog on the Kentish heights. Fog creeping into the cabooses of collier-brigs; fog lying out on the yards, and hovering in the rigging of great ships; fog drooping on the gunwales of barges and small boats. Fog in the eyes and throats of ancient Greenwich pensioners, wheezing by the firesides of their wards; fog in the stem and bowl of the afternoon pipe of the wrathful skipper, down in his close cabin; fog cruelly pinching the toes and fingers of his shivering little 'prentice boy on deck. Chance people on the bridges peeping over the parapets into a nether sky of fog, with fog all round them, as if they were up in a balloon, and hanging in the misty clouds.

Gas looming through the fog in divers places in the streets, much as the sun may, from the spongey fields, be seen to loom by husbandman and ploughboy. Most of the shops lighted two hours before their time – as the gas seems to know, for it has a haggard and unwilling look.

The raw afternoon is rawest, and the dense fog is densest, and the muddy streets are muddiest, near that leaden-headed old obstruction, appropriate ornament for the threshold of a leaden-headed old corporation: Temple Bar.

(*BH*, pp. 49–50)

London. This is the first word, the first 'sentence' of the novel. The word stands there before the reader as an unpassable, indefinable shibboleth or limit, defying definition and enunciation. It serves as an architectural fact, solid and immovable, invoking the most classical and conventional definitions in the history of architecture. Silencing the reader, the brute presence defies commentary and yet invites questioning. We desire to know more and yet do not know what to say, how to respond. The name of the city prohibits and renders mute. After this imposition of the proper name as edifice and monument, what can be said or known of the city? In this one name is everything against which Dickens's architexture militates, in the most English of fashions, by invoking the weather and the condition of the streets and giving them cultural and topographical specificity in the writing of the city *against* its name.

In writing against the monumental signature of the city this
passage emphasizes the random ordering of spatial logic according to what is being described; furthermore it displays the 'somewhat uneasy relationship between a certain kind of thinking and
a certain kind of space', spoken of by Wigley above. The imagined figure of the Megalosaurus estranges all possible identification of the city, and the prehistoric thus imagined offers to erase
the city as an organizable historical narrative (in *Dombey and Son*
London becomes 'the monster, roaring in the distance', at least
for Harriet Harker: *DS*, p. 563). Dogs cannot be seen, and horses
fare hardly any better, while umbrellas become confused. Dino-
saurs, soot, chimney-pots, dogs, horses and umbrellas: the condition of London and the details of the event frustrate every
attempt at ordering and mastery. Taxonomy, analogy, metaphor
all founder in the face of the event (we have already seen this
effect above in Esther Summerson's attempted description of
Krook's window). Dickens's random reading of the city, his
architextures, present us with a means of exposing the limits of
fixing meaning and, through this, the limits of the utterable. In
order to pursue this further in relation to other descriptions of
the city, seeing how London is such a determining yet unpredictable factor in Dickens's writing, we can usefully consider certain
misreadings of the passage itself (and, by extension, *Bleak House*),
which do not take the city and effect of the city either partially
or fully into account.

David Musselwhite understands *Bleak House* as a 'massively
closed edifice', a 'dreadful prison – a prison house of language,
a prison house of the soul'.[28] Certainly writing about a novel which
takes as its title the name of a house about which the novel concerns itself would seem to encourage architectural metaphors of
a particularly monumental kind. Musselwhite's description invites
images of the tomb and the prison, and we should hardly be
surprised at the latter metaphor of the two, given the text's interest
in the periphrastic functions of the Law as a form of imposing
institution and edifice. The Law can be said to take to the streets,
to take up street-walking (especially with the advent of Peel's
Bow Street Runners), in order that the streets of the city might
be rendered no longer lawless. Yet to take Musselwhite's position
is to ignore London, and especially its representation, reproduced
above, in the novel's powerful opening paragraphs. This is not
to deny that the text might come to figure in one possible reading

what Steven Connor describes as 'orderly closure'.[29] It is to be remembered, however, that this order and closure is opposable, as Connor tells us, with another spatial metaphor, that of 'sprawling openness'.[30] Such sprawling openness is figured in the passage above as the city resists all attempts to impose order on it, and, in return, affects the manner of writing about the city, and the shaping of narrative itself. Musselwhite's description only provides part of the picture, a picture delineated out of a desire on the part of the critic to impose and control, yet hiding that very desire – desire may well be already hidden as the unconscious of the critical subjectivity which seeks to decry the Law – to imagine the effects and the power of the Law as being present everywhere.

Such misrepresentation or partial representation is typical of New Historicism in its pseudo-Foucauldian excesses. Musselwhite's reading is at least attentive to certain textual nuances. D.A. Miller's criticism of *Bleak House*, on the other hand, succumbs to a practice of figural inversion in order to prove its case that the Law is wherever one looks (instead of recognizing that wherever one looks hard enough one will find the Law no matter what shape it seems to take). Miller's reading is a misreading if only because it does not understand that Chancery, while seeming to be everywhere, is in fact limited. Miller sees the fog, without seeing through it, and takes it to be merely some quasi-legal or judicial metaphor for the obfuscating nature of legal activity: 'Though the court is affirmed to be situated "at the very heart of the fog" ... this literally nebulous information only restates the difficulty of locating it substantially. Since there is "fog everywhere"'.[31] From this argument, Miller goes on to assert that Chancery's 'organization of power ... has become topography itself'.[32] Ignoring landscape, architecture, the city, mapping and all the other figures which are so prevalent a feature of the Dickensian architexture, Miller pursues the Law until it is part of the very air that all the characters breathe, until the streets and building themselves become permeated by juridical structure and the power it figures and disseminates.

If this is all *Bleak House* is about, then, to paraphrase J. Hillis Miller, why bother reading it?[33] If Chancery is all there is, as institution, location, discourse, representation, why so many houses, so many streets and locations which figure as serial reiterations of one another, despite their geographical and spatial identity and specificity, and despite such apparent acts of what Allon White calls 'discursive closure'?[34] The iterability of the serial city disjoints ahead of all reading the possibility of unity or identity. The 'merely thematic' reading[35] cannot, by the very necessity which drives it, take into account that which is anti- or a-thematic, such as an act of writing which attempts to write the city, an a-thematic space and architexture (unless one wishes to put the city to work for some particular purpose, which, of course, the city of London as the other of writing in the nineteenth century does not allow). Chancery may well seem to be everywhere, like the fog, but Chancery's only power is the power to maintain itself through obfuscation, like the Circumlocution Office in *Little Dorrit*. It shows its limits by being unable to resolve the case of Jarndyce vs Jarndyce; were it to do so, its purpose would evaporate, its power gone, and all revealed in the clear light of day. Chancery is then infected by the atmosphere of London, rather than the atmosphere of London being a metaphor for the Law and its 'power'. D. A. Miller's reading of the novel is a somewhat desperate attempt to fix meaning, which Dickens gives up on the first page, and which Esther gives up soon after. Miller's vague assertions about the 'institutional practice' of Chancery[36] (a comment unsupported by any historical or contextual material about Chancery's practices in the nineteenth century) merely displays a somewhat melodramatic discursive tendency towards rhetorical emotionalism as part of the effort to suppress the novel's own rhetorically vertiginous unfixity readable in the unknowability of London. Allon White speaks of locations being labyrinthine and maze-like; of all the novel's major locations being palimpsests of every other;[37] he speaks also of the drive to repetition in the text, a drive which 'marks style as well as narrative'.[38] This double marking echoes Tschumi's remarking of the event, where hierarchization and the idea of a fixed meaning collapse, while the acts of palimpsestic haunting are those traces in writing of the very condition of the city itself. In the fog lay Chancery and the Temple, swallowed up, obscured and thus traced ineffably. The fog is one figure of writing, of the city writing itself, tracing its contours otherwise, writing the city as that which cannot be written of directly. And even fog cannot dominate the writing for it too is replaced in Chapter 2 by the rain.

The condition of London affects therefore at the very moment in which the act of writing takes place; the foggy, abysmal, rainy weather affects and creeps into, traces everywhere. The fog is not a synecdochic figure for the Law, but one possible, unreadable figure of the city. London infects as well as affecting. It writes as well as being written on, even to the extent that the writing of the novel is dictated by the city. Were we to desire further evidence of the ways in which it is the city and not some particular power structure or discourse which determines the writing, we might do well to compare the passage above from *Bleak House* with the following passages from *Our Mutual Friend* and *Little Dorrit*:

It was a foggy day in London, and the fog was heavy and dark. Animate London, with smarting eyes and irritated lungs, was blinking, wheezing, and choking; inanimate London was a sooty spectre, divided in purpose between being visible and being invisible, and so being wholly neither. Gaslights flared in the shops with a haggard and unblest air, as knowing themselves to be night-creatures that had no business abroad under the sun; while the sun itself, when it was for a few moments dimly indicated through circling eddies of fog, showed as if it had gone out, and were collapsing flat and cold. Even in the surrounding country it was a foggy day, but there the fog was grey, whereas in London it was, at about the boundary line, dark yellow, and a little within it brown, and then browner, and then browner, until at the heart of the City – which call Saint Mary Axe – it was rusty-black. From any point of the high ridge of land northward, it might have been discerned that the loftiest buildings made an occasional struggle to get their heads above the foggy sea, and especially that the great dome of St Paul's seemed to die hard; but this was not perceivable in the streets at their feet, where the whole metropolis was a heap of vapour charged with muffled sounds of wheels, and enfolding a giant catarrh.

(*OMF*, p. 421)

It was a Sunday evening in London, gloomy, close, and stale. Maddening church bells of all degrees of dissonance, sharp and flat, cracked and clear, fast and slow, made the brick-and-mortar echoes hideous. Melancholy streets, in a penitential garb of soot, steeped the souls of the people who were condemned to look at them out of windows, in dire despondency. In every thoroughfare,

up almost every alley, and down almost every turning, some
doleful bell was throbbing, jerking, tolling, as if the Plague were
in the city and the dead-carts were going round. Everything
was bolted and barred that could by possibility furnish relief
to an overworked people. No pictures, no unfamiliar animals,
no rare plants or flowers, no natural or artificial wonders of
the ancient world – all *taboo* with that enlightened strictness,
that the ugly South Sea gods in the British Museum might have
supposed themselves at home again. Nothing to see but streets,
streets, streets, Nothing to breathe but streets, streets, streets.

(*LD*, pp. 67–8)

These passages both echo and haunt the opening of *Bleak House*.
In the passage from *Our Mutual Friend*, we are witness once again
to the fact that the fog is intrinsic to the writing of the city. Yet,
by its very nature, it would seem to forestall all conventional
discussion of London in hiding the city from view. Dickens seems
to deploy the fog in order to hide the city, yet revealing simultaneously to the reader all the more the very otherness of London
itself indirectly through such obscurity and ineffability. It might
well be argued that the fog *is* the city, except that this would be
to privilege its presence, fix its meaning, and accord it some architectural immovability. Instead, even where Dickens writes of
London at its most tedious, as in the passage from *Little Dorrit*,
there is, because of the movement of the writing, the absence of
a hierarchy or comprehensible taxonomy, a sense of 'delirious
spinning that creates both a spatial mirage and the illusion of
passing time'.[39] There is always rhythm and movement, even if
it is without discernible purpose or meaning. In constructing the
architextural event of London – the event requires both space
and time as necessary constituents, or at least their spectres –
Dickens is able to construct and obscure the city through principles
of unanticipated and unanticipatable disorganization: disorganization or disjointing as an organizing principle, no less.

In *Bleak House* and *Our Mutual Friend* fog, mud and rain disorganize throughout the city and throughout the text. The passage
from *Our Mutual Friend* reiterates the image of a dying sun found
in the opening of *Bleak House*, even as the fog causes the gaslights
to be lit during the day, a time not conventionally associated
with their lighting (Esther remarks elsewhere on the curiosity of
having candles lit during day). The fog thus disrupts even the

day itself, the order of things. London is disorganized to the extent that, despite its being a city composed of streets and buildings, it is rendered immaterial, set afloat in a 'foggy sea' and becoming nothing less than a 'sooty spectre' by the fog. This last image is itself disorganized, spectres not conventionally assumed to be dark of hue. There is no substance to the city and its state is purely liminal, being, as the passage informs us, neither wholly visible nor invisible. And as this passage and that passage from *Bleak House* inform the reader, the fog has qualities peculiar to the city, so that we read the city as informing the fog and the fog informing the city. But there are no easily defined boundaries or margins for the fog darkens almost imperceptibly as the reader travels into the centre of London. In both passages, the fog affects and infects the inhabitants to the extent that the city-as-event assumes the monstrous form of a wheezing, freezing, blackened, catarrh-ridden organism. In *Bleak House* the fog is at its densest at Temple Bar, while, in *Our Mutual Friend*, the heart of the city, St Mary Axe, is 'rusty-black'. Density, darkness and discolouration spread, like the fog, from novel to novel, as the respective texts imagine London, deconstructing all possibility of a thematic reading.

In *Little Dorrit*, it is the bells in the passage above which disorganize, bells which have no common organizing principle themselves. The bricks and mortar produce ghosts and palimpsests, curious, dissonant affirmations of the sound of the city, reverberation subsuming 'original' sound. In turn the passage becomes taken up with the endless streets, of which there is nothing either to see or to breathe except those streets, as their endless, reiterable figures take the place of the echoes and the church bells. There is at work the catachresis of violent displacement from one sensory perception to another, and the city becomes only that constant work of the supplement without recourse to an originary or stabilizing figure. Dickens further amplifies the effects of disorganization in creating the writing of the event through analogous anachronism and cultural estrangement in the images of the Plague and the South Sea Gods. Importantly, the Gods imagine 'themselves at home again', Dickens reinventing the space of London into something strange, unknowable, something not-London, while the Plague similarly removes London through space and time to an other more dangerous, 'delirious' version of itself. The last two sentences of the passage give way to a series of negations, as occurs so often in Dickens's descriptions of the city.

The fog is, then, merely one disorganizing trope among many within the city, as I have already suggested. Thomas Richards speaks of the fog as disorganization; disorganization not as the opposite of order but, as already implied, 'the very absence of comprehensible order'.[40] The fog is one trace dictated by and dictating London, part of a disorganizing principle of structure without or beyond structure, the 'place without place of deconstruction . . . where deconstruction inscribes itself'.[41] It speaks of what cannot be spoken, hiding, obscuring and dissolving the concrete, while providing provisional and equivocal 'structure' – *and* slippage – through reiteration. This reiteration, which is there all along in Dickens's writing of the city, from *Sketches by Boz* to the end of the writer's life, is always part of the deconstruction of system, and as part of the exposure of system to the random, the chance event, the ineffable articulation of the other.

Steven Connor writes of *Our Mutual Friend* as having an 'absence of any unified and visible representation of system'.[42] This absence is dictated, I would suggest, in part, because, in the words of David Trotter, 'Dickens knew only too well what the city looked like'.[43] However, it is because of familiarity that Dickens is led to find ways of saying the unsayable, of being true in the act of writing to the shapes and spaces of London. Trotter offers a reading of the spaces of London as constituting an enigma,[44] where characters pass through the streets, often unaware of their location (as in *Oliver Twist* or *Nicholas Nickleby*).[45] For Trotter, this enigma constitutes in turn 'the problem of the city'.[46] While I would certainly suggest – as I already have done – that there is an 'uneasy relationship' between Dickens's writing and the city, I would not go so far as to suggest that the city of London is a problem for Dickens. Trotter's acknowledgement of 'uncertainty of reference'[47] leads to a consideration of representation as the representation of dilemma on the part of characters. This is only true, however, for characters such as Pecksniff, as I will go on to suggest. For the moment, however, it is important to move away from the idea that the city is a problem, or that it is merely the place of particular oppressive forces. Rather, we should recognize, along with Dickens, that the city produces discourse as heterogeneously marked as itself. The nature of the city, its ability to mark language in particular, unexpected ways, registers even in the characters' speech. We see this in Esther Summerson's report of her first entry into, and first conversation in, London:

... it was time to watch for London.

I was quite persuaded that we were there, when we were ten miles off; and when we really were there, that we should never get there. However, when we began to jolt upon a stone pavement, and particularly when every other conveyance seemed to be running into us, and we seemed to be running into every other conveyance, I began to believe that we really were approaching the end of our journey.

(BH, p. 75)

I asked him whether there was any great fire anywhere? For the streets were so full of dense brown smoke that scarcely anything was to be seen.

'O dear no, miss,' he said. 'This is a London particular.'

I had never heard of such a thing.

'A fog, miss,' said the young gentleman.

(BH, p. 76)

We drove slowly through the dirtiest and darkest streets that ever were seen in the world (I thought), and in such a distracting state of confusion that I wondered how the people kept their senses, until we passed into sudden quietude under an old gateway, and drove into a silent square until we came to an odd nook in a corner, where there was an entrance up a steep, broad flight of stairs, like an entrance to a church.

(BH, p. 76)

Esther's language is affected as a result of her encounter with London, as Krook's window shows. But for now we see the early signs of the London-effect in Esther's descriptions and questions. The first passage is marked by confusion of location and movement. Esther cannot 'tell' what or where London is, and it is by this that we know her speech to be figured by the city. She then misunderstands the nature of the fog, and is informed that the fog is a variety particular to London, as the opening passage from *Bleak House* and the passage from *Our Mutual Friend* have already informed us. London names the fog and determines it apart from other fogs as being peculiar to the city. Londoners know the name and it is this knowledge, knowledge of how to describe the unspeakable which defines a Londoner as distinct from a visitor. The last passage records Esther's entrance into the courtyard and, with its suggestion of arches, passages, empty courtyards, and sudden quietness, anticipates David Copperfield's memory of entering Doctors' Commons (*DC*, p. 409). There is thus a linguistic register for legal-architectural spaces distinct from the language of the city. However, of immediate interest in the tone of these extracts from Esther's narrative is the relationship between language and the city, the negotiation between the event of the unexpected encounter and subsequent representation.

THE LIMINAL CITY AND ARCHITEXTURAL MEMORY

The relationships between writing and city, between form and space, texture and architexture can be seen throughout *Sketches by Boz*. From this early text we can understand how Dickens begins a process of writing the city which is continued throughout his work, without there necessarily being the transition desired by Eagleton (I have sought to explore certain passages from the later novels first in order to counter any notion of such a purely linear, progressive transition, as suggested by Eagleton). Of particular interest are the two sketches of the streets at morning and night (*SB*, pp. 49–61). Boz leads the reader through places where there is an 'air of cold, solitary desolation' (*SB*, p. 49). The streets are described as 'noiseless', as 'cold and lifeless', 'deserted', 'empty' and there is the 'stillness of death over the streets' (*SB*, p. 49). Later, such descriptions are amplified, the scene being described as a 'deserted prospect' with 'no signs of life, nor . . . habitation' (*SB*, p. 51). At this hour even the trinity of the 'drunken, the dissipated, the wretched have disappeared' (*SB*, p. 49). Only a solitary drunk and a homeless person, victim of both 'penury and police' (*SB*, p. 49), that is to say economics and the law, are left. This first description of London impresses by the sense it gives of reiterated negation and constant movement, a double movement throughout streets and time, as Boz focuses our attention on yet another negation, whilst calling to our attention the wearing away of another hour or half-hour (*SB*, pp. 51–3). London is a place without place, a place where everything is not, and this repeatedly so. The city is never fixed.

Even when life does come half-hour by half-hour to the streets, London is not so much a *tableau vivant*, as the place of 'decayed cabbage leaves' (*SB*, p. 51) and a discordant 'compound' of sounds

(*SB*, p. 52), which will later come to find themselves reverberating in *Dombey and Son*, when Florence encounters 'the rising clash and roar of the day's struggle' (*DS*, p. 758), or when she sets off across the city in the early morning sun, accompanied by the noises of London (*DS*, p. 759). Both sound and decay speak (of) the event and the city as event through the Dickensian attention to the details of process and a certain movement. And as people begin to fill the streets, Boz's description of the streets becomes more sketchy, vaguely and barely defined, as Londoners obscure and blur 'London', before its definition becomes too fixed. Description gives way to the image of a 'vast concourse of people' (*SB*, p. 54) engulfing the streets. Despite the fact that we can read a certain desire inscribed in the attempt to define the city, London clearly cannot be spoken of, except in the sketchiest of terms.

Boz seems to know the problem inherent in describing London. He appears to comprehend the way in which words will have already failed to capture a likeness, before that likeness is embarked upon, unless the writer resorts to cliché. The recognition of the problem is stated nowhere more lucidly than in the first sentence of the second sketch of the streets:

> But the streets of London, to be beheld in the very height of their glory, should be seen on a dark, dull, murky winter's night, when there is just enough damp gently stealing down to make the pavement greasy . . . .
>
> (*SB*, p. 55)

That insistent objection with which the sentence opens registers the impossibility of writing the city in any full, simple manner. It also begins an attempt to justify the writing of the city otherwise. Yet the ironic dimension is marked in the statement that, for the city to be viewed at its best, one should 'see' it through the atmospheric obstructions and lack of light that define a winter's night in London. The city can hardly be seen through the murk and the 'heavy lazy mist' (*SB*, p. 55), the 'cold, thin rain' (*SB*, p. 58) and the mud (*SB*, p. 59), the same mud which rises at the beginning of *Bleak House* and which is everywhere in *Our Mutual Friend*. All that does 'appear' to the eye is 'dirt and discomfort' (*SB*, p. 57), while glory, having departed, is only conspicuous by its absence (*SB*, p. 57). Even the lamps of the shops serve only to illuminate the enclosing and engulfing darkness (*SB*, p. 55). As in the daytime, discordant sound intrudes upon the 'melancholy stillness of the night' (*SB*, p. 58). What this scene and its companion piece illustrate is a city in process, in transition; a city, in short, composed of events, and London as existing as an architexture of events. Dickens can write only of a liminal city.[48] What is glaringly absent in and between these two chapters is the city of the daytime, the city in full view. Such a city is clearly ineffable.

Instead we see, yet again, fragments, fluid multiplicities of details which do not cohere, but which impress by their being so fragile, so tentatively drawn. And, to reiterate, Boz knows the difficulty; for, as he closes the night-time scene, he comments – defensively, wistfully – that scenes such as those we have been privileged to witness are so numerous, and replaced so endlessly by 'fresh ones', that 'a description of all of them, however slight, would require a volume' (*SB*, p. 60). Such a volume, we are assured, would be 'by no means pleasing' (*SB*, p. 60). So that which is unspeakable in and about London remains unspoken on the grounds of the author's reluctance to expend energy and the presumed issue of the audience's aesthetic sensibilities, even as the city's ephemera maintain a rhythm, taking place across the text and displacing presence and the present day in favour of those moments of transition. However, if Boz is unwilling or unable to go into greater detail, Dickens is not. Indeed, this reticence on Boz's part seems nothing less than the artist's coyness, given the already detailed performance of London's marginalia which entail the street scenes. If there is any perceptible shift between early and later Dickens, then that transition seems to be one where the verecund persona gives way to a performance imbued with Pancksian relish in the double face of wonder and monstrosity.

Inevitably, yet again, Dickens's architextures do not present us with a form – of a building, of the city – as a meaning, system or structure. Rather, we are presented with the architextural event as the impossible expression, writing at the very limit of possible representation. The reiteration of singular structure, where singularity is announced by and in the very act of reiteration, is simultaneously concerned with the announcement of that structure's fragility and ambiguous meaning. Reiteration, as Derrida has taught us, is the condition on which the thought of the singular, is possible. The fixing of meaning, the imposition of the law of the absolute, is resisted through the spatiotemporal movement of the event. The architecture of meaning may well be desired, hence the seemingly infinite repetitions; but the Dickensian architexture of the event 'reinvents architecture in a series of "only onces" which are always unique in their repetition'.[49] In Derrida's words again, 'the dimension of the event is subsumed in the very structure of the architectural apparatus: sequence, open series, narrativity'.[50] We see this in the transformations of Dombey's house, already mentioned. Each time the house is seen or described, the description is one of a series of 'only onces'. There is no 'original' to the house, from which the other descriptions are merely deviations. It is always the same house and yet also, always radically different and other than its other non-original versions.

There is even reiteration in the form of printed handbills, found in different novels. Both Arthur Clennam and Esther Summerson, in passages typical of the Dickensian architexture, come across handbills which announce from their 'mouldering', decaying walls 'FOUND DROWNED' (*LD*, pp. 70–1; *BH*, p. 827). Similarly, both texts reiterate architectural details which are 'rusty' (*BH*, p. 650; *LD*, p. 70) in appearance (Jarndyce also speaks of the rust: p. 147). The decay and the appearance of text drifts from text to text, repeated and yet not the same. Elsewhere the phrase 'carcasses of houses' is reiterated in different novels (*DC*, p. 747; *DS*, p. 289). Obviously enough, any walker in London, even today, might encounter repeated images, figures, architectural curiosities. But the context changes each time, even as each feature, in its singularity, suggests itself as the palimpsest or echo of countless other details. And all such details build into an unimaginable, undetectable, indescribable and unpredictable irregular 'structure'. And to take the question of structure further, it is not that there is what Steven Connor calls, in describing *Bleak House*, a '*problematic excess of metonymy*'.[51] As I hope has already been demonstrated, the excess is not necessarily problematic (unless seen from certain critical perspectives), when regarded as belonging to the architextural event, as described in this chapter. It is merely part of the narrative structuring, part of a strategy to accommodate the modern capital in a writing which comprehends London, without seeking to apprehend it.

Those who do seek out the definite place in 'Dickens's London', seeking to apprehend or arrest the movable feast of the capital, should take as a salutary warning against such a desire certain passages from *Martin Chuzzlewit*. When Mr Pecksniff and his daughters arrive in London, the city is shrouded in fog (once more), as though it were 'a city in the clouds' (*MC*, p. 180). The whole city is both afloat and insubstantial, rather than being marked by any oppressiveness. One of the outsiders on the coach is pronounced parenthetically as mad because he chances to give a firm definition to some indefinable substance, calling it snow (*MC*, p. 180). Pecksniff's relationship to and knowledge of the city is highly ambiguous, verging between confidence and despondence, 'thinking he had lost his way, now thinking he had found it' (*MC*, p. 180), as he seeks Todger's. The city slips out of Pecksniff's grasp, leaving him in a perpetual state of 'perspiration and flurry' (*MC*, p. 180). Even when Pecksniff seems assured of his knowledge, and tells his daughters confidently where they are, our narrator is obliged to point out that:

> . . . at length they stopped in a kind of paved yard near the Monument. That is to say, Mr Pecksniff told them so; for as to anything they could see of the Monument, or anything else but the buildings close at hand, they might as well have been playing blindman's buff at Salisbury.
>
> (*MC*, p. 180)

Absolute knowledge is subsumed by the dissolution of certainty. The paved yard cannot be defined except relatively, and Mr Pecksniff's arrogant authority is revealed as being its extreme limits. There is no truth to the city which can be fixed in place and the Monument[52] becomes a suitable figure and metaphor for architectural solidity and certainty undergoing deconstruction at Dickens's hand. Dickensian architexture clearly renounces any hierarchy or precedence, to invoke Bernard Tschumi once again, even at the moment in which it seems to have come to rest on a seemingly knowable, fixable feature. The text's architexture rejects any possible 'hierarchical cause-and-effect between function and form' (Tschumi's words already cited above) by making the certainty of the monument called the Monument merely an insupportable – and unsupported – assertion on the part of the perspiring Pecksniff, thereby placing the assertion at the level of one more contesting narrative strand, belonging to a general sequential structure.

When finally found, Todger's interiors are revealed. They are figured in a manner similar to other interiors already mentioned from *Our Mutual Friend* and *Master Humphrey's Clock* (*MC*, p. 182).

And, as is revealed in the aptly named Chapter 9, 'Town and Todger's', with its alliterative exchange, the lodging house is a figure of the event *par excellence* that is Dickens's London (and not 'Dickens's London' which is the fixation of a certain critical practice, most typically represented by a feature such as 'the Monument'). For London, as we are told, was worthy of Todger's (*MC*, p. 185). And yet for all its singularity, Todger's is resisted as a finite definition, being revealed as belonging to an 'odd family' of 'hundreds and thousands' (*MC*, p. 185). Todger's neighbourhood thus features as one of an undefined number of non-similar reiterations which make up the city. In this neighbourhood 'you' grope 'your way' 'through lanes and bye-ways, and court-yards, and passages; and you never once emerged upon anything that might reasonably be called a street' (*MC*, p. 185). Approximate definitions substitute themselves one for the other, indicating the principle of singular repetition which can mark the event, while it is noted that no one name can command definition, nor order the random movement into either a stable topographic feature or a taxonomic grouping. These are 'devious mazes' (*MC*, p. 185) belonging to a labyrinth 'whereof the mystery was known but to a chosen few' such as the postman apparently (although this is all told in a somewhat doxical and apocryphal register; *MC*, p. 185); and Todger's can never be found 'on a verbal direction, though given within a minute's walk of it' (*MC*, p. 185).[53]

Thus the city is never absolutely knowable, nor can one speak of its movements. But this is not a problem, for those who fail to find their way in the town around Todger's remain, in Dickens's words, 'tranquil and uncomplaining', and in a state of 'resigned distraction' (*MC*, p. 185). The city is ineffable, and only the Pecksniffs among us try to name it, to fix it and resist its constant re-figuring processes. For each figure is a figure for all other figures in the writing of the city. And this writing is what Allon White calls the 'insistent repetition'[54] of the palimpsest, where the writing of the city figures the city as writing, or, in Derrida's words, the 'architectural experience of memory'.[55] This is an apt approximation for Dickens's architextural memory of the ineffable city . . . .

... IN WHICH, DAVID COPPERFIELD MEETS PETER
EISENMAN

Memory and its written negotiations are the constant concerns
of *David Copperfield*, in some ways perhaps the most atypical of
Dickens's London narratives.[56] Esther Summerson's memory of
the city in *Bleak House* is not too far removed from that of Charles
Dickens, but David Copperfield, as the author of his own narrative, does not have the same focus. His attention is not drawn to
London as obsessively as Dickens's, and, subsequently, London
does not occupy so much of the novel. It does concern David
however, and in the concluding pages of the chapter I want to
turn my attention to *Copperfield* and its images of London, as
these can be read from the perspective of architect Peter Eisenman's
theoretical essays. It is necessary then to position this reading of
Copperfield, in relation to Dickens's writing on London, before
moving on to Eisenman and the novel's interpretation of the city.

London is a 'proper name' for a non-classical and essentially
'modern' architecture in and across Dickens's novels which gets
carried away from its self, not recognizing the limits of the novel
or the functions and limits of the realist narrative, and distribut-
ing, in Derrida's words (talking of Tschumi), 'a non-finite number
of elements in a space which it in fact spaces but does not fill'.[57]
London thus never comes to be finished. Writing about the
architecture and mapping of the city acknowledges the city as a
form of writing, a serialized form without closure or the promise
of an end (serial publication being the most appropriate expression for the 'architectural experience of memory'). Every description
of London implies and contains, while distancing itself from, every
other description, every other image, as I have already explored.
'London' names narrativity and open sequence. Its architexture
deconstructs architecture, even as the idea of the text in the broad
sense offers the possible deconstruction of the idea of the novel,
where the act of 'biography' becomes marked by the architextural
trace. In this gesture Dickens is directing us to rethink what it
means to inhabit the architecture and topography of the city, to
accommodate our narratives to its events and movements, in order
to rid ourselves of that fear of losing ourselves, so well known
to writers such as Wordsworth, De Quincey or Engels, who feel
themselves to be homeless, and, therefore, without identity, in a
space without end, a space which implies, *narrates*, the impossibility

of ending. The problem for these other writers is that London cannot be put to use, cannot be made to serve a particular end.

Dickens, on the other hand, can be read as not expecting this purpose or function to be found in 'London', which is nothing short of the function of classical architecture: to serve, to identify, to create meaning, as architect Peter Eisenman outlines in his essay 'The End of the Classical: The End of the Beginning, The End of the End'.[58] Dickens enters, and writes himself into, the city's condition. He thus indirectly rejects the notion of classical architecture through his relationship to London which, in responding to London-as-event, acknowledges a change in identity for the urban writer, brought about by the city itself. Peter Eisenman describes this shift, recalling for us the idea of the event:

> a not-classical architecture begins actively to involve an idea of a reader conscious of his own identity as a reader rather than as a user or observer. Such a reader brings no *a priori* competence to the act of reading other than an identity as a reader.... The competence of the reader ... comes from the capacity to read *per se*, to know how to read ... architecture as text. Thus the new 'object' [London] must have the capacity to reveal itself first of all as a text, as a reading event.[59]

The authors considered in the previous chapter are what Eisenman calls users or observers: not only do they not know how to read the city, they are not aware that the city should be read, rather than observed as a discrete, classical entity, with a fixed meaning. To a lesser, certainly less problematic, extent, Barbauld, Shelley and Byron are also users and observers, rather than readers. Dickens on the other hand knows that to comprehend the city, one must be aware of oneself, one's identity as a reader of the city's architextures. After Dickens, writers of London are invariably readers also. Dickens is first and foremost always a reader, an interpreter of what he loves most strongly and what he abhors most vehemently. Through Dickens's texts the city of London reveals itself, through Dickens's readings, as what Eisenman calls a reading event. It is for this reason that I have chosen to discuss *David Copperfield* last, as a text concerned with an identity, and the writing of an identity, always involved – and aware that it is involved, that a condition of its consciousness is that it is implicated – in acts of reading, and having difficulties in reading, as a result of necessary historical and cultural transitions.

In his theory of the history of architectural representation, Peter Eisenman argues that, since the Renaissance, architecture has been dominated by what he calls three 'fictions', regardless of styles and stylistic labels. This term 'fiction' clearly has importance for talking of architecture in narrative, and of narrative architecture. The 'fictions' are representation, reason and history.[60] Eisenman goes on to argue that each fiction has served a purpose within the modern history of architecture:

> representation was to embody the idea of a meaning; reason was to codify the idea of truth; history was to recover the idea of timelessness from the idea of change.[61]

It is these three ideas which serve to define for the architect the 'continuous mode of thought . . . referred to as the *classical*',[62] within which all stylistic markers, such as Gothic, Palladian, and so on are subsumed. All architecture from the Renaissance to the twentieth century has aspired to serve the classical mode.

This architectural ordering of elements and discourses into a metalanguage governed by the production of universality, meaning and truth bears certain resemblances to notions of the classic realist text in the nineteenth century.[63] While the classical model has persisted (according to Eisenman) in architecture until the second half of the twentieth century, writing such as Dickens's embodies a radical questioning of the classical structure, with regard to the 'representation' or the writing of the city. While narrative order and the production of a metalanguage may in the nineteenth century be analogous to, organized around, Eisenman's three 'fictions', the act of writing the city brings into question this epistemic model, once the shift has been made from being a user or observer to being a reader. Dickens's writing of the city inscribes within itself an undeniably readable 'necessary historicity', to use Eisenman's phrase,[64] which challenges indirectly the implicit claims to the paradigmatic in terms of truth and reason supposedly represented by the narrative ordering of its various discursive levels. In this, Dickens's acts of 'writing-the-city' can be read as be a modern – if not a *modernist* – form of writing (regardless of style or genre), concerned in its movements to bring out function through form, to collapse the one in to the other; so that the form of writing, in reproducing (though not representing or claiming to tell the 'truth' of) the city as text, does not seek to represent or imitate a knowable entirety. Rather, it conveys the transitions and movements of the urban event in the nineteenth century. In doing so it involves the production of identity, showing that production to be a profoundly textual affair.

We see this at work in the first passage from *David Copperfield* which is concerned with the city and its 'representation', when David first enters London:

> What an amazing place London was to me when I saw it in the distance, and how I believed all the adventures of all my favourite heroes to be constantly enacting and re-enacting there, and how I vaguely made it out in my mind to be fuller of wonders and wickedness than all the cities of the earth, *I need not stop to relate here.*
>
> (*DC*, p. 122; emphasis added)

> [the Inn in Whitechapel] I forget whether it was the Blue Bull, or the Blue Boar; but I know it was the Blue something, and that its likeness was painted up on the back of the coach.
>
> (*DC*, p. 122)

Both extracts stress the fundamentally fictive, signifying nature of the city, a place of narrative adventures from others' novels, recalled to the mind as a comparison for possible identities, which narratives are not to be related, being, strictly speaking, ineffable. David's identity is only indirectly compared with other fictional characters by reference to the indescribable qualities of the city. The city is read rather than observed, given a narrative, albeit one constructed out of a limited expression, which the writer strives to skip over through a sense of hurry and movement in the phrase emphasized from the first of the two quoted passages. One does notice the doubleness of the city, and its power to imply both wonder and wickedness, the alliterative phrase emphasizing the polarities contained within the same site at the same time, and enlarged beyond the capacities of any other urban location. Unspeakable, still the city is given a comparative expression, through a form of periphrastic indirection which affirms the nature of the city while simultaneously affirming its resistance to naming and description. This finds itself manifested in the slippage of the Inn's name, which can be represented and recalled only through a pictorial image, an approximation, a likeness, which is seen moving past the viewer, seen only ever in passing, on the back of a coach. This forgetting, the narrative incompletion, is reiterated later on by David when he forgets the name of yet another inn, in Chapter 11

> ... a miserable old public-house opposite our place of business, called the Lion, or the Lion and something else that I have forgotten.
>
> (*DC*, p. 215)

Forgetting the name in both instances, and the earlier, highlighted example of the avoidance of narrative (hiding perhaps the impossibility of narrative closure and completed representation of identity) suggests both narrative and architectural incompletion. The full, complete classical model is resisted in acts which expose the writing of representation as always unfinished acts. This is echoed in a later passage when David finds Traddles' lodgings in Camden Town, which have '[a]n *indescribable* character of faded gentility' (*DC*, p. 461; emphasis added). Once more, Copperfield writes of what he cannot write in relation to London architecture, this time with reference to a specific building which is, nonetheless, singled out as being a singularly idiomatic structure 'unlike all the other houses in the street' (*DC*, p. 461). The house is described, even though it is apparently indescribable, as well as being a narrative and architectural anomaly which breaks into the possibility of completed representation, finished, truthful description and universal, absolute imitation. Thus we read Copperfield reading uncertainly, at the global and local levels of the city and its dwellings, where everything remains incomplete. In a narrative full of letters, texts and Mr Dick's unfinished history, London is one more example of the unfinished textual form.

Yet form and function being related, the unending condition of the city is not merely one more example of textuality. Given its writing as event, with the unpredictable and chance encounters which this implies in Dickens's other novels, the writing of London becomes a figure of non-classical textual productivity. The city is the incomplete, unending (imperfect) paradigm – a non-paradigmatic paradigm, perhaps – which counters the classical mode. If a detail is forgotten, this also implies that it remains to be remembered and that, concomitantly, there will always be something left forgotten, remembered as forgotten. The structure remains to be finished, and is structured in a fragmentary fashion.

The form of the writing, then, assumes the functioning of the city, with the possibility of one more example, one more street, one more narrative, one more chance encounter, all of which serve to drive the narrative, even as the image of the inn is driven before the forgetful reader in a blurred impression. The city certainly overwhelms David on his first visit, yet the sense of resistance to the possibilities of classical representation and the fulfilment of the criteria of the three 'fictions' remains throughout. We see that this is so in another two scenes, both taking place in the same location, from Steerforth's house in Highgate. The first view of London comes when David first stays at the house:

> From the windows of my room I saw all London lying in the distance like a great vapour, with here and there some lights twinkling through it.
>
> (*DC*, p. 350)

The second image occurs when David visits Rosa Dartle to discuss Mr Littimer's information concerning Emily:

> She was sitting on a seat at one end of a kind of terrace, over-looking the great city. It was a sombre evening, with a lurid light in the sky; . . . I saw the prospect scowling in the distance, with here and there some larger object starting up into the sullen glare.
>
> (*DC*, p. 734)

The city on both occasions involves fragments, light, insubstantiality. The city is formed not as a representation in writing, but as a simulation. That is to say, the narrative, in both instances, figures the city constructed partially from signifiers which are there to be read as signs of the city, the whole city, the reality of the city being unrepresentable and always being somewhere other than in these fragmentary structures. In both instances the city is formed as oblique commentary on the situation of the narrative and Copperfield's identity as constituted at that moment. There is no meaning to the city other than Copperfield's 'meaning' at a given moment. This is not London either in or for itself but as a figure of a deferred identity. That it is a simulation is a key to the fragmentary, incomplete nature of David's knowledge.

Even as London is only simulated and only ever a simulation, so too David Copperfield is no more than a narrative, marked by gaps, absences, moments of forgetfulness. David, like the city, has no meaning other than his narrative. He simulates himself as the subject of his narrative fragments, and the act of writing the city signifies his own incompletion. The simulation of the city in David's mind is a form of writing which challenges the possibility of telling the complete truth.

In Dickens's texts the architecture of the city, like the writing of a fictive biography, exposes what Eisenman calls, talking of classical architectural form, 'a nostalgia for the security of knowing . . . and the need for verification'.[65] The city's identity is constructed out of the ineffable, from the provisionality of textual function, from the signs of lights and the occasional structural fragment. The city as narrative paradigm in *Copperfield* thus typifies architectural form described by Eisenman as 'a "place of invention" rather than . . . a subservient representation of another architecture'.[66] Eisenman continues:

> [t]his suggests the idea of architecture as 'writing' as opposed to architecture as image. What is being written, is not the object itself [in this case, the city of London] . . . but the *act* of massing. This idea gives a metaphoric body to the act of architecture. It then signals its reading through an other system of signs, called *traces*. Traces are not to be read literally, since they have no other value than to signal the idea that there is a reading event and that reading should take place . . . . Thus a trace is a partial or fragmentary sign; it has no objecthood. It signifies an action that is in process.[67]

Partial and fragmentary signs signifying an action in process and the event of reading the city are seen in the descriptions of Traddles's street in Camden:

> [the street was not only] rank and sloppy, but untidy too, on account of the cabbage-leaves. The refuse was not wholly vegetable either, for I myself saw a shoe, a doubled-up saucepan, a black bonnet, and an umbrella, in various stages of decomposition . . . .
>
> (*DC*, p. 461)

In one of the few passages in the novel to hint at the ungovernable taxonomies so typical of Dickens's descriptions of London
in other novels, we comprehend David attempting to remember
his being in the street, to compose a narrative from memory,
through his attempt to read what he sees. He is unable to describe
the image in full, unable also to make sense of what he encounters. He reads, yet what he reads of the street and in the street
has no narrative 'truth', merely being a number of chance, random
elements and signs. These in turn inform the reader indirectly of
the 'architectural experience of memory'. The act of writing the
city involves once again showing the city as an ungovernable
writing, where the signs neither point to nor can be assembled
so as to provide a greater meaning. David's description of the
area around Fleet Street and Covent Garden similarly involves
an act of reading recalled by memory on the narrator's part:

> I used to look at the venison-shop in Fleet Street; or I have
> strolled, at such a time, as far as Covent Garden Market, and
> stared at the pineapples. I was fond of wandering about the
> Adelphi, because it was a mysterious place, with those dark
> arches. I see myself emerging one evening from some of these
> arches, on a little public-house close to the river, with an open
> space before it, where some of the coal-heavers were dancing.
>
> (*DC*, p. 215)

This memory combines the knowable, prosaic and locatable with
the exotic, in the form of the pineapple and the strange image of
coal-heavers dancing, and the promise of the theatrical where
the dark arches also hint architecturally at the Inns of Court
(implying a 'performative' metaphor to the location of the Law).
What these traces of London suggest in David's memory and
narrative is that there is no 'truth', no absolutely stable representation, either to or for the city. The memory and narration of
the city always carry within them the possible reinvention, and
thus the reinvention of the reading subject. London's identity
cannot be fixed because its narratives are never finished. The
narratives of identity reinvent themselves in the act of writing,
as the city's narrative carries in it its other narratives, through
traces of simulation and dissimulation, iterability, undecidability
and supplementarity.

David Copperfield is a novel concerned with identity and memory and the admission of their provisional absence-marked condition. These 'acts' are shown composed only of traces. The novel is not then a 'biography' as such but a reading event in Eisenman's terms where a reading of the limits of urban 'representation' can be turned to understanding the limits of the biographical act in its efforts to construct a 'true' identity. David Copperfield (obviously) exists only to be read and only exists in the act of reading *David Copperfield*. 'David Copperfield' is a narrative of traces signifying an action in process. If Dickens does not concentrate so insistently on the city in this text it is because all that he has learned from the writing of the architextural event is now focused in the narrative place of invention, which is *David Copperfield*. 'London' for Dickens is a place of invention, rather than merely a reality, and his writing accommodates itself to this, being dictated by the city. If David does not write too much of the city, this is, we might suggest, only avoided by Dickens in order not to give the game away. The city, in *David Copperfield* as in Dickens's other novels, is a series of signals which suggest 'the idea that there is a reading event and that reading should take place'. Reading should take place. Dickens understands this about London, because, for him, London, there to be read but remaining unreadable, always *takes place*. Is this not what we, as readers, also come to understand, through being drawn, repeatedly, to the Dickensian architextures?

5

Fragments, supplements, palimpsests: a photo-essay

The following images from London have no other particular narrative than that which is imposed by wandering without any goal, collecting snapshots, visual fragments of the city. The pictures come from all over London, taken at different times. The city dictates the response which is the still-life image.

Similarly, in selecting the photographs which appear here, the choice of images for this photo-essay is not governed by any desire to create a narrative, although many possible narratives may emerge from viewing these city fragments, these supplements to the city-text.

Some of the images are mentioned or otherwise gestured towards indirectly in *Writing London*. The photograph of Copperfield Street taken in Southwark offers an interesting layering of the fictional text onto the texture of the so-called *real* city.

The architecture and other objects caught in the photographs are obviously not only nineteenth century or even 'Victorian' in origin. These are ghosts, traces of ghosts. They are what remains of countless other Londons.

Afterword:
'the only game in town' or,
London to come

With a logic for every contingency, every ability and need, the city is the only game in town.

Donald Preziosi

London is begging to be rewritten

Iain Sinclair

There is also a Narrative which is hidden so that none may see it. . . .

Peter Ackroyd

(RE:)WRITING LONDON

At first glance, if not in conclusion, it may seem anachronistic, not to say paradoxical or perverse, to insist on writing about the city as writing, to concentrate on the performance of the city through writing, where the constative and performative collapse in upon each other, at a point when the virtual space is celebrated or excoriated in relation to what is too glibly called the real, as though this banal binarism virtual/real had any force, any cogency. In the face of cyberspace and the investigation already underway into the possible 'conflation of electronic communication technologies and the space of the city',[1] to insist upon the immanence of the urban space haunting the scene of writing might be misconstrued as a last modernist gasp, a final hurrah of an outdated epistemology. Why write at all, why all this fuss about writing, or what writing can be read as effecting?

The problem is that, while virtuality in all its electronic and technological forms comes to impose itself on us, to occupy our interests, we've yet to find adequate means for discussing those

spaces and places we occupy. We have yet to catch up with the
network of the modern city in all its heterogeneity and otherness,
its condition of constant becoming. We have only recently begun
to come to terms with articulating what Klaus R. Scherpe describes
as the 'articulation of the complexity of cosmopolis'[2] through the
reconsideration of the city as, no longer, homogeneous space but
as the taking place of the event. Understanding the city in terms
of text, writing, networks appears to be the only option and one
dictated by the city itself. As with writing, the city offers us no
single mastering form or code, an understanding which would
allow us in turn to classify, systematize or thematize, as Alexander
Gelley reminds us.[3] And to keep the history of the city and the
history of writing separate is, in Donald Preziosi's words, futile:
'Indeed, to continue to pursue the history of writing and the
history of the city along separate avenues comes to be as futile
as trying to trace with a pencil the shadow of the tracing pencil.'[4]
Preziosi performs the interconnectedness between histories in his
metaphor of avenues and the image of the pencil, tracing and
the shadow, even as he speaks of the futility of seeking to keep
them apart. The figural exchange of Preziosi's statement bespeaks
the condition of our involvement with the urban with which we
have still to come to terms.

The city and writing are then intimately bound in a relationship, for which no merely sociological or architectural history can
account completely. Writing the city is not the same as writing
about the city. The former transforms and translates, responding
to its other, allowing the other to return in other words as the
trace of the city-text. The process of writing the city involves
both giving one's identity over to the urban other, while unsettling or estranging conceptions of how the city functions even,
especially, at its seemingly most quotidian or banal levels.

There are of course so many narratives possible in London,
that it's hard enough to know where to start, let alone finish.
This Afterword is concerned neither with neat conclusions nor
with having the last word on London. Indeed, its purpose is to
suggest that there is no such thing as a 'last word' on the city.
We cannot conclude that London is done with or that there is
only anxiety or pessimism concerning London's future, as Roy
Porter implies.[5] There is always something else to which we may
be obliged to respond. There is always that excess to the city,
already there as the haunting trace of its otherness, which disturbs

any neatly conceived literary approximations concerning London's identity. Indeed, London names excess. If the 'modern capital is always a monopoly of writing' as Jacques Derrida suggests in paraphrasing Rousseau's assessment of Paris,[6] then this monopoly is, in London's case, a heterogeneous monopoly, one which is composed of supplementarity, illegibility and undecidability.

With this excess, and with its relationship to writing in mind, I want to turn here to three narrative moments, from 1743, 1930, and 1997. These dates mark moments which are, strictly speaking, outside the frame of reference of *Writing London*. They disturb that frame, the narratives appended to these dates not quite belonging to what has been my ostensible interest in the preceding chapters, the tracing of the city in texts of the nineteenth century. These remarks are neither inside nor outside the book, even as this Afterword is not quite of the book itself. Appropriately, they are marginal commentaries, yet their concerns are with London. They point to issues of representation, performance, inscription, identity and definition, all of which are the issues, interests and concerns of the writers discussed in this book, albeit in different and differing fashions. If the question is one of disturbing the frame, then this question is dictated by London itself. The disruption of the representation *is* always, and in a certain manner, disruption *within* representation.

WRITING (AND) LONDON

The first two extracts are from Henry Fielding and Virginia Woolf.[7] They are brought together because both share the pretext of writing and reading as the departure points for their narratives. *A Journey From This World to the Next*[8] (1743), includes a brief preface, from which the following intriguing passage is drawn:

> Mr *Robert Powney*, Stationer, who dwells opposite to *Catherine Street* in the *Strand* a very honest Man, and of great Gravity of Countenance; who, among other excellent Stationary Commodities, is particularly eminent for his Pens, which I am abundantly bound to acknowledge, as I owe to their peculiar Goodness that my Manuscripts have by any means been legible: this Gentleman, I say, furnished me some time since with a Bundle of those Pens, wrapt up with great Care and Caution,

in a very large Sheet of Paper full of Characters, written as it seemed in a very bad Hand. Now I have a surprizing Curiosity to read every thing which is almost illegible; partly, perhaps, from the sweet Remembrance of the dear *Scrawls*, *Skrawls*, or *Skrales*, (for the Word is variously spelt) which I have in my youth received from that lovely part of the Creation for which I have the tenderest Regard.[9]

The play in this passage is quite dizzying. It moves from signature, address and character reference to an illegible text and the memory of the instability of writing. Honesty and gravity are situated against, and, perhaps, in anticipation of, that memory of spelling's waywardness which haunts Fielding and is made manifest in an anxiety over demonstrating the adult's control over various spellings of the same word.

The stationer, known for his pens, is located in the town as a constant, a standard or stable referent, while the pens themselves are praised for their quality and ability to render Fielding's prose legible in the first place. Yet the pens, the generators and producers of legible narrative, come wrapped in text which cannot be read. As Fielding recounts, it is the stationer, Robert Powney, who has wrapped the pens in illegible script. And there is that delightful play (impossible to say whether it is deliberate) in the term *stationery*, haunted by its double, *stationary*. The spelling of the two words seems not to have become fixed until either the end of the eighteenth or beginning of the nineteenth centuries. Fielding's use of *a* rather than *e* inscribes the movable feast of writing, the purely graphic difference doubling and unsettling the performance of either term. The play in writing disturbs fixity, permanence and, to use a now obscure word, *stationarity*.

The address of the stationer seems given by the author as if to make stationary the movement of writing *through* the paradoxical inscription. Fielding writes about the habitual purchase of pens, no doubt writing with one of those pens, from a fixable, knowable location in London, from which location comes the disturbance in writing which, by chance, sets the novelist off in different directions, recalling his own past as a childish writer, and directing him towards the possible deciphering of an enigmatic text. London is not the subject here, of course. It does, however, provide the unlooked-for opportunity for writing on writing, and this is identified as a destabilizing and specifically urban activity.

Almost two hundred years later, in 1930, it is the desire for a pencil as the pretext for walking the city and allowing chance narratives to unfold which encourages the act of writing London, in Virginia Woolf's 'Street Haunting: A London Adventure':

> No one perhaps has ever felt passionately towards a lead pencil. But there are circumstances in which it can become supremely desirable to possess one; moments when we are set upon having an object, an excuse for walking half across London between tea and dinner . . . when the desire comes upon us to go street rambling the pencil does for a pretext, and getting up we say: 'Really I must buy a pencil,' as if under cover of this excuse we could indulge safely in the greatest pleasure of town life in winter – rambling the streets of London . . . . The evening hour . . . gives us the irresponsibility which darkness and lamp-light bestow. We are no longer quite ourselves . . . we shed the self our friends know . . . .[10]

Writing and walking are both forms of trace here. They are never merely themselves, but become doubled within writing and through the recall of desire. Memory is the written trace where walking and writing collapse into each other, the performance of the latter re-marking the movement of the former. Both place the walking/writing subject in a place from which to observe and respond, at the margin of events. As if to develop this, the chosen time of day is crepuscular, promising to dissolve the writer/walker into the scene, displacing and even erasing identity as a response to the liminal condition of London. The city, a place of writing implements the access to which allows the writing of London to take place, implicates itself in complex narrative webs. In the case of both Woolf and Fielding, narrative is the unlooked-for event as a result of the subject's relationship to the city. In the city the other returns to tell us a tale, transforming our encounter with London. The city traces itself onto our perceptions even as it returns as its own doubled trace in the narratives we write. London doubles itself, becoming other than it is in a continuous process and thereby making its meaning undecidable. If these two passages suggest a connection, a cross-contamination between writing *and* London, they also speak of a double, disjointing articulation: London *is* writing, writing *is* London. The city is a text, inescapably so, performed from traces, marks, citations, narratives legible and illegible. The only way to be faithful to these traces is to respond in writing, a writing alive to the event, to that which takes place as the condition of London. To reiterate: both Fielding and Woolf understand, each in their own way, that London is the possibility of the unexpected inscription.

There are, however, those who dislike the unexpected, the undecidable. They would like the writing of the city set in stone. Which brings me to the third narrative.

NEW LABOUR, NEW LONDON?

In 'The Culture of Blairism', Adam Gopnik makes the following, trenchant claim: 'Terence Conran's vast Bluebird complex on the King's Road . . . is to New Labour what the Crystal Palace was to High Victorianism'.[11] The article, ostensibly concerned with the mood of Britain under Blair, has a quiet subtext running through it about the ideological refashioning of the capital (ideology being less costly than architecture, the investors more ready to spend). Gopnik asserts, quite correctly in my view, that this New (Labour) Mood is, in fact, a continuation, rather than a breach, of certain Thatcherite strands. The article is accompanied by a Gerald Scarfe cartoon, entitled 'Tony Blair and the Ghost of Conservatism'. Scarfe's cartoon depicts Tony Blair as Prince Hamlet, the skull of Yorick seemingly intoning, 'Alas. Poor Labour!' Next to Tony, Prince of Islington (you know, one of those sites from which the New Jerusalem would be built; or so William Blake believed), stands a reeking spectre, a green helmeted Margaret Thatcher. Her spirit rises from the New Globe or, to give it its proper title, William Shakespeare's Globe, just in case you thought it belonged to anybody else. (Given this proprietorial nomenclature, by the way, can any living descendants of the Bard – supposing some to exist – claim ground rent? and what if the tenants make too much noise? The potential for real estate/legal disputes is enough to convince almost anyone that the ghost of the Thatcherite past still has yet to be sufficiently exorcised.) The question of spectrality and its relation to the city is an important one to which I will return.

One of Gopnik's foci is the New Globe itself, the idea for which has been around since the 1890s as Raphael Samuel reminds us.[12] Gopnik uses this icon (or Trojan horse?) of English Heritage in

order to show how the Globe (the old one) was not so much an
English Tudor building as a product (culturally, aesthetically) of
the Renaissance, via Northern, largely Protestant, entrepreneurial
Europe of the fifteenth century. The Globe is of course only the
most visible London reclamation project – or, at least, the selec-
tive reclamation of a certain London which has never existed. It
is merely part of a pre-millennial fervour/anxiety which desires
the paradoxical construction of a New London founded on the
imagined presence and permanence, formed from so many fictions
of the old: a New London in which to enter the New Millen-
nium, though not the New Jerusalem (unless this is a yet-to-be-
thought-of shopping mall somewhere near the Elephant and
Castle).

Just along from the theatre a disused power station is being
converted into the permanent home for the Tate Gallery's modern art collection, while, near to this, the Oxo building has been
converted into part of a complex of condominiums and a variety
of shops. The spectres of beef-stock-cube makers and sugar mag-
nates aside, the South Bank is being reinvented, as if to lay to
rest other spirits, the ghosts of work and the working classes
who occupied much of London, south of the Thames. This area,
comprising the boroughs of Southwark and Lambeth (see the
photo-essay preceding this Afterword), which even at the time
of the publication of *Our Mutual Friend*, was still part of Surrey
and not London as such, is being given a soft-focus aesthetic, an
urban makeover which speaks to the new urbanites' right – or
will – to pleasure (providing that the urbanites have the right
income).

The impulses behind the current redevelopment, behind cultural
reclamation and reinvention are considerably more subtle, more
insidious, than the Thatcherite revivification of Docklands and
the building of Canary Wharf, which now stands as a huge
mausoleum without a corpse but with ghosts – the 'ghosts of
labour' is Iain Sinclair's appropriate phrase[13] – enough to rival
the Victorian Valhalla, Highgate Cemetery. Now, as we approach
the end of the 1990s, we can pretend we are no longer interested in making money (unlike those *dreadful* Victorians); we just
want to spend it. And there's the shift. Gopnik's comparison
between Terence Conran's upmarket shopping mall and Crystal
Palace marks the transition very economically indeed. In response
to the games being played with London and, if the city is the

only game in town, as Donald Preziosi claims,[14] then it's time we raised the stakes as well as raising the dead.

RAISING THE STAKES: THE SPECTRAL GAMBIT

Behind the counter a poster of the Italian team Torino was faring little better. The players had lost the glossy Mediterranean health of a few months ago, the combined forces of heat, moisture and light turning them to anaemic, dough-faced London ghosts.

Greg Williams, Diamond Geezers

London.

This is not a new London we're encountering. It's a very old one in particular ways, even though it has never been present as such and is always marked by the possibility of a certain future London, a 'London to come' as I put it in part of the title to this Afterword. I'm referring indirectly to a moment of torque, a spectral habitation within the phrase 'l'avenir/l'à venir', employed by Derrida on a number of occasions: a future for London, a future moment always to come, always as a particular retreating horizon, never to be present or to have presence, fully or finally. London, not as a monumental place, but as the spectral which *takes place, which is always already taking place within the name.*

London.

There is in this name, as the ghostly architexture of its installation, the constant return of countless spectral traces temporally and spatially, (and multiplied by technology) as the play within the French announces; as, on the one hand, the textual affirmation of that taking place; while, on the other hand, a resistance to the imposition of a single identity. London names a certain imagined totality which can never be presented, yet which is composed from a network of traces worked up into a narrative which most suits the storyteller.

London.

Am I recalling the opening gambit of *Bleak House* (which title, we may suggest a little fancifully, provides almost an anagram for 'Blake's House')? Or is this merely to name what this proper-improper name has always improperly anticipated about the modern city? Which is, that the 'city is no longer organized into a localized and axial estate', to quote Paul Virilio.[15] 'London' names the fact that London never was so organized. Even today, with the proliferation of technological surveillance devices, the city's present is never a presence, never present as such but rendered ever more spectral. It is always already fragmented, made ghostly, composed of optical illusions and divided subjects, as Virilio and Iain Sinclair discuss, each in their own fashion: 'As a unity of place without any unity of time, the City has disappeared into the heterogeneity of that regime comprised of the temporality of advanced technologies';[16] and '[s]urveillance abuses the past while fragmenting the present. The subject is split, divided from itself.'[17]

These are typical of the issues concerning the city. The anti-heritage polemicists don't necessarily always appreciate spectral or textual concerns, any more than their pro-heritage counter-parts. The anti-heritage lobbyists appear never to be self-consciously aware enough of their own stake in the narratives they oppose, or in the narratives they see being erased (the narratives they tell about narratives being erased). The pro- and anti-heritage language is charmingly – or alarmingly – disingenuous. Both camps speak for permanence rather than productivity and performativity. Both address the city according to preferred typologies of monumentalization, entombment, and architectural space which is conceived as being static. They cannot comprehend that the city is comparable with, comprehensible only as, what Ignasi de Solà-Morales describes as 'a culture of the event: a culture that',

in the moment of fluidity and decomposition leading towards chaos, is capable of generating instants of energy that from certain chaotic elements construct ... a new fold in multiple reality .... The event is a *vibration* ... a point of encounter, a conjunction whereby the lines of a limitless itinerary cross with others to create nodal points of outstanding intensity ... It is a subjective action, producing a moment of pleasure and fragile plenitude.[18]

The culture of the event is the culture of the city properly understood, and returned to us through a revaluation of the city-texts
of the nineteenth century, which, each in their own singular fashion, respond to 'instants of energy', multiple realities, 'fragile
plenitude'. For the writers of the nineteenth century, London-
as-event is always already in a 'situation of permanent transition'.[19] To understand this further, it is necessary to concede that
the city today is best described by Alexander Gelley, who suggests
that it 'represents one of those nodes or points of confluence
where the status of textuality is today being articulated'.[20] To know
this is to respond to the flow, technological and spectral –
spectrotechnological – which is encountered in the city. This
articulation belongs to the game, where the heritage narrative
and its various oppositional disclaimers are locked into their
respective poker faces concerning the city's truth, whatever that
might be, and always supposing such a thing exists. Despite this,
what the constant reconfiguration of the city involves (and invokes)
though, as its reshapings flow through those various points of
confluence, is that the city itself is what Donald Preziosi calls

> ... a topology of irony, situating us in only one place at a
> time while endlessly drawing us on to other places, other
> desires .... It is both the trace left by ... alterations and the
> trace that engenders them.[21]

Any astute reader of Anthony Trollope would immediately
recognize the cogency of this remark, particularly if one were to
take it as a statement concerning the narratives of *The Way We
Live Now* or *The Three Clerks*. In both novels, the city is understood not as the sum of its buildings, properties, streets, nor as
the fixed space of the combination of these features, but as the
confluence and clash of power flows and fluxes of subversion,
along with the tidal rhythms of discursive activity, relating at
the most obvious levels to economics and politics, fiction and
desire. As Trollope's or Dickens's characters show us, however,
the city leads astray, enticing us with its confusions and excesses.
The fact that the city can so draw us, can leave its trace on us
even as we attempt to trace its contours, is what those who resist
London find so disturbing.

The traces spoken of by Preziosi above are spectral through
and through: they are the marks of already retreating ghosts who

disturb any certain perception we may think we have concerning the city's identity. The disturbance of this ghostly trace means
that, to quote Alexander Gelley again, '[w]hat is evoked does not
quite match what is shown'.[22] This is seen constantly throughout
Iain Sinclair's response to London in his *Lights Out for the Territory*, especially in the first essay 'Skating on Thin Eyes: The First
Walk' which deals with Sinclair's encounters with the capital's
graffiti. Graffiti is, for the author, a spectral form of textuality
transforming its reader into a ghost and described as 'the trum-
peting exotica in the encyclopaedia of the city'.[23] Graffiti, for both
Sinclair and Gelley, is 'legible but not meaningful'[24] and thus is
particularly attuned to the very different modalities of the city's
poetics, modalities which do not rely on narrativization but which
dissonantly articulate the condition of the city as a textual network,
never quite at home with itself. The heritage and anti-heritage
narratives want equally to calm down the city's spectral dissonance, where the imagined identity is disturbed from within itself
by its other, the other having arrived, not only to distort the
model of identity which we may have sought to impose, but also
to displace our sense of our identity or location within the city-
text. It is an effect of skewed citation, where the citation comes
back as never quite what we had believed it to be, unsettling
'the signifying or indexical function'.[25]

Those who argue for *and* against heritage projects in any simply
sociological or ideological fashion fail to comprehend how cities
such as London 'endlessly . . . replicate, and palimpsest . . . ', to
borrow once more from Preziosi: 'The truth of the city is that it
is forever false. A city is not a city unless it occludes the laws of
its composition and the rules of its game'.[26] Such occlusion and
the concomitant unsettling of the signifying or indexical function can be witnessed at work in a poem by Arthur Hugh Clough,
To The Great Metropolis (1841). The sonnet demonstrates how the
city is 'false', how it doesn't appear to 'play the game' when
viewed from a preconceived perspective which involves an
assumption about playing by the rules. The sonnet is worth quoting
in extenso:

> Traffic, to speak from knowledge but begun,
> I saw, and travelling much, and fashion – Yea,
> And if that Competition and Display
> Make a great Capital, then thou art one,

One, it may be, unrivalled neath the Sun.
But sovereign symbol of the Great and Good,
True Royalty, and genuine Statesmanhood,
Nobleness, Learning, Piety was none.
If such realities indeed there are
Working within unsignified, 'tis well;
The stranger's fancy of the thing thou art
Is rather truly of a huge Bazaar,
A railway terminus, a gay Hotel,
Anything but a mighty Nation's heart.[27]

Clough's sonnet, written in response to Wordsworth's 'Westminster Bridge', expresses the desire for a certain image or identity for London, which is found wanting for the poet. Clough's disingenuous response is clearly marked by particular philosophical-ideological concerns, for he upbraids the city's material and visible condition for not making manifest those more abstract qualities which, in his mind's eye, should comprise the ideal identity for London. This much is clear from the poem. What is interesting, however, is the assumption that a city should be a certain experience or expression in the first place, that it should in some manner conform to the eye or perception of the beholder. Clough appears to have much invested in his organic vision of the capital, and is thwarted from the first line by motion, transport, contest and specularity. The city disturbs, and is most disturbing by appearing to be materially what it is.

That London is, then, a privileged site involving the playing out of a range of ideological and philosophical contests (which it always sidesteps) is without doubt, as we see in Clough's sonnet. The game currently involves the cleaning up of the past, giving the city a face-lift, or otherwise editing it. This is merely one form of what has always been the case, or at least since the first Globe was recognized retrospectively as the 'birth-place' of 'British Theatre'. On the one hand, the question of London is one concerned with the forging of definite, stable identities, as I have suggested. On the other hand, writing the city often can mean the abandonment of identification, of giving up oneself, going with the flow, that 'ebb and flow' spoken of by Baudelaire and cited in the Introduction to *Writing London*. To abandon the desire for identity, identification, mastery, control, is to raise the stakes with regard to one's own ability to respond, to be responsible to what takes place between self and other in the urban space, and what is inscribed on the self by the other. Giving up the ghost of a chance for control means acknowledging that the city-text's condition is one of constantly becoming, as well as being constantly to-come; it means giving ourselves to the spectral alterity of the city, that which breaks all the rules of the game, before the game has even begun.

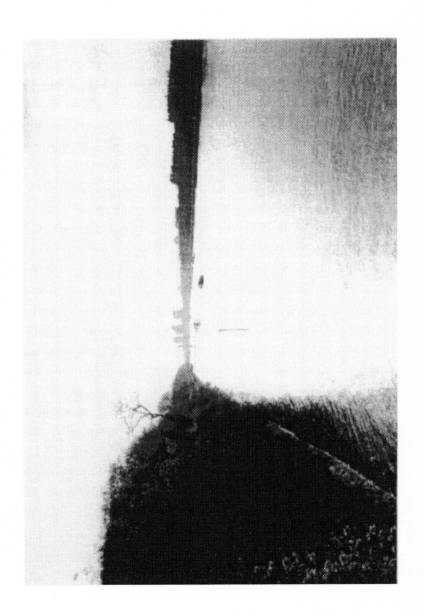

Notes

INTRODUCTION: IMAGINING LONDON OR, RAINBIRD WAS SURE OF IT

1. Charles Baudelaire, *The Poems in Prose* and *La Fanfarlo*, introd. and trans. Francis Scarfe (London: Anvil Press Poetry, 1989), pp. 24, 25.
2. Marc Augé, *Non-places: Introduction to an Anthropology of Supermodernity* (1992) trans. John Howe (London: Verso, 1995).
3. Augé, *Non-places*, p. 118.
4. Hana Wirth-Nesher, *City Codes: Reading the Modern Urban Novel* (Cambridge: Cambridge University Press, 1996). Wirth-Nesher's chapter on Virginia Woolf's *Mrs. Dalloway* is particularly informative about modernist representations of the city and the experience of being one of its inhabitants.
5. Richard Jefferies, 'The Lions in Trafalgar Square', in Richard Jefferies, *The Toilers of the Field* (1892) (London: Longmans Green, 1894; pp. 321–7), pp. 326–7.
6. Arthur Symons, 'London: A Book of Aspects', in *Cities and Sea-Coasts and Islands* (London: Collins, 1918), p. 155.
7. Symons, 'London', p. 137.
8. Jonathan Raban, *Hunting Mr Heartbreak* (1990) (London: Picador, 1991), pp. 357–8.
9. I draw this distinction from the work of Pierre Macherey in his *A Theory of Literary Production* (1966) trans. Geoffrey Wall (London: Routledge and Kegan Paul, 1978), pp. 75–81.
10. Alan Sandison, *Robert Louis Stevenson and the Appearance of Modernism* (Basingstoke: Macmillan, 1996). Sandison points to a quality of city-writing in Stevenson which distinguishes the writers being read in this book and those of the second half of the nineteenth century. From Blake to Dickens, the concern is with the city as city. As we move into the second half of the century, let us say from Wilkie Collins and Anthony Trollope onwards, it is arguable that the writing of the city assumes an ever greater function not only as backdrop or stage, but as psychic context. Certainly, Sandison reads Stevenson's London as a mediator and corollary of Jekyll/Hyde's personalities, where the urban proximity of urbanity and squalor reflect the dual character of the narrative's principal agents. Similarly, Oscar Wilde writes the London of *The Picture of Dorian Gray*, while Arthur Conan Doyle works this London also. Henry James in *The Princess Casamassima* and Joseph Conrad in *The Secret Agent* both make explicit the relationship between character or psyche, and space or site. Clearly such gestures anticipate modernist novels such as *Mrs. Dalloway* or *Ulysses*, or T.S. Eliot's London in *The Waste Land*.

Although Dickens could be said to have begun the exploration of such relationships, however tentatively, in *Oliver Twist*, we would argue that around the middle of the century – let us call this moment 'after Dickens' as an imprecise phrase which gestures towards aesthetic redirection – there occurs something akin to an epistemic shift in the comprehension of the uses of the city in writing. The writers of this study are fascinated with exploring London itself through the written trace, whereas those who come after tend to employ stock images of the city without necessarily allowing it to transform their texts.

11. Sandison, *RLS*, Chapter 6, '*Jekyll and Hyde*: The Story of the Door', pp. 215–69.
12. Sandison, *RLS*, p. 223.
13. Sam Selvon, *The Lonely Londoners* (1956) introd. Kenneth Ramchand (London: Longman, 1994), p. 23.
14. J.B. Priestley, *Angel Pavement* (1930) (Harmondsworth: Penguin, 1968), pp. 14–16, 21.
15. Richard Jefferies, 'A Wet Night in London', in Richard Jefferies, *The Open Air* (London: J.M. Dent and Sons, 1914), pp. 250–6.
16. Elizabeth Gaskell, *Mary Barton* (1848) ed. Edgar Wright (Oxford: Oxford University Press, 1987), pp. 114, 115.
17. Twilight London is a favourite scene with nineteenth- and early twentieth-century writers. Even when it is not twilight, the effect is of partial and obscured vision, with writing attempting to render in words the painterly effects of chiaroscuro lighting. All of *The Secret Agent* seems to be crepuscular, and the following passages from James's *The Princess Casamassima*, Stevenson's *Jekyll and Hyde*, and Wells' *Ann Veronica* respectively, are just three of many such typical, strangely familiar liminal London scenes:

> . . . the dusky multitude of chimney-pots and the small black houses, roofed with grimy tiles. The thick, warm air of a London July floated beneath them, suffused with the everlasting uproar of the town . . . (James, *The Princess Casamassima*, p. 216)

> The dismal quarter of Soho . . . with its muddy ways, and slatternly passages, and its lamps, which had never been extinguished, seemed, in the lawyer's eyes, like a district of some city in a nightmare . . . (Stevenson, *Jekyll and Hyde*, p. 27)

> The afternoon has passed now into twilight. The shops were lighting up in gigantic lanterns of colour, the street lamps were glowing into existence, and she had lost her way. She had lost her sense of direction, and was among unfamiliar streets. She went on from street to street, and all the glory of London departed. Against the sinister, the threatening, monstrous inhumanity of the limitless city, there was nothing now but this supreme, ugly fact of a pursuit – the pursuit of the undesired, persistent male. (Wells, *Ann Veronica*, pp. 87–8).

Notes

18. Jean Baudrillard, *Simulations* (1981) trans. Paul Foss, Paul Patton and Philip Beitchman (New York: Semiotext(e), 1983), p. 2. See also Geoff King, *Mapping Reality: An Exploration of Cultural Cartographies* (Basingstoke: Macmillan, 1996).
19. Mark Wigley, *The Architecture of Deconstruction: Derrida's Haunt* (Cambridge, MA: MIT Press, 1993), p. 106.
20. Elizabeth Grosz, *Space, Time, and Perversion: Essays on the Politics of Bodies* (New York: Routledge, 1995), p. 105.
21. There is further brief discussion of these issues at the beginning of Chapter 2 and in n.1 and n.3 of that chapter.
22. The clamour for political change, and the voices of religious dissent are only two possible discourses which unsettle conceptions of identity during the period in question. Charles Tilly interestingly addresses the various transformations in collective political action in British culture of the period 1758–1834, in his *Popular Contention in Great Britain 1758–1834* (Cambridge, MA: Harvard University Press, 1995). As he points out, London workers of the period were significantly organized and offered support to radical and reformist politics (p. 267). As we know from any contextual study of Blake's poetry, often such London workers were also members of radical dissenting religious groups.
23. Matthew Arnold, 'West London', in *The Poems of Matthew Arnold*, 2nd ed., ed. Miriam Allott (London: Longman, 1979), p. 526. See also 'East London', p. 525. I discuss both poems at length in my *Being English: Narratives, Idioms, and Performances of National Identity from Coleridge to Trollope* (Albany: State University of New York Press, 1994), pp. 35–54.
24. Peter Ackroyd, *Milton in America* (London: Sinclair Stevenson, 1996). Curiously, Milton's interior monologue, in which there are memories of London on the first page (p. 5), bears a resemblance to Blake's city-scenes, in their abrupt, staccato delivery of proper names.
25. Greg Williams, *Diamond Geezers* (London: Fourth Estate, 1997). Two examples of Williams' response to the trace will suffice:

> And this was February, maybe not the coldest but certainly the bleakest month of the year: the month when the sky was so low across London that it looked like it had fallen from above and settled on the rooftops . . .
>
> (p. 15)

> Russell thought it best not to wake him and slipped quietly out the front door, making sure that it was locked behind him, and into the London babble.
>
> (p. 24)

The effect of writing the city combines with city writing to produce a doubling, haunting effect. It is impossible to decide, strictly speaking, whether these passages are responses to the city or to the traces of the city already inscribed in others' texts. What we may propose is that Williams' text effectively ensures that the city can only be understood as being always and only comprehensible as the disseminated trace, prior to any supposed reality on which we may choose to speculate.

26. Priestley, *Angel Pavement*, p. 22.
27. Charlotte Riddell, *Mitre Court. A Tale of the Great City* (London: Richard Bentley and Son, 1885), p. 60. Charlotte Riddell wrote over 50 novels and collections of short stories, many set in London. In *Mitre Court* and other novels of the 1880s, such as *George Geith of Fen Court* (London: Richard Bentley and Son, 1886) and *The Government Official* (London: Richard Bentley and Son, 1887), she bemoans the indiscriminate, often wholesale, architectural destruction of 'beautiful' buildings in favour of 'mere aggregation[s] of offices and warehouses' (*Mitre Court*, p. 68) brought about through the vested interest of businessmen who allegedly have the ear of politicians and can bring about Acts of Parliament for the purpose of urban planning (*Mitre Court*, pp. 51–2; *Government Official*, p. 1). Another favourite theme of Riddell's is that of being able hide oneself in London more completely than in the country. Interestingly, Riddell's London, compared with contemporaries such as Bram Stoker, Richard Jefferies, R.L. Stevenson, and Oscar Wilde, is not a place of exotic and dangerous proximity, a place where the monstrous which the city embodies is always likely to overwhelm us. Riddell's vision of London is more akin to descriptions of late nineteenth-century New York as found, for example, in novels by Horatio Alger.

    I am very grateful to Helen Debenham for mentioning Riddell in a passing email message.
28. Riddell, *George Geith*, p. 1.
29. M. Christine Boyer, *The City of Collective Memory: Its Historical Imagery and Architectural Entertainments* (Cambridge, MA: MIT Press, 1994), pp. 279–80. See also her study of cyberspace and its possible relation to the urban imaginary, *Cybercities: Visual Perception in the Age of Electronic Communication* (New York: Princeton Architectural Press, 1996), particularly Chapter 2, 'Labyrinths of the Mind and the City – Real and Virtual', pp. 45–72.
30. Riddell, *Mitre Court*, p. 67.
31. Nicholas Royle, *After Derrida* (Manchester: Manchester University Press, 1995), pp. 2–5.
32. The miraculous and monstrous are of course never entirely distinct; the one contaminates the other perpetually, as that necessity of its supposed opposite which makes it possible in the first place.
33. Carol L. Bernstein, *The Celebration of Scandal: Toward the Sublime in Victorian Urban Fiction* (University Park, PA: Pennsylvania State University Press, 1991), p. 172.
34. Bernstein, *Celebration*, p. 45.
35. Bernard Tschumi, *Architecture and Disjunction* (Cambridge, MA: MIT Press, 1994), p. 48.
36. Tschumi, *Architecture*, p. 49.
37. Tschumi, *Architecture*, p. 49.

38. H.G. Wells, *Love and Mr Lewisham* (1900) (Harmondsworth: Penguin, 1946), p. 236.
39. The Sealy Tomb, St Mary's Lambeth, and the dentated snake first came to my attention in Iain Sinclair's *Lights Out for the Territory: 9 Excursions in the Secret History of London* (London: Granta, 1997), pp. 170–84, which includes a photograph of the snake, taken by Marc Atkins. My own photograph came about by accident when taking photographs for this book. Walking in Lambeth, with the intention of getting to Southwark (which never happened), I came by accident on St Mary's, and could not resist this image, as though it were to become an improper citation, if not of London, then of Atkins' photograph.
40. Neil Hertz, *The End of the Line: Essays on Psychoanalysis and the Sublime* (New York: Columbia University Press, 1985), p. 55.
41. I take this phrase 'theatre of memory' from Samuel's book, *Theatres of Memory: Volume 1 – Past and Present in Contemporary Culture* (London: Verso, 1994).
42. On this relationship see Walter Benjamin, *Charles Baudelaire: A Lyric Poet in the Era of High Capitalism*, trans. Harry Zohn (London: New Left Books, 1973), pp. 128–31. The epigraph to Ch. 3, below, is taken from this discussion (p. 131).
43. Bernard Tschumi, *Event-Cities (Praxis)* (Cambridge, MA: MIT Press, 1994), p. 157.
44. Henry James, 'London', in *London Stories and Other Writings*, ed. David Kynaston (Padstow: Tabb House, 1989; pp. 241–70), p. 261.

1 BLAKE'S LONDON • LONDON'S BLAKE: AN INTRODUCTION TO THE SPIRIT OF LONDON OR, ON THE WAY TO APOCALYPSE

1. Jacques Derrida, 'Remarks on Deconstruction and Pragmatism', trans. Simon Critchley, in *Deconstruction and Pragmatism*, ed. Chantal Mouffe (London: Routledge, 1996; pp. 77–88), p. 85.
2. Vincent De Luca, 'A Wall of Words: The Sublime as Text', in *Unnam'd Forms: Blake and Textuality*, ed. Nelson Hilton and Thomas A. Vogler (Berkeley: University of California Press, 1986; pp. 218–41), p. 232. Also of interest with regard to Blakean archetectonics is Morton Paley's *The Continuing City: William Blake's Jerusalem* (Oxford: Clarendon Press, 1983). Paley's discussion lights upon various 'real' London sites and determinate material urban referents as a means of explaining certain references within *Jerusalem*, although he ultimately subordinates London to a mere reality and template for Blake's Golgonooza, which is where we part company. While London 'and its associated symbols are the central embodiment of Blake's millenarian theme. . . . [Blake's Golgonooza] combines the quotidian reality of Blake's London, its streets, buildings, and public places, with the visionary New Jerusalem' (136). I would suggest that Blake's is no mere combination but a reciprocal discursive interchange and overlay; even 'the quotidian reality' of London is profoundly textual for William Blake.

3. David E. Wellbery, *The Specular Moment: Goethe's Early Lyric and the Beginnings of Romanticism* (Stanford: Stanford University Press, 1996), p. 3.

4. Palmer, quoted in Alexander Gilchrist's biography, *Life of William Blake* (2nd ed., 1880), ed. Ruthven Todd (New York: Dutton, 1942), p. 77.

5. On the possible relationship between Blake and Derrida's writing, see Peter Otto, *Constructive Vision and Visionary Deconstruction: Los, Eternity, and the Productions of Time in the Later Poetry of William Blake* (Oxford: Clarendon Press, 1991), pp. 19–21, 24–27.

6. Dan Miller, 'Blake and the Deconstructive Interlude', in *Critical Paths: Blake and the Argument of Method*, ed. Dan Miller, Mark Bracher, and Donald Ault (Durham: Duke University Press, 1987; pp. 139–67), p. 155.

7. Simon Critchley, *The Ethics of Deconstruction: Derrida and Levinas* (Oxford: Blackwell, 1992), p. 13.

8. Derrida, 'Deconstruction and Pragmatism', p. 85.

9. Peter Ackroyd, *Blake* (London: Sinclair Stevenson, 1995), p. 92. Ackroyd's own passionate obsession with the sublime aspects of London (manifested repeatedly in his novels) makes him in some ways the ideal biographer of Blake, even though he can be accused of ignoring certain facets of Blake's writing, as Helen Bruder has done in the introduction to her *William Blake and the Daughters of Albion* (Basingstoke: Macmillan, 1997), pp. 14–15. In many ways *Blake* is as much the biography of a city at a given moment, as it is the biography of one of its inhabitants.

10. Henry James, 'Preface', *The Princess Casamassima* (1886) ed. and introd. Derek Brewer, notes by Patricia Crick (London: Penguin, 1987; pp. 33–48), p. 33.

11. William Blake, *The Complete Poems*, ed. Alicia Ostriker (London: Penguin, 1977). All references to these poems will be taken from this edition and will be cited parenthetically, following quotation in the text.

12. Ackroyd, *Blake*, p. 92.

13. Particularly interesting is Jon Mee's *Dangerous Enthusiasm: William Blake and the Culture of Radicalism in the 1790s* (Oxford: Clarendon Press, 1992). See also, Iain McCalman's essay, 'The Infidel as Prophet: William Reid and Blakean Radicalism', in *Historicising Blake*, ed. Steve Clark and David Worrall (Basingstoke: Macmillan, 1994), pp. 24–42, and Jon Mee's essay in the same collection 'Is there an Antinomian in the House? William Blake and the After-Life of a Heresy', pp. 43–58.

14. For more detail, refer to Ackroyd, *Blake*, pp. 42–6. As Ackroyd points out, Basire's antiquarian interests provided Blake with a quite arcane and 'other-worldly' experience of image-making. Furthermore, while apprenticed to Basire, Blake came into regular contact with the Freemasons, whose meeting place was immediately opposite Basire's home in Great Queen Street (p. 45). Ackroyd points out that the Masons 'bore affinities with the Dissenting tradition' of Blake's family (pp. 45–6). For further information on Blake's engraving and book-making

techniques, refer to Joseph Viscomi, *Blake and the Idea of the Book* (Princeton: Princeton University Press, 1993) and to Ruth Robbins, 'William Blake', in *Dictionary of Literary Biography, Volume 154: The British Literary Book Trade, 1700–1820*, ed. James K. Bracken and Joel Silver (Detroit: Gale Research Inc., 1995), pp. 26–32.

15. Arthur Symons, 'London: A Book of Aspects', in *Cities and Sea-Coasts and Islands* (London: Collins, 1918; pp. 137–87), p. 173.
16. Jacques Derrida, *The Truth in Painting* (1978) trans. Geoff Bennington and Ian McLeod (Chicago: University of Chicago Press, 1987), p. 377.
17. Derrida, *Truth in Painting*, p. 338.
18. Marilyn Butler, 'Art for the People in the Revolutionary Decade: Blake, Gillray and Wordsworth', in *Romantics, Rebels and Revolutionaries: English Literature and its Background 1760–1830* (Oxford: Oxford University Press, 1981), pp. 39–68.
19. Butler, *Romantics*, p. 41.
20. Butler, *Romantics*, p. 43.
21. Steven Goldsmith, *Unbuilding Jerusalem* (Ithaca: Cornell University Press, 1993), p. 137. The understanding of Blake's political, radical sympathies is central to E.P. Thompson's *Witness Against the Beast: William Blake and the Moral Law* (Cambridge: Cambridge University Press, 1993). I am indebted to this work for its sensitive analysis of Blake's 'London' from *Songs of Experience* in Chapter 11 (pp. 174–94), to which I shall refer further on in this chapter.
22. On these plans, see Linda Colley, *Britons: Forging the Nation 1707–1837* (1992) (London: Pimlico, 1994), pp. 215, 231–2. The most immediate reference to the monarchy is the violently architectural image of blood running down palace walls in 'London' of course. But we could argue that Blake writes and revises *Jerusalem* and *Milton* as acts of imaginary and symbolic counter-architecture, as if such writing were an attempt to unbuild and rebuild the spiritual London in the face of the commercial capital's simultaneous reinvention on the part of the Georges. See also Roy Porter, *London: A Social History* (London: Hamish Hamilton, 1994; pp. 126–30) on John Nash's urban redevelopment and its social context in the first decades of the nineteenth century. Less than a mile from South Molton Street, Nash's ordered repetitive stucco and *faux-palazzo* sensibility of Regent Street is everything which Blake's London is not, and to which Blake's writing of London may be opposed.
23. J. Hillis Miller, *Topographies* (Stanford: Stanford University Press, 1995), p. 276.
24. Goldsmith, *Unbuilding Jerusalem*, p. 14. In his introduction, Goldsmith discusses briefly Derrida's analysis of the ideological interests hidden within apocalyptic discourses, in his 'Of an Apocalyptic Tone Recently Adopted in Philosophy', *Oxford Literary Review* 6 (1984) (subsequently reprinted and retranslated as 'On a Newly Arisen Apocalyptic Tone in Philosophy', trans. John P. Leavey, Jr, in *Raising the Tone of Philosophy*, ed. Peter Fenves (Baltimore: Johns Hopkins, 1993; pp. 117–72)). Goldsmith ultimately argues against Derrida's claims that apocalyptic discourse in its formal concerns is transformative.

Goldsmith comments that Derrida can only make such a gesture by retreating from historical questions into formalist concerns with language, so that, ultimately, Derrida's insistence on constant wariness in the face of hidden ideological structures in apocalyptic discourses is itself undermined by the apparently apocalyptic tone of much of Derrida's own writing; what is initially discernible as a progressive politics in Derrida's writing gives way in American practices of 'deconstructive criticism' to what Goldsmith terms a 'mere political phantazia' as the 'by-product of ahistorical linguistic and phenomenological necessities' (p. 16).

Of course it can be argued, equally, that Goldsmith's own reading of Derrida – though not necessarily deconstruction as an institutional critical practice in the US – is a mis-reading, based on the narrow understanding of the uses of terms 'text' and 'writing'. Certainly Goldsmith seems keen to situate the formal/political, text/history binarisms without much preliminary distrust of the 'truth' of such positions; and such an understanding of the narrow uses of terms such as 'text' is clearly there in Goldsmith's critique, especially when he moves, all too easily it seems, from the (partly justified) critique of deconstructive formalism to Northrop Frye's own formalistic desires as embodied in Frye's use of Mallarmé's comment 'Tout, au monde, existe pour aboutir à un livre' ('everything in the world exists in order to end up in a book'). Goldsmith gives the translation as 'All earthly existence must ultimately be contained in a book'.

While Goldsmith's point concerning the political abandonment inherent in formalist acts may well be made economically, the shift between text and book implicit in his argument is far too violent and suspect. Such criticisms, and other related issues arising out of such discussion, might well be directed towards or oriented around Blake himself in a certain reading of *Jerusalem*. From a different critical orientation, it certainly seems to be part of Marilyn Butler's criticism of the later Blake (*Romantics*, pp. 41–52). For further comparison of Blake and Derrida, see W.J.T. Mitchell's 'Visible Language: Blake's Wond'rous Art of Writing' in *Romanticism and Contemporary Criticism*, ed. Morris Eaves and Michael Fischer (Ithaca: Cornell University Press, 1986). See also, David Simpson, 'Reading Blake and Derrida – Our Caesars Neither Praised nor Buried', in *Unnam'd Forms: Blake and Textuality*, ed. Nelson Hilton and Thomas Vogler (Berkeley: University of California Press, 1986). Both Mitchell and Simpson's essays are reprinted in *William Blake*, ed. David Punter (Basingstoke: Macmillan, 1996), pp. 123–48, 149–64 respectively. See also those works referred to in notes 2, 5, and 6, above.

25. Given Blake's apparent reworking of certain material from *Milton* in *Jerusalem*, or what is at the very least an obviously reciprocal intertextuality so that images appear transposed, inverted, re-ordered, the intertextual paraphrasing may well be part of Blake's way of figuring or 'building' London otherwise; each text is readable today as quoting, misquoting, paraphrasing, citing, annotating, pastiching and parodying the other.

26. This seems to be very much the problem with Peter Ackroyd's vision

of Blake's London, which is really Ackroyd's vision of London. The form and tone of this vision appears so regularly in Ackroyd's work that it erases the very difference of the city, the difference which articulates London for writers such as Blake and Dickens, and which is still to be found in Iain Sinclair's writing, which juxtaposes the banal and the esoteric in endlessly inventive ways.

27. See Goldsmith, *Unbuilding Jerusalem*, Ch. 3, 'Apocalypse and Representation: Blake, Paine, and the Logic of Democracy', pp. 135–64. On the subject of Apocalypse in Blake's writing, see Northrop Frye, *Fearful Symmetry: A Study of William Blake* (Princeton: Princeton University Press, 1947), and Harold Bloom, *Blake's Apocalypse: A Study in Poetic Argument* (Garden City, NY: Anchor, 1959).

28. Thompson, *Witness Against the Beast*, Ch. 11, p. 173.

29. Thompson, *Witness*, p. 181.

30. Thompson, *Witness*, p. 174. Curiously, Thompson contradicts his own comment on the poem being an image of the human condition, when he writes, '"London" is not about the human condition but about a particular condition or state, and a way of seeing this' (p. 192).

31. Thompson, *Witness*, pp. 181, 187–8.

32. Deborah Epstein Nord, *Walking the Victorian Streets: Women, Representation, and the City* (Ithaca: Cornell University Press, 1995). On the relationship between the sublime and the urban experience in Victorian fiction, see Carol L. Bernstein, *The Celebration of Scandal: Toward the Sublime in Victorian Urban Fiction* (University Park, PA: Pennsylvania State University Press, 1991). I discuss Bernstein's readings of the city in the chapter on Dickens, below.

33. Thompson makes a similar point, when he says that we 'have been wandering, with Blake, into an ever more dense immersion' (p. 188).

34. Thompson, *Witness*, p. 187.

35. Thompson, *Witness*, p. 190.

36. Thompson, *Witness*, p. 190.

37. Harold Bloom, *Poetry and Repression* (New Haven: Yale University Press, 1976).

38. Bloom, *Poetry and Repression*, p. 37.

39. Bernstein, *Celebration*, p. 9.

40. Nord, *Victorian Streets*, p. 1.

41. Nord offers readings of a number of now largely neglected female writers of the nineteenth century in her study of the female spectator, particularly Elizabeth Gaskell, Flora Tristan, Margaret Harkness, Amy Levy, Maud Pember Reeves, Beatrice Webb and Helen Bosanquet, while considering also Virginia Woolf and George Orwell. Bernstein provides readings of George Gissing's and Henry James's representations of urban spaces and sites.

42. Thomas De Quincey, 'Confessions of an English Opium-Eater' (1821), in *Confessions of an English Opium-Eater and Other Writings*, ed. Grevel Lindop (Oxford: Oxford University Press, 1985; pp. 1–80), pp. 16–37. It is not difficult to work out that De Quincey is as addicted to London as he is to opium, devoting one quarter of the 'Confessions' to his experience of the city.

43. Bernstein, *Celebration*, p. 21.

44. 'Songs of Experience', p. 124.
45. Thompson, *Witness*, p. 190.
46. Thompson, *Witness*, pp. 175–6.
47. Thompson, *Witness*, p. 175.
48. The phrase 'marriage hearse' also functions as a resistance to unity, with its various spectres all of which bear a certain relationship to one another, while yet retaining an affirmative heterogeneity, which speaks of a certain temporal experience. We hear in this phrase 'marriage hearth'; we can hear also 'carriage' in 'marriage', while 'hearse' conveys in itself 'horse'. This is, of course, highly speculative, but Blake's image of the 'marriage hearse' is a catachrestic figure appropriate to the construction of London, as I discuss in the next chapter.
49. Thompson, *Witness*, pp. 182–3.
50. Derrida, 'On a newly Arisen Apocalyptic Tone', p. 136.
51. Bill Readings, 'Mobile supplement II: work', in *Introducing Lyotard: Art and Politics* (London: Routledge, 1991), pp. 140–53.
52. Readings, 'Mobile supplement', p. 140.
53. Readings, 'Mobile supplement', pp. 148–9.
54. Readings, 'Mobile supplement', p. 141.
55. Readings, 'Mobile supplement', p. 149.
56. Readings, 'Mobile supplement', p. 152.
57. Readings, 'Mobile supplement', p. 150.
58. Readings, 'Mobile supplement', p. 150.
59. On catachresis and its importance to the structuring of London in Romantic poetry see Chapter 2, below.
60. Jerome J. McGann, *Social Values and Poetic Acts* (Cambridge, MA: Harvard University Press, 1988), cit. Goldsmith, p. 135.
61. On singularity and iterability in Derrida's work, see principally Jacques Derrida, *Limited Inc*, trans. Samuel Weber and Jeffrey Mehlman (Evanston: Northwestern University Press, 1988); see also the section on 'The Signature', and also those on 'The Proper Name', 'The Title', 'The Series', in Geoffrey Bennington and Jacques Derrida, *Jacques Derrida* (1991) trans. Geoffrey Bennington (Chicago: University of Chicago Press, 1993), pp. 148–65, 104–13, 241–57, 267–83. See as well Samuel Weber, 'After Deconstruction' in *Mass Mediauras: Form Technics Media*, ed. Alan Cholodenko (Stanford: Stanford University Press, 1996), pp. 129–51.
62. Thompson, *Witness*, p. 58.
63. Blake's citing /siting of Primrose Hill and St John's Wood as the location of 'Jerusalems pillars' may well be read as an attempt once more to anticipate and oppose John Nash's eventual developments of villas and stuccoed terraces. Building London otherwise in his imagination, Blake resists Regency affluence and the territorialization which accompanies it.
64. Jacques Derrida, *On the Name* (1993) ed. Thomas Dutoit, trans. David Wood, John P. Leavey, Jr, and Ian McLeod (Stanford: Stanford University Press, 1995), p. 28.
65. Derrida, *On the Name*, p. 29.

66. Robert N. Essick, *William Blake and the Language of Adam* (Oxford: Clarendon Press, 1989), p. 174.
67. Essick, *William Blake and the Language of Adam*, p. 174.
68. Jacques Derrida, *Of Spirit: Heidegger and the Question* (1987) trans. Geoffrey Bennington and Rachel Bowlby (Chicago: University of Chicago Press, 1989), p. 113.

2 'HALF LOST IN NIGHT': ENVISIONING LONDON OR, ROMANTIC POETRY'S CAPITAL SNAPSHOTS

1. Alexander Pope, *The Dunciad Variorum*, in *The Poems of Alexander Pope*, ed. John Butt (London: Methuen, 1963), pp. 317–59. See, for example, the description of the 'endless band', described also as a 'motley mixture' in Book II (p. 372; ll. 15, 17). See also, in Book II, the description of the babble of a 'thousand tongues' (p. 390; l. 227) which discordantly rattle around various areas of London.
2. Tobias Smollett, *The Expedition of Humphrey Clinker* (1771) ed. Angus Ross (Harmondsworth: Penguin, 1983).

    While a good number of letters are written from London, Matthew Bramble's and Lydia Melford's (May 24, 31) are the two which deal at any length with the city (1983, pp. 117–26).
3. Bramble comments on the report that 11,000 houses have been built in seven years (p. 117), and describes London as an 'unwieldy metropolis' (p. 117), an 'overgrown monster' (p. 118), and an 'immense wilderness' (p. 118), which phrase anticipates De Quincey. With something which today seems like prescience, he comments that, if things continue as they are, Middlesex will one day be covered in houses (p. 118). Despite the fact that the streets are 'spacious and regular, and airy' (p. 118; a definition not found in nineteenth-century accounts), the principal threat to Bramble in the growth of London is that 'there is no distinction or subordination left – The different departments of life are jumbled together' (p. 119). Clearly, Smollett's character feels the threat to class distinctions apparently posed by a large and rapidly developing city such as London in the 1770s.

    Lydia Melford comments similarly on the spread of London, talking of the 'swarm' and 'human tide' of the capital (p. 122). Her collective noun for the city's transportation is 'an infinity' (p. 123). The city dazzles and confounds her (p. 124) with its 'infinite number of lamps', and, like a number of later city-writers such as those considered in *Writing London*, she resorts to a list of effects (p. 124).

    Smollett is clearly setting the scene in these two letters for narrative developments, rather than allowing the city to become part of the narrative itself. While each character does in certain ways speak of London in a manner common in the texts of the first half of the nineteenth century, the brevity of their discourse on the city indicates that London is merely employed by Smollett in order to further the reader's comprehension of Bramble's and Melford's characters, the former somewhat misanthropic, the latter somewhat awe-struck.

Those texts which appear from the turn of the century onwards attempt to engage with the city in a more sustained, complex, even ambiguous fashion.

4. Peter Wagner, *Reading Iconotexts: From Swift to the French Revolution* (London: Reaktion Books, 1995), pp. 120–31. For a discussion of Hogarth's influence (along with that of other illustrators) on Dickens, see Harry Stone, *The Night Side of Dickens: Cannibalism, Passion, Necessity* (Columbus: Ohio State University Press, 1994), pp. 35–55.

5. Peter Stallybrass and Allon White, *The Politics and Poetics of Transgression* (Ithaca: Cornell University Press, 1986), p. 125.

6. Joseph Conrad, *The Secret Agent* (1907) ed. and introd. Martin Seymour-Smith (London: Penguin, 1990), p. 117.

7. Jerome J. McGann, *The Romantic Ideology: A Critical Investigation* (Chicago: University of Chicago Press, 1983), p. 41.

8. T. Ashe, ed., *The Table Talk and Omniana of S.T. Coleridge* (London: Bohn's Popular Library, 1923).

9. Coleridge, *Table Talk*, pp. 136–7, cit. McGann, p. 41.

10. Gas lamps were introduced onto the streets of London in 1812.

11. George Gordon, Lord Byron, *Don Juan*, in *Poetical Works* (1904) ed. Frederick Page, corrected John Jump (Oxford: Oxford University Press, 1970), pp. 635–859; Percy Bysshe Shelley, *Peter Bell the Third*, in *Poetical Works* (1905) ed. Thomas Hutchinson, corrected G.M. Matthews (Oxford: Oxford University Press, 1970), pp. 346–61; Anna Laetitia Barbauld, *The Poems of Anna Laetitia Barbauld*, ed. William McCarthy and Elizabeth Kraft (Athens, GA: University of Georgia Press, 1994), pp. 152–60 ('Eighteen Hundred' etc.), p. 141 ('Songs for' etc.), p. 142 ('West End Fair'). All further references to these texts will be cited by line, or, where appropriate, canto and verse, parenthetically following quotation. I would like to thank Jane Stabler for suggesting certain passages to me.

12. Roy Porter, *London: A Social History* (London: Hamish Hamilton, 1994), p. 160.

13. Jacques Derrida, 'Deconstruction and the Other', an interview with Richard Kearney, in Richard Kearney, ed. *Dialogues with Contemporary Continental Thinkers: The Phenomenological Heritage* (Manchester, Manchester University Press, 1984; pp. 107–26), p. 123.

14. Derrida, 'Deconstruction and the Other', p. 126.

15. Paul Virilio, *The Vision Machine* (1988) trans. Julie Rose (London: British Film Institute, 1994), p. 14.

16. Frances Ferguson, *Solitude and the Sublime: Romanticism and the Aesthetics of Individuation* (New York: Routledge, 1992), p. 19.

17. With London and Britain becoming in Barbauld's poem a wasteland, this provides the reader today with an interesting moment of coincidental relation between Barbauld and T.S. Eliot, with his own ironic reference to the 'Sweet Thames'.

18. Another felicitous coincidence. Barbauld's reeds and sedge along the Thames can be seen to anticipate the weeds and waste of Richard Jefferies' vision of a post-apocalyptic London in his novel, *After London*.

19. The moribund quality of empty architecture is referred to by Byron in *Don Juan*:

In deserts, forests, crowds, or by the shore,
There solitude, we know, has her full growth in
The spots which were her realms for evermore;
But in a mighty hall or gallery, both in
    More modern buildings and those built of yore,
A kind of death comes o'er us all alone

(Canto V, LVII)

20. Shelley's poem is 'Peter Bell the Third' because it comes after Wordsworth's *Peter Bell* and John Hamilton Reynolds' *Peter Bell, a Lyrical Ballad*. Written in October 1819, its dedicatory letter, signed by Shelley as Miching Mallecho, is dated December 1, 1819, coincidentally being the date on which Anna Laetitia Barbauld completed the composition of 'Eighteen Hundred and Eleven', in that year.
21. Steven Goldsmith, *Unbuilding Jerusalem* (1993), p. 216. See the previous chapter on Blake for further discussion of Goldsmith's book.
22. Shelley, dedication to *Peter Bell the Third*, in *Poetical Works*, p. 347. The figure of a London covered by marshes, rushes and weeds is a favourite one of naturalist and novelist Richard Jefferies, as I have already pointed out above. On this aspect of Jefferies' writing, see Jessica Maynard's fine essay in *Literary Theories: A Case Study in Critical Performance* ed. Julian Wolfreys and William Baker (Basingstoke: Macmillan, 1996), pp. 129–56.
23. On this subject, see for example, Goldsmith's chapter in *Unbuilding Jerusalem*, 'Apocalypse and Politics: Percy Bysshe Shelley's 1819', pp. 209–60.
24. Timothy Morton, *Shelley and the Revolution in Taste: The Body and the Natural World* (Cambridge: Cambridge University Press, 1994), p. 3.
25. Goldsmith, *Unbuilding Jerusalem*, p. 214.
26. Nicholas Abraham, *Rhythms: On the Work, Translation, and Psychoanalysis* (1985) collected and presented by Nicholas T. Rand and Maria Torok, trans. Benjamin Thigpen and Nicholas T. Rand (Stanford: Stanford University Press, 1995), p. 123. Here, Abraham is discussing a poem of Goethe's, *The Sorcerer's Apprentice*, and what he terms the psychoanalysis of rhythm. It is the rhythm of the text to which Abraham is referring in the quotation above, but I have borrowed the remark because of its pertinence to Shelley's London, which must be seen as a fictive construct rather than a representation of particular empirical realities. My reason for drawing on Abraham's work in this somewhat violent manner is because my reading of the poem suggests that what we read when we read of 'London' is a series of phenomenological images affecting and affected/effected by the mind. The text's jump-cut imagery constructs London as a range of psychic phenomena being the products of a particular psyche, in this case Peter Bell's, as I show above. But what I want to suggest is that, all which is contained in the poem is contained in the mind, hence my reference in the main body of the text to '*Peter Bell* and Peter Bell'. The poem is clearly not a reflection of a certain reality, and just because it names London we should not mistake Shelley's

work as suddenly becoming a *merely* sociological critique or contemporary satire. London is a fiction of the psyche and that psyche is that of both the character Peter Bell, and of the text *Peter Bell.* In Abraham's terms Bell's and the poem's unconscious, ego and superego are played out by and through the text, through its rhythms, allusions, images and tropes, and this is mapped particularly clearly in the third part which is concerned with London, and in the fourth part, which is concerned with Peter's being in London, or, to use an awkwardly quasi-Heideggerian construction, Peter's-Being-in-London. On the mind's productions, see Byron's *Don Juan,* Canto X, XX.

27. Andrew Elfenbein, *Byron and the Victorians* (Cambridge: Cambridge University Press, 1995), p. 19.
28. Michel Foucault, *The Order of Things: An Archeology of the Human Sciences* (1966) (New York: Random House, 1973). Elfenbein, *Byron and the Victorians,* p. 19.
29. Elfenbein, 19.
30. Foucault, *Order of Things,* p. 44.
31. Foucault, *Order of Things,* pp. 30, 34, 42.
32. *Don Juan* was published serially, Cantos VI–XIV published in 1823, XV and XVI in 1824.
33. This forward-looking quality is captured in the opening verses of the Dedication of Canto I, as Byron derisorily distances himself from Wordsworth, Coleridge, Southey, and the other 'Lakers' (l. 14). Verses XI–XVII pick up Barbauld and Shelley's political critique. Byron does align himself with the eighteenth-century tradition also, in his rejection of the 'Lakers', but, arguably, this is not a simple alignment, so much as an ironic reinvention.
34. Charles Dickens, *Sketches by Boz and Other Early Papers 1833–39,* ed. Michael Slater (London: J.M. Dent, 1994), p. 55. For more on this passage and the *Sketches* see the final chapter, below.
35. Nicola J. Watson, 'Trans-figuring Byronic Identity', in *At the Limits of Romanticism: Essays in Cultural, Feminist, and Materialist Criticism,* ed. Mary A. Favret and Nicola J. Watson (Bloomington: Indiana University Press, 1994; pp. 185–206), p. 192. Watson's essay convincingly explores 'Byronic poetic identity' (p. 197) and its functions in the literary marketplace. Given the Don's entrance into the *demimonde* of London's literary society in Canto XI, it is not unreasonable to assume, as others have before me, that the Don is one possible mask for Byron, an Oriental, exotic Other, always desired by Byron. 'Poetic identity' is, I would suggest, an effect of the city's social life upon the subject. This does perhaps suggest a reading of Canto XI along such lines.
36. McGann, *Romantic Ideology,* p. 132. McGann argues this point in relation to 'Romantic poetry in general'. Certainly my reading of the Romantics' vision of London bears out the assertion, because London is perceived as composed only of displacements and illusions. Without a centre or origin, without a physically locatable centre or a metaphysical truth, the nature of the city would seem to give the lie implicitly to the idea that London was the 'heart' of the empire,

for how is it possible to have a heart without a heart, to have a centre which has no dominant ordering principle?
37. Virilio, *Vision Machine*, p. 61.

3 *CITEPHOBIA*: THE ANXIETY OF REPRESENTATION OR, FEAR AND LOATHING IN LONDON: THOMAS DE QUINCEY, FRIEDRICH ENGELS, AND WILLIAM WORDSWORTH

1. Jeremy Tambling, *Dickens, Violence and the Modern State: Dreams of the Scaffold* (Basingstoke: Macmillan, 1995), p. 75.
2. Anthony Vidler, *The Architectural Uncanny: Essays in the Modern Unhomely* (Cambridge, MA: MIT Press, 1992), p. 3.
3. Vidler, *The Architectural Uncanny*, pp. 3–4.
4. Sigmund Freud, 'Anxiety', in *Introductory Lectures on Psychoanalysis*, Penguin Freud Library, Vol. 1, trans. James Strachey, ed. James Strachey and Angela Richards (Harmondsworth: Penguin, 1982), pp. 440–60. The earlier work referred to is the paper entitled 'On the Grounds for Detaching a Particular Syndrome from Neurasthenia under the Description "Anxiety Neurosis"', and is to be found in Volume 10, *On Psychopathology*, trans. James Strachey, ed. Angela Richards (London: Penguin, 1993), pp. 35–63, which volume also contains 'Inhibitions, Symptoms and Anxiety' (1926; pp. 237–334) to which I will be referring below.
5. Sigmund Freud, 'Anxiety and Instinctual Life', in *New Introductory Lectures on Psychoanalysis*, Penguin Freud Library, Vol. 2, trans. James Strachey, ed. Angela Richards (London: Penguin, 1991), pp. 113–44. Referred to in footnotes as AIL, followed by page number.
6. Freud, 'Inhibitions', pp. 237–334.
7. Freud, 'Inhibitions', p. 263.
8. Freud, 'Inhibitions', p. 264.
9. Freud, 'Inhibitions', pp. 324–5.
10. Freud, 'Inhibitions', p. 325.
11. Freud, 'Inhibitions', pp. 325–7.
12. Raymond Williams, *The Country and the City* (Oxford: Oxford University Press, 1973), p. 186.
13. Celeste Langan, *Romantic Vagrancy: Wordsworth and the Simulation of Freedom* (Cambridge: Cambridge University Press, 1995), p. 182. Comparing l. 540 with ll. 158–60 of Book VII of *The Prelude*, Langan makes the point that the poem registers a 'catalogue of London recreations, whose discursive form . . . mirrors the practice of urban walking' (p. 182).
14. Boyer, *The City of Collective Memory*, p. 280.
15. Freud, 'Inhibitions', p. 327.
16. Freud, 'Inhibitions', p. 328.
17. See, for example, Mary Ann Caws, ed., *City Images: Perspectives from Literature, Philosophy, and Film* (Langhorne: Gordon and Breach, 1993); Deborah Epstein Nord, *Walking the Victorian Streets: Women, Representation, and the City* (Ithaca: Cornell University Press, 1995); Carol

T. Christ and John O. Jordan, eds, *Victorian Literature and the Victorian Visual Imagination* (Berkeley and Los Angeles: University of California Press, 1995). The importance of vision and visual figures and tropes in relation to concepts of modernity in the nineteenth century is explored by Jonathan Crary in his influential *Techniques of the Observer: On Vision and Modernity in the Nineteenth Century* (Cambridge MA: MIT Press, 1992).

18. Crary, *Techniques*, pp. 118–25.
19. Boyer, *The City of Collective Memory*, p. 285. See also, Peter Stallybrass and Allon White, 'The City: the Sewer, the Gaze and the Contaminating Touch', in *The Politics and Poetics of Transgression* (Ithaca: Cornell University Press, 1986), pp. 125–48.
20. Boyer, *The City of Collective Memory*, pp. 278–89.
21. Kojin Karatani, *Architecture as Metaphor: Language, Number, Money*, trans. Sabu Kohso, ed. Michael Speaks (Cambridge MA: MIT Press, 1995), p. 83.
22. Iain Chambers, *Migrancy, Culture, Identity* (London: Routledge, 1994), p. 10. Chambers is here quoting De Certeau's *The Practice of Everyday Life* (Berkeley and Los Angeles: University of California Press, 1988), p. xxi. In this chapter, 'Migrant Landscapes', Chambers goes on to say that 'Writing depends on the support of the "I".... Yet in the provisional character or writing this structure oscillates' (p. 10). Here he is describing how the very act of writing is a form of travel which, in its act, deconstructs the premise of stability and unity. For me, the act of writing the city in the nineteenth century is one provisional, yet highly visible, starting point for the act of identity's self-deconstruction.
23. Bernstein, *Celebration*, p. 13.
24. Vidler, *Architectural Uncanny*, p. ix.
25. Mary Jacobus, *Romanticism, Writing, and Sexual Difference: Essays on The Prelude* (Oxford: Clarendon Press, 1989), p. 208.
26. Thomas De Quincey, *Confessions of an English Opium-Eater and Other Writings*, ed. Grevel Lindop (Oxford: Oxford University Press, 1985), p. 20.
27. Vidler, *Architectural Uncanny*, pp. 37–8.
28. Vidler, *Architectural Uncanny*, p. 57.
29. Freud, AIL, p. 113.
30. De Quincey, *Confessions*, p. 27.
31. De Quincey, *Confessions*, p. 27.
32. John Barrell, *The Infection of Thomas De Quincey: A Psychopathology of Imperialism* (New Haven: Yale University Press, 1991), p. 2.
33. Barrell, *Infection*, p. 5.
34. De Quincey, *Confessions*, p. 23.
35. Barrell, *Infection*, p. 3.
36. Barrell, *Infection*, p. 2. On the uses of opium, Englishness and the fear of the Oriental Other in Coleridge, see my *Being English: Narratives, Idioms, and Performances of National Identity from Coleridge to Trollope* (Albany: State University of New York Press, 1994), pp. 15–33.

37. M. Christine Boyer makes a similar point concerning the relation between terror and magnitude (p. 280).
38. Grosz, *Space*, p. 104.
39. Grosz, *Space*, p. 110.
40. Grosz, *Space*, p. 108.
41. Jacques Lacan, *Écrits: A Selection*, trans. Alan Sheridan (New York: W.W. Norton and Company, 1977), p. 4.
42. Lacan, *Écrits*, p. 4.
43. De Quincey, *Confessions*, p. 17.
44. De Quincey, *Confessions*, p. 16.
45. De Quincey, *Confessions*, p. 25.
46. De Quincey, *Confessions*, pp. 16, 21–2.
47. De Quincey, *Confessions*, p. 17.
48. De Quincey, *Confessions*, p. 27.
49. De Quincey, *Confessions*, p. 26.
50. De Quincey, *Confessions*, p. 24.
51. De Quincey, *Confessions*, p. 24.
52. De Quincey, *Confessions*, p. 27.
53. De Quincey, *Confessions*, p. 27; emphasis added.
54. De Quincey, *Confessions*, p. 27.
55. De Quincey, *Confessions*, p. 27.
56. De Quincey, *Confessions*, p. 33.
57. De Quincey, *Confessions*, p. 33; emphasis added.
58. De Quincey, *Confessions*, p. 34.
59. De Quincey, *Confessions*, p. 34.
60. De Quincey, *Confessions*, p. 34.
61. De Quincey, *Confessions*, p. 36.
62. De Quincey, *Confessions*, p. 37.
63. Avital Ronell, *Crack Wars: Literature, Addiction, Mania* (Lincoln: University of Nebraska Press, 1992), p. 121. See also pp. 119–25, which is particularly suggestive for a reading of De Quincey.
64. De Quincey, *Confessions*, p. 38.
65. De Quincey, *Confessions*, p. 38.
66. Friedrich Engels, *The Condition of the Working Class in England* (1845) trans. Florence Kelley-Wischnewetsky, revised Engels (1887), ed. and introd. David McLellan (Oxford: Oxford University Press, 1993), p. 36.
67. Engels, *Condition*, p. 5.
68. Engels, *Condition*, p. 36.
69. Engels, *Condition*, p. 36.
70. Engels, *Condition*, pp. 36, 37.
71. Engels, *Condition*, p. 37.
72. Engels, *Condition*, p. 40.
73. My main concern here is with the rhetoric of statistics, mathematics and numeracy. However the language of proximity offers the reader the startling revelation that 'poverty often dwells in hidden alleys close to the palaces of the rich; but in general a separate territory has been assigned to it' (Engels, *Condition*, p. 39); or there is the description of the slum of St Giles, at the heart of 'the gay

world of London' (p. 40). Engels's language of proximal relationships is a somewhat melodramatic, but nonetheless effective, device to force a certain recognition on the reader about the nature of London and social relations. Certainly, it works far more effectively to create an effect of uncomfortable understanding on the reader than all the statistical and numerical information which pervades this description of London. However, Engels does not pursue this gesture of economic deterritorialization, hence my reason for not concentrating in this chapter on this moment. It does, though, have potential which Engels does not recognize, but which potential is further explored, later in the century, by Stevenson in *Dr Jekyll and Mr Hyde* and Oscar Wilde in *Dorian Gray*, amongst others.

74. Engels, *Condition*, p. 36.
75. Freud, AIL, pp. 114–16.
76. Freud, 'Anxiety', p. 446.
77. Engels, *Condition*, p. 36.
78. The figures and facts are taken from Roy Porter, Ch. 9, '"The Contagion of Numbers": The Building of the Victorian Capital 1820–1890', in *London: A Social History*, pp. 205–39.
79. Immanuel Kant, *Critique of Judgment*, trans. J.H. Bernard (New York: Hafner, 1966).
80. Neil Hertz, *The End of the Line: Essays on Psychoanalysis and the Sublime* (New York: Columbia University Press, 1985), p. 40.
81. Engels, *Condition*, p. 41.
82. Engels, *Condition*, p. 41.
83. An irony which today, writing in May 1996, seems all the more appropriate, following the recent revelations about the 'homes for votes' scandal engineered in the Borough of Westminster by Dame Shirley Porter and other Tory councillors, a London narrative surely worthy of Dickens or Trollope.
84. Engels, *Condition*, pp. 41–2.
85. Engels, *Condition*, p. 42.
86. Engels, *Condition*, p. 42.
87. Engels, *Condition*, pp. 42–3.
88. Engels, *Condition*, p. 43.
89. Engels, *Condition*, p. 44.
90. Engels, *Condition*, p. 44–5.
91. Engels, *Condition*, p. 44.
92. Engels, *Condition*, p. 45.
93. Engels, *Condition*, p. 45.
94. Karl Marx, *Early Writings*, trans. Rodney Livingstone and Gregor Benton, introd. Lucio Coletti (New York: Vintage, 1975), p. 421. Marx wrote this in 1845, the same year that Engels wrote *The Condition of the Working Class in England*.
95. Gilles Deleuze and Félix Guattari, *Anti-Oedipus: Capitalism and Schizophrenia* (1972) trans. Robert Hurley, Mark Seem, and Helen R. Lane, preface Michel Foucault (Minneapolis: University of Minnesota Press, 1983). See in particular Pt. 3, Ch. 10, 'Capitalist Representation', pp. 240–62.

96. The edition of *The Prelude* referred to throughout is the 'four-text' edition, edited by Jonathan Wordsworth (London: Penguin, 1995), pp. 250–96. All references are designated by year and line number following quotation.

97. William Wordsworth, 'Composed upon Westminster Bridge, September 3, 1802', in *Poetical Works* (1904), new edn rev. Ernest de Selincourt (Oxford: Oxford University Press, 1988), p. 204.

98. Philip Cox, 'William Wordsworth: Constructions of the "self" in *The Prelude*', in *Gender, Genre and the Romantic Poets* (Manchester: Manchester University Press, 1996; pp. 58–80), p. 58. On the relationship between gender and genre, see Mary Jacobus, *Romanticism*, Ch. 7: 'Genre, Gender, and Autobiography', pp. 187–205.

99. Cox, *Gender*, p. 58.

100. Cox, *Gender*, p. 58.

101. Alan Liu, '"Shapeless Eagerness": The Genre of Revolution in Books 9–10 of *The Prelude*', *Modern Language Quarterly*, 43.1 (1982: 3–28), p. 6. Again, see Jacobus, Ch. 7, cited in n. 30. The confusion of genres that marks *The Prelude* (discussed by Cox, *Gender*, pp. 58–80), confusing the autobiographical with the epic, dislocates the very possibility of a single identity, whether personal or literary.

102. Cox, *Gender*, p. 58.

103. Antony Easthope, *Wordsworth Now and Then: Romanticism and Contemporary Culture* (Buckingham: Open University Press, 1993), p. 27.

104. Geoffrey H. Hartman, *Wordsworth's Poetry 1787–1814* (1964) (Cambridge, MA: Harvard University Press, 1971), p. 239.

105. Hartman, *Wordsworth's Poetry*, p. 239.

106. Jacobus, *Romanticism*, p. 111; emphasis added.

107. Jacobus, *Romanticism*, p. 113.

108. Jacobus, *Romanticism*, p. 111.

109. Hertz, *End of the Line*, pp. 55–6; emphasis added.

110. Bernstein, *Celebration*, p. 29.

111. Bernstein, *Celebration*, p. 1.

112. Bernstein, *Celebration*, p. 172.

113. Hertz, *End of the Line*, p. 56.

114. Hertz, *End of the Line*, pp. 56–7; emphases added.

115. Bernstein, *Celebration*, p. 172.

116. Hertz, *End of the Line*, p. 58.

117. Bernstein, *Celebration*, p. 172.

118. Jacobus, *Romanticism*, p. 210.

119. Jacobus, *Romanticism*, p. 214.

120. Bernstein, *Celebration*, p. 82.

121. Jacobus, *Romanticism*, p. 111.

122. Bernstein, *Celebration*, p. 45.

123. Bernstein, *Celebration*, p. 82.

124. Langan, *Romantic Vagrancy*, p. 182.

125. Langan, *Romantic Vagrancy*, p. 182.

126. Jacques Derrida, 'Différance', in *Margins of Philosophy* (1972) trans. Alan Bass (Chicago: University of Chicago Press, 1982; pp. 1–29), p. 21.

127. Derrida, 'Différance', pp. 20–1.
128. Jacques Derrida, 'Structure, Sign, and Play in the Discourse of the Human Sciences', in *Writing and Difference* (1967) trans. Alan Bass (London: RKP, 1981, pp. 278–95), p. 286.
129. Derrida, 'Structure', p. 286.
130. Forest Pyle, *The Ideology of the Imagination: Subject and Society in the Discourse of Romanticism* (Stanford: Stanford University Press, 1995), p. 60.
131. Pyle, *Ideology*, p. 60.
132. Slavoj Žižek, *The Indivisible Remainder: An Essay on Schelling and Related Matters* (London: Verso, 1996), p. 190. All further reference to this book is taken from the same passage as the first quotation.
133. I have already argued above that London is not an object. Wordsworth mistakenly takes the city to be of the order of objects, hence his frustration and the constant, often furious attempts to describe and define the city, which fail and so lead to the final rejection of the city in favour of 'Composure and ennobling harmony' (1805: 740). Is it any wonder that, after the exhaustion of the self in Book VII, Book VIII should be concerned with a 'Retrospect – Love of Nature Leading to Love of Mankind'? Nature puts everything in perspective.
134. Giorgio Agamben, *Stanzas: Word and Phantasm in Western Culture* (1977) trans. Ronald L. Martinez (Minneapolis: University of Minnesota Press, 1993), p. 33. Agamben is writing here of Freud's theory of fetishes. A more sustained, fully psychoanalytic reading of Book VII might give attention to the city as fetish.
135. Freud, AIL, p. 114.
136. Porter, *London*, Chs. 8–12, pp. 185–305. A quarter of Porter's book is given over to the history of Victorian London, which is a sign perhaps that, despite its longer history, London is, principally, a Victorian city, and the nineteenth century serves to define the city as much as the city defines Victorian life in all its complexity. Porter's is an astute and comprehensive social history, and merits careful consideration. If I have not referred to it further, this is only because my prime concern is not with 'history' or 'reality' as such, but with rhetoric and the architecture of nineteenth-century writing about the city, as I have already discussed in my 'Introduction'. Another fascinating study of London is David Kynaston's *The City of London: Volume I, A World of its Own 1815–1890* (London: Chatto and Windus, 1994), which provides a history of the rise of the City as the key financial centre of the world in the Victorian period.
137. Thomas Carlyle, letter to his brother, 1824, cited in Porter, p. 257.
138. Samuel Weber, *Return to Freud: Jacques Lacan's Dislocation of Psychoanalysis* (1978) trans. Michael Levine (Cambridge: Cambridge University Press, 1991), p. 110.
139. Weber, *Return to Freud*, p. 112.

4 DICKENSIAN ARCHITEXTURES OR, THE CITY AND THE INEFFABLE

1. Wherever I have quoted from or referred to Dickens's novels I have referred to them parenthetically with abbreviations for titles, as follows:

   MHC   *Master Humphrey's Clock*
   OMF   *Our Mutual Friend*
   DC   *David Copperfield*
   OT   *Oliver Twist*
   BH   *Bleak House*
   SB   *Sketches by Boz*
   MC   *Martin Chuzzlewit*
   LD   *Little Dorrit*
   DS   *Dombey and Son*
   NN   *Nicholas Nickleby*

   Full bibliographical details for these and other novels by Dickens are found in the Bibliography at the end of the book. There is, as any reader of Dickens will be aware, too much London in Dickens's novels for a single chapter (even a somewhat lengthy chapter, such as this). I have tried to give the reader a sense of Dickens writing the city across a wide range of texts. I would suggest also the description of 'Quilp's Wharf' in *The Old Curiosity Shop* (*DS*, p. 73), the two lengthy descriptions of Staggs's Gardens from *Our Mutual Friend* (pp. 20–1; 289–90) and Captain Cuttle's accommodation (*DS*, pp. 178–9); the description of Arthur Clennam's and Meagles's search for Miss Wade (*LD*, pp. 373–4), or the various descriptions of Bleeding Heart Yard in *Little Dorrit*; also, the description of the district of Clerkenwell and Gabriel Varden's shop and house in *Barnaby Rudge* (pp. 75–7); and Tom-all-Alone's (*BH*, Ch. 16).
2. Paul Virilio, *The Vision Machine* (1988) trans. Julie Rose (London: British Film Institute, and Bloomington: Indiana University Press, 1994), p. 10.
3. The standard studies are, of course, Alexander Welsh's *The City of Dickens* (Oxford: Clarendon Press, 1971) and Raymond Williams's *The Country and the City* (Oxford: Oxford University Press, 1973). Perhaps the most important study of the figure of the city in nineteenth-century fiction in recent years is that of Carol Bernstein's *The Celebration of Scandal*, already drawn upon and referred to in previous chapters, which touches in several places on my own study, in its uses of Derrida's writing in relation to the trope of the city. Drawing on Georg Lukács, Michel Foucault and Walter Benjamin, Bernstein works through readings of the immaterial city, producing a negative urban sublime and a failure to represent the modern city. Where our studies diverge most consistently and repeatedly is precisely over the question of 'failure'. In terms of the aesthetics of the study, Bernstein is markedly modernist in her reading of the

failure of representation. My argument focuses more on a Dickensian celebration of provisionality and ineffability, as well as the architectural condition of writing. Perhaps it may be argued that the difference in tone between Bernstein's and my project is a difference which is marked by the the fact that, while I focus on texts in the earlier half of the century, she pays attention to those of the second half.

4. Tschumi, *Architecture and Disjunction*, p. 255.

5. Tschumi, *Architecture and Disjunction*, p. 255. See also the discussion of Peter Eisenman's architectural theory in the final section of this chapter.

6. Tschumi, *Architecture and Disjunction*, p. 255.

7. Dickens's iterable structures and the rhetorical frequency of negation and the undecidable which arise through such encounters anticipate both Conrad's writing in *Heart of Darkness* in certain ways, and, in another manner, Derrida's understanding of writing's operations. In relation to this, see my discussion of iterability, undecidability and writing in *Heart of Darkness* in the final chapter of my *Deconstruction • Derrida* (Basingstoke: Macmillan, 1998).

8. Tschumi, *Architecture and Disjunction*, pp. 255, 257.

9. Derrida, cit. Tschumi, *Architecture and Disjunction*, p. 257.

10. Tschumi, *Architecture and Disjunction*, p. 257.

11. Jacques Derrida, 'Point de folie – maintenant l'architecture', trans. Kate Linker, in Bernard Tschumi, *La Case Vide La Villette 1985* (London: Architectural Association, Folio VIII, 1987; pp. 4–20), p. 5.

12. Peter Ackroyd, *Dickens* (1990) (London: Minerva, 1991), p. 161.

13. Ackroyd, *Dickens*, p. 679.

14. F. S. Schwarzbach, *Dickens and the City* (London: Athlone Press, 1979), p. 48. Schwarzbach's study is perhaps the most thorough of its kind. If I cite it hardly at all in this chapter this is due to our different concerns. Schwarzbach is rigorous in his detailing of the relationships between text and context, between novel and social order; also he is concerned to demonstrate a process of progression, transition and change on Dickens's part. Principally, Schwarzbach's interest is in the representation of the real, which is a notion I finally challenge at the end of the chapter, not with regard to Schwarzbach's arguments in particular but as part of a more general rejection of the idea of representation in relationship to Dickens's urban rhetoric.

15. F.S. Schwarzbach has also commented on the fact that Oliver and the Dodger wait until after dark (p. 46). He observes also, in his chapter on *Oliver Twist*, that, despite the naming of streets as the two boys enter, Dickens does not heighten the realism; instead, naming serves merely to distance us even further, because no other details than names are provided (pp. 45–53). Schwarzbach's study is impressive in its attention to detail and the paradoxes and contradictions which arise out of the Dickensian concatenation of minutiae. The question of naming is one to which Schwarzbach repeatedly returns. One curiosity concerning street or place names is worth noting. When Oliver is arrested and taken to prison by the police, the one street named is a Mutton Hill (see the discussion of the

arrest and its scene in the main body of this essay). As far as I have been able to ascertain from maps of London dating between 1813 and 1888 no Mutton Hill existed. In Clerkenwell, the district adjacent to Islington, there was a Mutton Lane leading onto Clerkenwell Green, and there still is a Muswell Hill. It would appear then that Mutton Hill did not exist, and Dickens's conflation of place names only serves to heighten the ambiguity surrounding what we can say we know of 'Dickens's London' with any certainty.

16. See also the description of the Six Jolly Fellowship-Porters, where words such as 'dropsical', 'lopsided', 'toppling', 'corpulent', and phrases such as 'hale infirmity', 'confused memories', and 'toppling oranges' confuse the whole, while foregrounding the somewhat anarchic construction of the event of the tavern (*DS*, p. 61).

17. Terry Eagleton, *Criticism and Ideology: A Study in Marxist Literary Theory* (London: Verso, 1976), p. 127.

18. Eagleton, *Criticism and Ideology*, p. 130.

19. Eagleton, *Criticism and Ideology*, p. 130.

20. Allon White, *Carnival, Hysteria and Writing: Collected Essays and Auto-biography*, introd. Stuart Hall (Oxford: Clarendon Press, 1993), p. 103.

21. On this subject see Derrida's reading of Walter Benjamin in 'Force of Law: The "Mystical Foundation of Authority"', in *Deconstruction and the Possibility of Justice*, ed. Drucilla Cornell, Michael Rosenfeld, and David Gray Carlson (London: Routledge, 1992), pp. 3–68. This essay is of particular interest for the ways in which it counters arguments that deconstruction has no ethics, and for the difference which is opened up between notions of justice and the Law. Also of interest is the way in which the essay can be read as a scene of complication to the subject of the Law, which Derrida's earlier essay on the parable *Vor dem Gesetz* in Kafka's *The Trial* (Derrida, 'Before the Law', *Acts of Literature*, ed. Derek Attridge [London: Routledge, 1992], pp. 181–221; also in the same volume, see 'The Law of Genre', pp. 221–53) had instituted. 'Force of Law' complicates the discourse on the Law at many levels, not least in the ways in which it provides an implicit critique of certain (mis-)readings of 'Before the Law'.

22. Again, the imprecise nature of this analogy which relies on the roughest of fits might be read as anticipating the rhetoric of modernist novels such as Conrad's *Heart of Darkness*.

23. Comparable passages from Engels, already discussed in the previous chapter, are instructive and reveal the domestic, rather than carceral, context to Dickens's description:

> These slums . . . with cellars used as dwellings, almost always irregularly built . . . The streets are generally unpaved, rough, dirty, filled with vegetable and animal refuse . . . foul, stagnant pools . . . narrow, crooked, filthy, crooked streets . . . The houses are occupied from cellar to garret, filthy within and without . . . dwellings in the narrow courts and alleys between the streets, entered by covered passages between the houses, in which the filth and tottering ruin surpass all description. Scarcely a whole window

pane can be found, the walls are crumbling, door-posts and window-frames loose and broken, doors of old boards nailed together . . . Heaps of garbage and ashes lie in all directions, and the foul liquids emptied before the doors gather in stinking pools. Here live the poorest of the poor. . . . (Friedrich Engels, *The Condition of the Working Class in England*, [1845] ed. and introd. David McLellan [Oxford: Oxford University Press, 1993], pp. 39–40).

Engels is of course only interested in revealing the poorest of the working classes. An interesting comparison may be made by comparing Engels's description with a passage from a novel, *Paved with Gold*, by Henry Mayhew's brother, Augustus, who describes a costermongers' community near Drury Lane:

It was one of those streets which, were it not for the paved cartway, would be called a court. . . . This street is like the descriptions travellers have given of thoroughfares in the East. Opposite neighbours cannot exactly shake hands out of the windows, but they can chat together very comfortably; and indeed, all day long, women are seen with their arms folded up like cats' paws, leaning from the casements and conversing with their friends over the way . . . . On entering the place, it gives you the notion of belonging to a distinct colony, or as if it formed one large home, or private residence; for everybody seems to be doing just what he or she likes and the way in which any stranger who passes is stared at, proves that he is considered in the light of an intruder. . . . The parlour windows which look into the street have all of them wooden shutters as thick and clumsy as the flaps to a kitchen table, and the paint is turned to the dull colour of a greased slate. Some of these shutters are evidently never used as a security for the dwelling, but only as a table upon which to chalk the accounts of the day's street-sale. (Augustus Mayhew, *Paved with Gold or, the Romance and Reality of the London Streets* [Glasgow: The Grand Colosseum Warehouse Co., 1858], pp. 92–3).

As Augustus Mayhew acknowledges (p. iii), some of the descriptions of street scenes such as this were undertaken for inclusion in his brother's *London Labour and the London Poor*. The combination of the documentary use of present tense and the tendency to exoticize is typical.

24. Derrida, 'Force of Law', pp. 14–15.
25. Derrida, 'Force of Law', pp. 14–15.
26. Mark Wigley, *The Architecture of Deconstruction: Derrida's Haunt* (Cambridge, MA: MIT Press, 1993), p. xi.
27. Wigley, *Architecture of Deconstruction*, p. 155.
28. David E. Musselwhite, *Partings Welded Together: Politics and Desire in the Nineteenth-Century English Novel* (London: Methuen, 1987), p. 225.
29. Steven Connor, *Charles Dickens* (Oxford: Basil Blackwell, 1985), p. 59. Connor has recently produced an essay on architecture and

the architectural metaphor in *Martin Chuzzlewit*, 'Babel Unbuilding: the anti-archi-rhetoric of *Martin Chuzzlewit*' (*Dickens Refigured: Bodies, Desires and Other Histories*, ed. John Schad [Manchester: Manchester University Press, 1996], pp. 178–200), in which he supplies a useful corrective to a number of previous works (including Schwarzbach's) which 'considerably misconstrue the architectural ethics which are developed through the book...' and which '... collapse together too many important architectural and spatial differences' (p. 179). In particular, Connor resists the critical assumption that there is a 'single labyrinthine "architectural city" of commercial corruption' (p. 179). Like Connor, I also resist such a notion, not only in *Chuzzlewit* (which I leave largely to Connor's fine reading), but also throughout all of Dickens's city-texts. Importantly, and interestingly, Connor in this essay makes similar claims for the figure of the wind in *Chuzzlewit* to those which I make for the fog in *Bleak House*. In a gesture similar to my notion of the Dickensian 'architexture', Connor describes the wind as contributing to the 'anti-architectural design of the book... [it is] the air which moves through and across spatial distinctions' (p. 196). Connor's use of the prefix 'anti-' is too simply dialectic for me, however, and his use of terms such as 'through' and 'across' can be read as picking up the textural and textile metaphor which I have been employing.

30. Connor, *Charles Dickens*, p. 59.
31. D.A. Miller, *The Novel and the Police* (Berkeley and Los Angeles: University of California Press, 1988), p. 60.
32. D.A. Miller, *The Novel and the Police*, p. 61.
33. J. Hillis Miller, *Hawthorne and History: Defacing It* (Oxford: Blackwell, 1991), p. 151.
34. White, *Carnival*, p. 99.
35. J. Hillis Miller, *Hawthorne*, p. 151.
36. D.A. Miller, *The Novel and the Police*, p. 67.
37. White, *Carnival*, p. 100.
38. White, *Carnival*, p. 103.
39. Celeste Olalquiaga, *Megalopolis: Contemporary Cultural Sensibilities* (Minneapolis: University of Minnesota Press, 1992), p. 3.
40. Thomas Richards, *The Imperial Archive: Knowledge and the Fantasy of Empire* (London: Verso, 1993), p. 86.
41. Jacques Derrida, 'A Letter to Peter Eisenman', trans. Hilary P. Hanel, in *Assemblage: A Critical Journal of Architecture and Design Culture*, 12 (1990): 11–12.
42. Connor, *Charles Dickens*, p. 145. F.S. Schwarzbach writes of *Our Mutual Friend* that it has 'too much exciting material, too many centres of attention, too many modes of apprehension, and even too much overwriting' (p. 215). While Schwarzbach intends this as an aesthetic criticism of Dickens's last completed novel, I would suggest that he inadvertently hits on a possible description – or criticism, from some perspectives – of London itself. This only is a problem (with the novel, with London) if one cannot accommodate excess in terms other than negative ones.

43. David Trotter, *Circulation: Defoe, Dickens, and the Economics of the Novel* (London: Macmillan, 1988), p. 85.
44. Trotter, *Circulation*, p. 88.
45. This lack of awareness as to location is more marked in the earlier novels. Were we to desire a novel in which there is a perceptible shift from unawareness to nonchalance, we might suggest *Dombey and Son* as the novel of transition. Certainly by the time of *Bleak House*, *Little Dorrit*, and *Our Mutual Friend*, characters traverse the city with ease (mostly) or are happy to wander either aimlessly or, as in the case of Martha in *David Copperfield*, in curiously circuitous and devious routes which bespeak the unpredictable nature of the city itself. See the passage from Jonathan Raban's *Hunting Mr Heartbreak*, in the Introduction, above.
46. Trotter, *Circulation*, p. 88.
47. Trotter, *Circulation*, p. 86.
48. Liminality is a spatial, as well as temporal, concern for Dickens in the act of writing the city, as the following passage from *Nicholas Nickleby* shows:

> Cadogan Place is the one slight bond that joins two great extremes; it is the connecting link between the aristocratic pavements of Belgrave Square and the barbarism of Chelsea. It is in Sloane Street, but not of it. The people in Cadogan Place look down upon Sloane Street, and think Brompton low. They affect fashion too, and wonder where the New Road is. Not that they claim to be on precisely the same footing as the high folks of Belgrave Square and Grosvenor Place, but that they stand with reference to them rather than in the light of those illegitimate children of the great who are content to boast about their connexions, although their connexions disavow them. Wearing as much as they can of the airs and semblances of loftiest rank, the people of Cadogan Place have the realities of the middle station. It is the conductor which communicates to the inhabitants of regions beyond its limit, the shock of pride of birth and rank, which it has not within itself, but derives from a fountain-head beyond; or, like the ligament which unites the Siamese twins, it contains something of the life and essence of two distinct bodies, and yet belongs to neither.
> Upon this doubtful ground lived Mrs Wititterly. . . .
>   (*NN*, p. 339)

Dickens employs topography and geography as markers of class, but chooses to describe that which links and is at the margins of supposedly definable class-oriented boundaries given name in street and place-names, rather than describing a supposedly discrete area. Choosing terms such as 'conductor' and 'ligament', the latter with reference to Siamese twins, Dickens reinvents the supposedly static city space in terms which suggest the twin Victorian interests of Science and the Freak show, thereby rendering London in a singularly idiomatic manner. Furthermore, he calls the very idea of the knowability – or locatability – of the site into question through the phrase 'doubtful ground'. If we cannot understand topography through rigid social classification, then where are we, precisely?

49. Derrida, 'Point de folie', p. 13.
50. Derrida, 'Point de folie', p. 5. Derrida's phrase can be said to apply equally to the city and to Dickens's narratives.
51. Connor, *Charles Dickens*, p. 65; emphasis added.
52. The name of the monument – the Monument – serves as both proper name and generic definition, and this doubling seems to strain at the limits of what monumentalization can achieve in terms of identification and fixity. As with the name of the City of London, also known as the City (as opposed to 'the city'), the act of naming erases, or puts under erasure, specificity supposedly guaranteed by the proper name, even at the moment of naming. We may wish to observe this double and contrary process at work in the naming of *Bleak House*, a novel named after a house which is but one of many 'bleak houses' in that novel. And certainly, critics such as Musselwhite, Connor, and White, seem to understand the novel as a written form of the house itself, the house rebuilt in writing.
53. Another location which is hard to find is Boffin's Bower in *Our Mutual Friend*. Silas Wegg inquires for the precise location six times without luck (*OMF*, p. 54).
54. White, *Carnival*, p. 102.
55. Derrida, 'Letter', p. 11.
56. This atypicality is registered by F.S. Schwarzbach in his *Dickens and the City*, by there being no chapter devoted to *David Copperfield*.
57. Derrida, 'Point de folie', p. 7.
58. Peter Eisenman et al., *Re: Working Eisenman* (London: Academy Editions, 1993), pp. 24–31. This collection includes several essays and lectures by Eisenman, as well as a correspondence between Derrida and Eisenman, which is of particular interest for its discussion of the possible relation between architecture and deconstruction, and the conclusion on Eisenman's part (quite correctly), that the only possibility for architecture to be faithful to 'deconstruction' is in acts of betraying it and inventing something new and unexpected.
59. Eisenman, *Re: Working Eisenman*, pp. 30–1.
60. Eisenman, *Re: Working Eisenman*, p. 24.
61. Eisenman, *Re: Working Eisenman*, p. 24.
62. Eisenman, *Re: Working Eisenman*, p. 24.
63. On the subject of the classic realist text and the idea of a meta-language, see Colin MacCabe, *James Joyce and the Revolution of the Word* (Basingstoke: Macmillan, 1979), pp. 13–38.
64. Eisenman, *Re: Working Eisenman*, p. 24.
65. Eisenman, *Re: Working Eisenman*, p. 26.
66. Eisenman, *Re: Working Eisenman*, p. 30.
67. Eisenman, *Re: Working Eisenman*, p. 30.

236 *Notes*

AFTERWORD: 'THE ONLY GAME IN TOWN' OR, LONDON TO COME

1. M. Christine Boyer, *Cybercities: Visual Perception in the Age of Electronic Communication* (New York: Princeton Architectural Press, 1996), p. 242.
2. Klaus R. Scherpe, cit. Alexander Gelley, 'City-Texts: Representation, Semiology, Urbanism', in *Politics, Theory, and Contemporary Culture*, ed. Mark Poster (New York: Columbia University Press, 1993; pp. 237–61), p. 257 n.2.
3. Gelley, 'City-Texts', pp. 241, 243.
4. Donald Preziosi, 'Between Power and Desire: The Margins of the City', in *Glyph Textual Studies 1* (1986): 237–52, p. 252.
5. Porter, *London*, p. 385.
6. Jacques Derrida, *Of Grammatology* (1967) trans. Gayatri Chakravorty Spivak (Baltimore: The Johns Hopkins University Press, 1974), p. 302.
7. As a chance commentary between the narratives of Fielding and Woolf, we might insert Lucy Snowe's unexpected encounter with a bookseller's shop, after she has commented that 'London seemed of itself an adventure' and that she has found herself in Paternoster-row by accident (Brontë, *Villette*, p. 109).
8. Henry Fielding, *A Journey From This World to the Next and The Journal of A Voyage to Lisbon*, ed. Ian A. Bell and Andrew Varney (Oxford: Oxford University Press, 1997).
9. Fielding, *Journey*, p. 3.
10. Woolf, 'Street Haunting', p. 23. Rachel Bowlby's 'Walking, Women and Writing: Virginia Woolf as *Flâneuse*', in *New Feminist Discourses: Critical Essays on Themes and Texts*, ed. Isobel Armstrong (London: Routledge, 1992; pp. 26–47) offers the most complete and sensitive reading of this essay and Woolf's other considerations of walking/writing London.
11. Adam Gopnik, 'The Culture of Blairism', *The New Yorker*, 73:18 (7 July 1997): 26–32, p. 28.
12. Samuel, *Theatres of Memory*, p. 247. Samuel's is the most interesting sustained critique of the heritage industry in late twentieth-century Britain that I know. Its subtitle might well be 'the Victorianization of Britain'. As Samuel points out, the Globe is only one project among countless heritage ventures, belonging as he suggests to what Frank Parkin called 'middle-class radicalism' (p. 247). Such radicalism, whether of a left- or right-wing variety, has more to say about constructions of national identity in the twentieth century through our attitudes to the past which we call 'ours', than it can tell us about the past itself and all its various narratives. London is merely one focal point for heritage activity, and the fact that it can be understood as a city-text, a place which constantly takes place and is always undergoing reinvention, suggests that it might survive in some spectral fashion, despite whatever happens to be the *ideology-du-jour*.
13. Sinclair, *Lights Out*, p. 91.

14. Preziosi, 'Between Power and Desire', p. 238.
15. Paul Virilio, 'The Overexposed City', trans. Daniel Moshenberg, in *Rethinking Architecture: A Reader in Cultural Theory*, ed. Neil Leach (London: Routledge, 1997; pp. 381–90), p. 382.
16. Virilio, 'The Overexposed City', p. 383.
17. Sinclair, *Lights Out*, p. 106. It is interesting to compare Sinclair's understanding of the effects of surveillance technology in the third essay of *Lights Out* – 'Bulls & Bears & Mithraic Misalignments: Weather in the City' (pp. 89–132) – with Virilio's discussion of the proliferating technologies of the modern city, in the essay cited in n. 5, above. Sinclair's discussion is always more overtly spectral than that of Virilio, though both can be read as comprising a fascinating potential debate with Derrida's discussions of the spectral and technology, particularly those impromptu remarks made by Derrida in Ken McMullen's film, *Ghost Dance*, a film concerned not only with the relationship between the spectral and the technological, but also with the modern city. If, as Virilio suggests, the city is no longer an 'estate' or place, then it is certainly a transmission, a taking place of transportation. Understanding the condition of writing the city in the nineteenth century as a series of singular responses to its fragments and ghosts is perhaps to begin to comprehend that spectral immanence which technology is only now beginning to make apparent to us.
18. Ignasi de Solà-Morales, *Differences* (1995) trans. Graham Thompson, ed. Sarah Whiting (Cambridge, MA: MIT Press, 1997), p. 102.
19. de Solà-Morales, *Differences*, p. 102.
20. Gelley, 'City-Texts', p. 240.
21. Preziosi, 'Between Power and Desire', p. 238.
22. Gelley, 'City-Texts', p. 238.
23. Sinclair, *Lights Out*, p. 16. On the relationship between spectrality, writing, walking, the city, see my essay on Sinclair, 'The Hauntological Example: the City as the Haunt of Writing in the Texts of Iain Sinclair', in *Deconstruction • Derrida* (Basingstoke: Macmillan, 1998).
24. Gelley, 'City-Texts', p. 238.
25. Gelley, 'City-Texts', p. 238.
26. Preziosi, 'Between Power and Desire', p. 237.
27. Arthur Hugh Clough, 'To The Great Metropolis', in *Selected Poems*, ed. Jim McCue (London: Penguin, 1991), p. 9.

Bibliography

Abraham, Nicholas. *Rhythms: On the Work, Translation, and Psychoanalysis*. (1985). Collected and presented by Nicholas T. Rand and Maria Torok. Trans. Benjamin Thigpen and Nicholas T. Rand. Stanford: Stanford University Press, 1995.

Ackroyd, Peter. *Hawksmoor*. (1985) London: Abacus, 1988.

———. *Blake*. London: Sinclair Stevenson, 1995.

———. *Dickens*. (1990) London: Minerva, 1991.

———. *Milton in America*. London: Sinclair Stevenson, 1996.

Agamben, Giorgio. *Stanzas: Word and Phantasm in Western Culture*. (1977) Trans. Ronald L. Martinez. Minneapolis: University of Minnesota Press, 1993.

Appignanesi, Lisa, ed. *Postmodernism: ICA Documents*. London: FAB, 1989.

Arnold, Matthew. *The Poems of Matthew Arnold*. 2nd ed. Ed. Miriam Allott. London: Longman, 1979.

Ashe, T., ed. *The Table Talk and Omniana of S.T. Coleridge*. London: Bohn's Popular Library, 1923.

Augé, Marc. *Non-places: Introduction to an Anthropology of Supermodernity*. (1992) Trans. John Howe. London: Verso, 1995.

Barbauld, Anna Laetitia. *The Poems of Anna Laetitia Barbauld*. Ed. William McCarthy and Elizabeth Kraft. Athens, GA: University of Georgia Press, 1994.

Barrell, John. *The Infection of Thomas De Quincey: A Psychopathology of Imperialism*. New Haven: Yale University Press, 1991.

Baudelaire, Charles. *The Poems in Prose and La Fanfarlo*. Int. and trans. Francis Scarfe. London: Anvil Press Poetry, 1989.

Baudrillard, Jean. *Simulations*. (1981) Trans. Paul Foss, Paul Patton and Philip Beitchman. New York: Semiotext(e), 1983.

Bell, Walter George. *Unknown London*. London: John Lane, the Bodley Head, 1920.

Benjamin, Walter. *Charles Baudelaire: A Lyric Poet in the Era of High Capitalism*. Trans. Harry Zohn. London: New Left Books, 1973.

Bennington, Geoffrey, and Jacques Derrida. *Jacques Derrida*. (1991) Trans. Geoffrey Bennington. Chicago: University of Chicago Press, 1993.

Bernstein, Carol L. *The Celebration of Scandal: Toward the Sublime in Victorian Urban Fiction*. University Park, PA: Pennsylvania State University Press, 1991.

Blake, William. *The Complete Poems*. Ed. Alicia Ostriker. London: Penguin, 1977.

Bloom, Harold. *Blake's Apocalypse: A Study in Poetic Argument*. Garden City, NY: Anchor, 1959.

———. *Poetry and Repression*. New Haven: Yale University Press, 1976.

Bowlby, Rachel. 'Walking, Women and Writing: Virginia Woolf as *Flâneuse*'.

New Feminist Discourses: Critical Essays on Themes and Texts. Ed. Isobel Armstrong. London: Routledge, 1992, pp. 26–47.

Boyer, M. Christine. *The City of Collective Memory: Its Historical Imagery and Architectural Entertainments.* Cambridge, MA: MIT Press, 1994.

——. *Cybercities: Visual Perception in the Age of Electronic Communication.* New York: Princeton Architectural Press, 1996.

Brontë, Charlotte. *Villette.* (1853) Ed. Mark Lilly, introd. Tony Tanner. London: Penguin, 1985.

Bruder, Helen P. *William Blake and the Daughters of Albion.* Basingstoke: Macmillan, 1997.

Butler, Marilyn. *Romantics, Rebels and Revolutionaries: English Literature and its Background 1760–1830.* Oxford: Oxford University Press, 1981.

Byron, George Gordon, Lord. *Poetical Works.* (1904) Ed. Frederick Page, corrected John Jump. Oxford: Oxford University Press, 1970.

Calvino, Italo. *Invisible Cities.* (1974) Trans. William Weaver. London: Picador, 1979.

Caws, Mary Ann, ed. *City Images: Perspectives from Literature, Philosophy, and Film.* Langhorne: Gordon and Breach, 1993.

Chambers, Iain. *Migrancy, Culture, Identity.* London: Routledge, 1994.

Christ, Carol T., and John O. Jordan, eds. *Victorian Literature and the Victorian Visual Imagination.* Berkeley: University of California Press, 1995.

Clark, Steve, and David Worrall, eds. *Historicising Blake.* Basingstoke: Macmillan, 1994.

Clough, Arthur Hugh. *Selected Poems.* Ed. Jim McCue. London: Penguin, 1991.

Colley, Linda. *Britons: Forging the Nation 1707–1837.* (1992) London: Pimlico, 1994.

Connor, Steven. *Charles Dickens.* Oxford: Basil Blackwell, 1985.

——. 'Babel Unbuilding: the Anti-archi-rhetoric of *Martin Chuzzlewit*'. *Dickens Refigured: Bodies, Desires, and other Histories.* Ed. John Schad. Manchester: Manchester University Press, 1996, pp. 178–200.

Conrad, Joseph. *The Secret Agent.* (1907). Ed. and introd. Martin Seymour-Smith. London: Penguin, 1990.

Cox, Philip. 'William Wordsworth: Constructions of the "self" in *The Prelude*'. *Gender, Genre, and the Romantic Poets.* Manchester: Manchester University Press, 1996, pp. 58–80.

Cox, Stephen. *Love and Logic: The Evolution of Blake's Thought.* Ann Arbor: University of Michigan Press, 1992.

Crary, Jonathan. *Techniques of the Observer: On Vision and Modernity in the Nineteenth Century.* Cambridge, MA: MIT Press, 1992.

Critchley, Simon. *The Ethics of Deconstruction: Derrida and Levinas.* Oxford: Blackwell, 1992.

De Certeau, Michel. *The Practice of Everyday Life.* Berkeley: University of California Press, 1988.

Deleuze, Gilles, and Félix Guattari. *Anti-Oedipus: Capitalism and Schizophrenia.* (1972) Trans. Robert Hurley, Mark Seem, and Helen R. Lane. Preface Michel Foucault. Minneapolis: University of Minnesota Press, 1983.

——. *What is Philosophy?* (1991) Trans. Graham Burchell and Hugh Tomlinson. London: Verso, 1994.

De Luca, Vincent. 'A Wall of Words: The Sublime as Text'. *Unnam'ed Forms: Blake and Textuality*. Ed. Nelson Hilton and Thomas A. Vogler. Berkeley: University of California Press, pp. 218–41.

De Quincey, Thomas. *Confessions of an English Opium-Eater and Other Writings*. Ed. Grevel Lindop. Oxford: Oxford University Press, 1985.

Derrida, Jacques. *Of Grammatology*. (1967) Trans. Gayatri Chakravorty Spivak. Baltimore: The Johns Hopkins University Press, 1974.

——. *Writing and Difference*. (1967) Trans. Alan Bass. London: Routledge and Kegan Paul, 1981.

——. *Margins of Philosophy*. (1972) Trans. Alan Bass. Chicago: University of Chicago Press, 1982.

——. 'Deconstruction and the Other' *Dialogues with Contemporary Continental Thinkers: The Phenomenological Heritage*. Ed. Richard Kearney. Manchester: Manchester University Press, 1984, pp. 107–26.

——. 'Point de folie – maintenant l'architecture'. Trans. Kate Linker. *La Case Vide La Villette 1985*. Bernard Tschumi. London: Architectural Association, Folio VIII, 1987, pp. 4–20.

——. *The Truth in Painting*. (1978) Trans. Geoff Bennington and Ian McLeod. Chicago: University of Chicago Press, 1987.

——. *Limited Inc*. Trans. Samuel Weber and Jeffrey Mehlman. Evanston, Ill: Northwestern University Press, 1988.

——. *Of Spirit: Heidegger and the Question*. (1987) Trans. Geoffrey Bennington and Rachel Bowlby. Chicago: University of Chicago Press, 1989.

——. 'A Letter to Peter Eisenman'. Trans. Hilary P. Hanel. *Assemblage: A Critical Journal of Architecture and Design Culture* 12 (1990): 11–12.

——. 'Before the Law'. *Acts of Literature*. Ed. Derek Attridge. London: Routledge, 1992, pp. 181–221.

——. 'Force of Law: The "Mystical Foundation of Authority"'. *Deconstruction and the Possibility of Justice*. Ed. Drucilla Cornell, Michael Rosenfeld, David Gray Carlson. London: Routledge, 1992, pp. 3–68.

——. 'The Law of Genre', in *Acts of Literature*. Ed. Derek Attridge. London: Routledge, 1992, pp. 221–53.

——. 'Of an Apocalyptic Tone Recently Adopted in Philosophy'. *Oxford Literary Review* 6 (1984). Subsequently reprinted and retranslated as 'On a Newly Arisen Apocalyptic Tone in Philosophy'. Trans. John P. Leavey, Jr. *Raising the Tone of Philosophy*. Ed. Peter Fenves. Baltimore: The Johns Hopkins University Press, 1993, pp. 117–72.

——. *On the Name*. (1993). Ed. Thomas Dutoit. Trans. David Wood, John P. Leavey, Jr, and Ian McLeod. Stanford: Stanford University Press, 1995.

——. 'Remarks on Deconstruction and Pragmatism'. Trans. Simon Critchley. *Deconstruction and Pragmatism*. Ed. Chantal Mouffe. London: Routledge, 1996, pp. 77–88.

de Solà-Morales, Ignasi. *Differences*. (1995) Trans. Graham Thompson. Ed. Sarah Whiting. Cambridge, MA: MIT Press, 1997.

Dickens, Charles. *Sketches by Boz and Other Early Papers 1833–39*. Ed. Michael Slater. London: J.M. Dent, 1994.

——. *Master Humphrey's Clock and A Child's History of England*. Introd. Derek Hudson. Oxford: Oxford University Press, 1987.

——. *Our Mutual Friend.* (1864–5) Ed. Michael Cotsell. Oxford: Oxford University Press, 1991.

——. *David Copperfield.* (1850) Ed. Trevor Blount. London: Penguin, 1985.

——. *Oliver Twist.* (1837–9) Ed. Peter Fairclough. Introd. Angus Wilson. London: Penguin, 1986.

——. *Bleak House.* (1853) Ed. Nicola Bradbury. London: Penguin, 1996.

——. *Martin Chuzzlewit.* (1843–4) Ed. P.N. Furbank. London: Penguin, 1986.

——. *Little Dorrit.* (1857) Ed. John Holloway. London: Penguin, 1988.

——. *Dombey and Son.* (1848) Ed. Raymond Williams. London: Penguin, 1985.

——. *Nicholas Nickleby.* (1839) Ed. Michael Slater. London: Penguin, 1986.

Eagleton, Terry. *Criticism and Ideology: A Study in Marxist Literary Theory.* London: Verso, 1976.

Easthope, Antony. *Wordsworth Now and Then: Romanticism and Contemporary Culture.* Buckingham: Open University Press, 1993.

Eisenman, Peter et al. *Re: Working Eisenman.* London: Academy Editions, 1993.

Elfenbein, Andrew. *Byron and the Victorians.* Cambridge: Cambridge University Press, 1995.

Engels, Friedrich. *The Condition of the Working Class in England.* (1845) Trans. Florence Kelley-Wischnewetsky. Revised 1887. Ed. and introd. David McLellan. Oxford: Oxford University Press, 1993.

Essick, Robert N. *William Blake and the Language of Adam.* Oxford: Clarendon Press, 1989.

Ferguson, Frances. *Solitude and the Sublime: Romanticism and the Aesthetics of Individuation.* New York: Routledge, 1992.

Fielding, Henry. *A Journey from This World to the Next and The Journal of A Voyage to Lisbon.* Ed. Ian A. Bell and Andrew Varney. Oxford: Oxford University Press, 1997.

Fletcher, Geoffrey. *The London Nobody Knows.* (1962) Harmondsworth: Penguin, 1966.

Foucault, Michel. *The Order of Things: An Archeology of the Human Sciences.* (1966) New York: Random House, 1973.

Frampton, Kenneth. 'Some Reflections on Postmodernism and Architecture', in *Postmodernism: ICA Documents,* pp. 75–88.

Freud, Sigmund. 'Anxiety'. *Introductory Lectures on Psychoanalysis.* Vol. 1, Penguin Freud Library. Trans. James Strachey. Ed. James Strachey and Angela Richards. Harmondsworth: Penguin, 1982, pp. 440–60.

——. 'On the Grounds for Detaching a Particular Syndrome from Neurasthenia under the Description "Anxiety Neurosis"'. *On Psychopathology.* Vol. 10, Penguin Freud Library. Trans. James Strachey. Ed. Angela Richards. London: Penguin, 1993, pp. 35–63.

——. 'Inhibitions, Symptoms and Anxiety'. *On Psychopathology.* Vol. 10, Penguin Freud Library. Trans. James Strachey. Ed. Angela Richards. London: Penguin, 1993, pp. 237–334.

——. 'Anxiety and Instinctual Life'. *New Introductory Lectures on Psychoanalysis.* Vol. 2, Penguin Freud Library. Trans. James Strachey. Ed. Angela Richards. London: Penguin, 1991, pp. 113–44.

Frye, Northrop. *Fearful Symmetry: A Study of William Blake*. Princeton: Princeton University Press, 1947.

Gaskell, Elizabeth. *Mary Barton*. (1848) Ed. Edgar Wright. Oxford: Oxford University Press, 1987.

Gelley, Alexander. 'City-Texts: Representation, Semiology, Urbanism', in *Politics, Theory, and Contemporary Culture*. Ed. Mark Poster. New York: Columbia University Press, 1993, pp. 237–61.

Gilchrist, Alexander. *Life of William Blake*. (2nd ed., 1880) Ed. Ruthven Todd. New York: Dutton, 1942.

Goldsmith, Steven. *Unbuilding Jerusalem*. Ithaca, NY: Cornell University Press, 1993.

Gopnik, Adam. 'The Culture of Blairism'. *The New Yorker*, 73:18 (7 July 1997): 26–32.

Grosz, Elizabeth. *Space, Time, and Perversion: Essays on the Politics of Bodies*. New York: Routledge, 1995.

Hartman, Geoffrey H. *Wordsworth's Poetry 1787–1814*. (1964) Cambridge, MA: Harvard University Press, 1971.

Hertz, Neil. *The End of the Line: Essays on Psychoanalysis and the Sublime*. New York: Columbia University Press, 1985.

Jacobus, Mary. *Romanticism, Writing, and Sexual Difference: Essays on The Prelude*. Oxford: Clarendon Press, 1989.

James, Henry. 'London'. *London Stories and Other Writings*. Ed. David Kynaston. Padstow: Tabb House, 1989, pp. 241–70.

——. *The Princess Casamassima*. (1886) Ed. and introd. Derek Brewer, notes Patricia Crick. London: Penguin, 1987.

——. *English Hours*. (1905) Ed. Alma Louise Lowe. London: Heinemann, 1960.

Jefferies, Richard. 'The Lions in Trafalgar Square', in *The Toilers of the Field*. (1892) London: Longmans Green, 1894, pp. 321–7.

——. 'A Wet Night in London', in *The Open Air*. (1885) London: J.M. Dent and Sons, 1914, pp. 250–6.

Kant, Immanuel. *Critique of Judgment*. Trans. J.H. Bernard. New York: Hafner, 1966.

Karatani, Kojin. *Architecture as Metaphor: Language, Number, Money*. Trans. Sabu Kohso. Ed. Michael Speaks. Cambridge, MA: MIT Press, 1995.

King, Geoff. *Mapping Reality: an Exploration of Cultural Cartographies*. Basingstoke: Macmillan, 1996.

Kynaston, David. *The City of London: Volume I, A World of its Own 1815–1890*. London: Chatto and Windus, 1994.

Lacan, Jacques. *Écrits: A Selection*. Trans. Alan Sheridan. New York: W.W. Norton and Company, 1977.

Langan, Celeste. *Romantic Vagrancy: Wordsworth and the Simulation of Freedom*. Cambridge: Cambridge University Press, 1995.

Leach, Neil, ed. *Rethinking Architecture: A Reader in Cultural Theory*. London: Routledge, 1997.

Liu, Alan. '"Shapeless Eagerness": The Genre of Revolution in Books 9–10 of *The Prelude*', in *Modern Language Quarterly*, 43.1 (1982): 3–28.

MacCabe, Colin. *James Joyce and the Revolution of the Word*. Basingstoke: Macmillan, 1979.

Macherey, Pierre. *A Theory of Literary Production.* (1966) Trans. Geoffrey Wall. London: Routledge and Kegan Paul, 1978.

Marx, Karl. *Early Writings.* Trans. Rodney Livingstone and Gregor Benton. Int. Lucio Coletti. New York: Vintage, 1975.

Mayhew, Augustus. *Paved with Gold or, the Romance and Reality of the London Streets.* Glasgow: The Grand Colosseum Warehouse Co., 1858.

Maynard, Jessica. 'Agriculture and Society: A Marxist Reading of Richard Jefferies' "Snowed Up"'. *Literary Theories: A Case Study in Critical Performance.* Ed. Julian Wolfreys and William Baker. Basingstoke: Macmillan, 1996, pp. 129–56.

McCalman, Iain. 'The Infidel as Prophet: William Reid and Blakean Radicalism', in Clark and Worrall, 24–42.

McGann, Jerome J. *Social Values and Poetic Acts.* Cambridge, MA: Harvard University Press, 1988.

——. *The Romantic Ideology: A Critical Investigation.* Chicago: University of Chicago Press, 1983.

Mee, Jon. *Dangerous Enthusiasm: William Blake and the Culture of Radicalism in the 1790s.* Oxford: Clarendon Press, 1992.

——. 'Is there an Antinomian in the House? William Blake and the After-Life of a Heresy', in Clark and Worrall, pp. 43–58.

Miller, D.A. *The Novel and the Police.* Berkeley: University of California Press, 1988.

Miller, Dan. 'Blake and the Deconstructive Interlude', in *Critical Paths: Blake and the Argument of Method.* Ed. Dan Miller, Mark Bracher, and Donald Ault. Durham, NC: Duke University Press, 1987, pp. 139–67.

——. *Hawthorne and History: Defacing It.* Oxford: Blackwell, 1991.

Miller, J. Hillis. *Topographies.* Stanford: Stanford University Press, 1995.

Mitchell, W.J.T. 'Visible Language: Blake's Wond'rous Art of Writing', in *Romanticism and Contemporary Criticism.* Ed. Morris Eaves and Michael Fischer. Ithaca: Cornell University Press, 1986. Reprinted in Punter, ed., pp. 123–48.

Morton, Timothy. *Shelley and the Revolution in Taste: The Body and the Natural World.* Cambridge: Cambridge University Press, 1994.

Musselwhite, David. *Partings Welded Together: Politics and Desire in the Nineteenth-Century English Novel.* London: Methuen, 1987.

Nord, Deborah Epstein. *Walking the Victorian Streets: Women, Representation, and the City.* Ithaca, NY: Cornell University Press, 1995.

Olalquiaga, Celeste. *Megalopolis: Contemporary Cultural Sensibilities.* Minneapolis: University of Minnesota Press, 1992.

Otto, Peter. *Constructive Vision and Visionary Deconstruction: Los, Eternity, and the Productions of Time in the Later Poetry of William Blake.* Oxford: Clarendon Press, 1991.

Paley, Morton D. *The Continuing City: William Blake's Jerusalem.* Oxford: Clarendon Press, 1991.

Pope, Alexander. *The Poems of Alexander Pope.* Ed. John Butt. London: Methuen, 1963.

Porphyrios, Demetri. 'Architecture and the Postmodern Condition', in Appignanesi, ed., *Postmodernism: ICA Documents*, pp. 89–91.

Porter, Roy. *London: A Social History.* London: Hamish Hamilton, 1994.

Pratt, Alfred T. Camden. *Unknown London: Its Romance and Tragedy: A Contribution to the History of London; And a Guide to Places Generally Unknown.* London: Neville Beeman, 1897.

Preziosi, Donald. 'Between Power and Desire: The Margins of the City', in *Glyph Textual Studies 1* (1986): 237–52.

Priestley, J.B. *Angel Pavement.* (1930) Harmondsworth: Penguin, 1968.

Punter, David, ed. *William Blake.* Basingstoke: Macmillan, 1996.

Pyle, Forest. *The Ideology of the Imagination: Subject and Society in the Discourse of Romanticism.* Stanford: Stanford University Press, 1995.

Raban, Jonathan. *Hunting Mr Heartbreak.* (1990) London: Picador, 1991.

Readings, Bill. *Introducing Lyotard: Art and Politics.* London: Routledge, 1991.

Réda, Jacques. *The Ruins of Paris.* (1977) Trans. Mark Treharne. London: Reaktion Books, 1996.

Richards, Thomas. *The Imperial Archive: Knowledge and the Fantasy of Empire.* London: Verso, 1993.

Richey, William. *Blake's Altering Aesthetic.* Columbia: Missouri University Press, 1996.

Riddell, Charlotte. *Mitre Court. A Tale of the Great City.* London: Richard Bentley and Son, 1885.

——. *George Geith of Fen Court.* London: Richard Bentley and Son, 1886.

——. *The Government Official.* London: Richard Bentley and Son, 1887.

Robbins, Ruth. 'William Blake'. *Dictionary of Literary Biography, Volume 154: The British Literary Book Trade, 1700–1820.* Ed. James K. Bracken and Joel Silver. Detroit: Gale Research Inc., pp. 26–32.

Ronell, Avital. *Crack Wars: Literature, Addiction, Mania.* Lincoln: University of Nebraska Press, 1992.

Royle, Nicholas. *After Derrida.* Manchester: Manchester University Press, 1995.

Samuel, Raphael. *Theatres of Memory: Volume I – Past and Present in Contemporary Culture.* London: Verso, 1994.

Sandison, Alan. *Robert Louis Stevenson and the Appearance of Modernism.* Basingstoke: Macmillan, 1996.

Schwarzbach, F.S. *Dickens and the City.* London: Athlone Press, 1979.

Selvon, Sam. *The Lonely Londoners.* (1956) Introd. Kenneth Ramchand. London: Longman, 1994.

Shelley, Percy Bysshe. *Poetical Works.* (1905) Ed. Thomas Hutchinson, corrected G.M. Matthews. Oxford: Oxford University Press, 1970.

Simpson, David. 'Reading Blake and Derrida – Our Caesars Neither Praised nor Buried'. *Unnam'd Forms: Blake and Textuality.* Ed Nelson Hilton and Thomas A. Vogler. Berkeley: University of California Press, 1986. Reprinted in Punter ed., pp. 149–64.

Sinclair, Iain. *Lights Out for the Territory: 9 Excursions in the Secret History of London.* London: Granta, 1997.

Smollett, Tobias. *The Expedition of Humphrey Clinker.* (1771) Ed. Angus Ross. Harmondsworth: Penguin, 1983.

Stallybrass, Peter, and Allon White. *The Politics and Poetics of Transgression.* Ithaca, NY: Cornell University Press, 1986.

Stevenson, Robert Louis. *The Strange Case of Dr Jekyll and Mr Hyde and*

Weir of Hermiston. Ed. Emma Letley. Oxford: Oxford University Press, 1990.

Stone, Harry. *The Night Side of Dickens: Cannibalism, Passion, Necessity.* Columbus: Ohio State University, 1994.

Symons, Arthur. *Cities and Sea-Coasts and Islands.* London: Collins, 1918.

Tambling, Jeremy. *Dickens, Violence and the Modern State: Dreams of the Scaffold.* Basingstoke: Macmillan, 1995.

Thompson, E.P. *Witness Against the Beast: William Blake and Moral Law.* Cambridge: Cambridge University Press, 1993.

Tilly, Charles. *Popular Contention in Great Britain 1758–1834.* Cambridge, MA: Harvard University Press, 1995.

Trotter, David. *Circulation: Defoe, Dickens, and the Economics of the Novel.* London: Macmillan, 1988.

Tschumi, Bernard. *Architecture and Disjunction.* Cambridge, MA: MIT Press, 1994.

——. *Event-Cities (Praxis).* Cambridge MA: MIT Press, 1994.

Vidler, Anthony. *The Architectural Uncanny: Essays in the Modern Unhomely.* Cambridge, MA: MIT Press, 1992.

Virilio, Paul. *The Vision Machine.* (1988) Trans. Julie Rose. London: British Film Institute, 1994.

Viscomi, Joseph. *Blake and the Idea of the Book.* Princeton: Princeton University Press, 1993.

Wagner, Peter. *Reading Iconotexts: From Swift to the French Revolution.* London: Reaktion Books, 1995.

Watson, Nicola J. 'Trans-figuring Byronic Identity', in *At the Limits of Romanticism: Essays in Cultural, Feminist, and Materialist Criticism.* Ed. Mary A. Favret and Nicola J. Watson. Bloomington: Indiana University Press, 1994.

Weber, Samuel. *Return to Freud: Jacques Lacan's Dislocation of Psychoanalysis.* (1978) Trans. Michael Levine. Cambridge: Cambridge University Press, 1991.

——. *Mass Mediauras: Form Technics Media.* Ed. Alan Cholodenko. Stanford: Stanford University Press, 1996.

Wellbery, David E. *The Specular Moment: Goethe's Early Lyric and the Beginnings of Romanticism.* Stanford: Stanford University Press, 1996.

Wells, H.G. *Love and Mr Lewisham.* (1900) Harmondsworth: Penguin, 1946.

——. *Ann Veronica.* (1909) Harmondsworth: Penguin, 1968.

Welsh, Alexander. *The City of Dickens.* Oxford: Clarendon Press, 1971.

White, Allon. *Carnival, Hysteria and Writing: Collected Essays and Autobiography.* Introd. Stuart Hall. Oxford: Clarendon Press, 1993.

Wigley, Mark. *The Architecture of Deconstruction: Derrida's Haunt.* Cambridge, MA: MIT Press, 1993.

Williams, Greg. *Diamond Geezers.* London: Fourth Estate, 1997.

Williams, Raymond. *The Country and the City.* Oxford: Oxford University Press, 1973.

Wirth-Nesher, Hana. *City Codes: Reading the Modern Urban Novel.* Cambridge: Cambridge University Press, 1996.

Wolff, Janet. 'The Invisible *Flâneuse:* Women and the Literature of Modernity'. *Theory, Culture and Society.* 2:3 (1985): 37–46.

Wolfreys, Julian. *Being English: Narratives, Idioms, and Performances of National Identity from Coleridge to Trollope*. Albany: State University of New York Press, 1994.

Woolf, Virginia. 'Street Haunting: A London Adventure', in *The Death of the Moth and Other Essays*. (1942) Harmondsworth: Penguin, 1965, pp. 23–36.

——. *The Essays of Virginia Woolf*. Vol. III. Ed. Andrew McNeillie. London: Hogarth Press, 1987, pp. 404–5.

Wordsworth, William. *The Prelude*. Ed. Jonathan Wordsworth. London: Penguin, 1995.

——. *Poetical Works*. (1904) New edition, rev. Ernest De Selincourt. Oxford: Oxford University Press, 1988.

Žižek, Slavoj. *The Indivisible Remainder: An Essay on Schelling and Related Matters*. London: Verso, 1996.

Index of Proper Names

Main discussions are printed in **bold** type.

Printed in the United States
39115LVS00001B